D0563305

Boston

Patricia Harris and David Lyon

Photography by Joel Sartore, Robert Holmes,
and James Marshall

COMPASS AMERICAN GUIDES
An Imprint of Fodor's Travel Publications

Boston

Third Edition
Copyright © 2001 Fodor's Travel Publications
Maps Copyright © 1998, 2001 Fodor's Travel Publications

Compass American Guides and colophon are trademarks of Random House, Inc.
Fodor's is a registered trademark of Random House, Inc.
ISBN 0-676-90132-8

All rights reserved. No part of this publication may be translated, reproduced, or transmitted in any form or by any means, electronic or mechanical, including photocopying and recording, or by any information storage and retrieval system, without the written permission of the Publisher, except brief extracts by a reviewer for inclusion in critical articles or reviews.

Although the Publisher and the Authors of this book have made every effort to ensure the information was correct at the time of going to press, the Publisher and the Authors do not assume and hereby disclaim any liability to any party for any loss or damage caused by errors, omissions, misleading information, or any potential travel disruption due to labor or financial difficulty, whether such errors or omissions result from negligence, accident, or any other cause.

Editors: Thomas N. Brown, Kit Duane, Julia Dillon, Pennfield Jensen, Beth Burleson
Designers: Christopher Burt, Julia Dillon
Managing Editor: Kit Duane
Photography Editor: Christopher Burt
Map Design: Mark Stroud, Moon Street Cartography
Cover Design: Siobhan O'Hare

Compass American Guides, 5332 College Avenue, Suite 201, Oakland, CA 94618
Production House: Twin Age Ltd., Hong Kong   Manufactured in China

10 9 8 7 6 5 4 3 2 1

THE PUBLISHER GRATEFULLY ACKNOWLEDGES THE following institutions and individuals for the use of their photographs and/or illustrations on these pages: All photos are by **Joel Sartore** unless otherwise noted: **Robert Holmes,** pp. 12 (middle), 30, 52, 60, 66, 74, 75, 90, 94, 119, 162 (both photos), 169, 173, 187, 195, 204, 206, 228, 229, 237, 250, 254, 255, 316 (all photos), 320; **Boston Public Library,** pp. 93, 120, 206; **Connecticut Historical Society,** p. 253; **Isabella Stewart Gardner Museum,** pp. 47, 178, 179; **Library of Congress,** pp. 21, 25, 53, 40, 81, 102, 137, 152, 153; **Patricia Harris,** p. 239; **James Marshall,** cover, pp. 5, 59, 63, 72, 101, 103, 112, 138, 141, 150, 151, 155, 156, 158, 160, 194, 198, 211, 242; **Massachusetts Historical Society,** pp. 26, 31, 35, 57, 70, 95, 225, 260; **Museum of Fine Arts, Boston,** pp. 42, 43, 174-175, 176; **Peabody-Essex Museum,** p. 259; **The Bostonian Society,** pp. 18, 39, 111; **Underwood Photo Archives, San Francisco,** pp. 48, 83, 99, 217.

THE PUBLISHER would also like to thank the following for their contributions to this book: **Holly Cratsley** for her architecture essay; **Lesley Bonnet** for indexing; and **Ellen Klages** for proofreading.

To generous friends

AUTHORS' ACKNOWLEDGMENTS

FROM START TO FINISH this book has represented the efforts of many people determined to see Boston get its due. We are deeply grateful to the staff of Compass American Guides: Chris Burt for championing the project, Kit Duane for her enthusiastic guidance in the conceptual stage of the book, and Julia Dillon for careful and imaginative editing. We would also like to thank historian Thomas N. Brown for leavening some of our readings of events with his broader, more clear-eyed vision of the uses of history. Mark Stroud has untangled the legendary labyrinth of Boston's streets with maps that enable the reader to claim the length and breadth of the city. Photographer Joel Sartore has furnished the splendid images which compensate a thousand-fold for the failings of the words. And, finally, we wish to thank our friends and colleagues for their suggestions and support.

C O N T E N T S

Literary Extracts

Topical Essays & Timelines

Maps

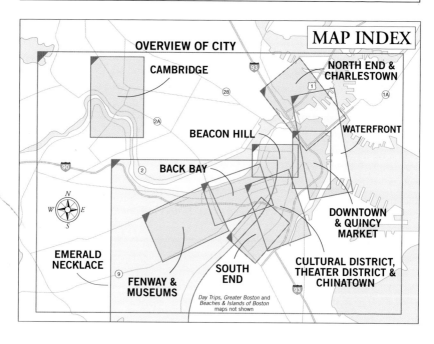

MAP INDEX

OVERVIEW OF CITY

CAMBRIDGE

NORTH END & CHARLESTOWN

BEACON HILL

WATERFRONT

BACK BAY

DOWNTOWN & QUINCY MARKET

EMERALD NECKLACE

FENWAY & MUSEUMS

SOUTH END

CULTURAL DISTRICT, THEATER DISTRICT & CHINATOWN

Day Trips, Greater Boston and Beaches & Islands of Boston maps not shown

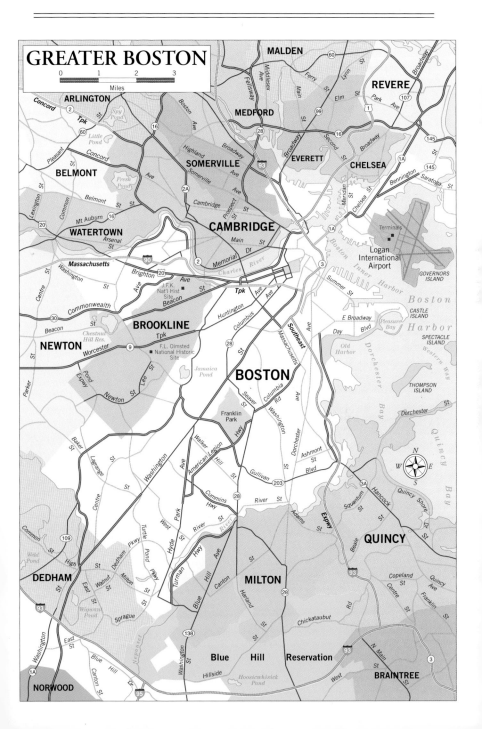

GREATER BOSTON

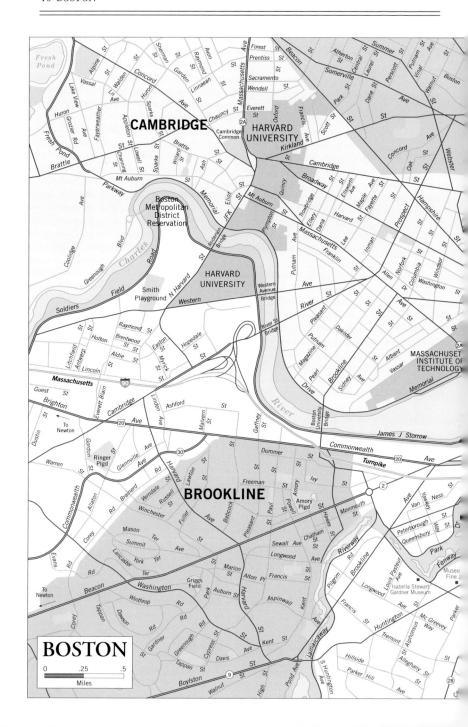

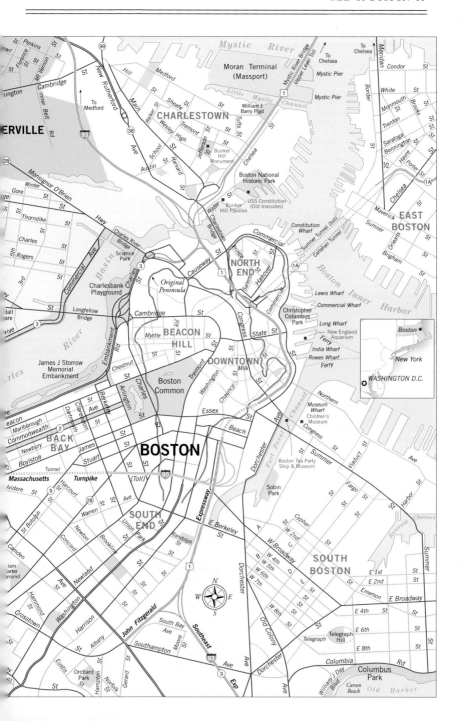

OVERVIEW

BOSTON'S HISTORY IS AMERICA'S STORY writ small. From daring Puritans who sought a New Jerusalem in the wilderness to the patriots who willed a country out of a colony, Boston has been where America happened first. The evidence is all still here, from Paul Revere's house to Frederick Law Olmsted's Emerald Necklace to Isabella Stewart Gardner's scandalous portrait. Meet the people and places of the Athens of America.

BEACON HILL   *pages 56–78*

The "City on a Hill" is literally the loftiest perch in Boston. It remains a showpiece of Federal-era architecture, with brick sidewalks, gaslights, and cobblestone alleys. Many a storied Boston character—from Louisa May Alcott to Ted Kennedy—has lived here.

DOWNTOWN BOSTON   *pages 79–106*

Downtown begins at the Common, the green heart of the city. It encompasses several of the most important sites of the American Revolution, and is the seat of Boston finance. Faneuil Hall, the "Cradle of Liberty," serves as a gate to Boston's great festival marketplace.

NORTH END   *pages 107-126*

The old North End, home to Paul Revere and Rose Fitzgerald Kennedy, remains a warren of 17th-century streets lined now with the bustling trattorias and caffes of Boston's Italian population, just one of the city's vibrant immigrant groups.

CULTURAL DISTRICT   *pages 127-143*
The district contains the thriving remains
of Boston's commercial theater district as
well as the pan-Asian dining of Chinatown and the resurgent cultural activity
and street life of the South End.

BACK BAY   *pages 144-179*
Not only does the neighborhood boast a
virtual catalog of Victorian architecture
styles, it also has some of sharpest shopping and hippest dining in the city.

EMERALD NECKLACE   *pages 180-189*
The city is ringed with spectacular parks and green
spaces designed by Frederick Law Olmsted. These outdoor riches are precious heirlooms in this age of
heightened ecological awareness.

WATERFRONT   *pages 190-217*
Boston's waterfront is the city's birthplace and
birthright. With the cleanup of Boston Harbor and the
redevelopment of the old wharves and piers, Boston is
again an energetic city at the edge of a great ocean.

CAMBRIDGE   *pages 218-247*
Cambridge lies on the other side of the Charles River
from Boston, and has influenced its larger sibling from
the outset. As the intellectual capital of the Boston area, Cambridge offers great bookstores, a bustling street scene, and the life of the mind. And, oh yes, there's Harvard.

DAY TRIPS   *pages 248-261*
Three day trips from Boston amplify a
sense of the political, religious, seafaring,
and intellectual heritage of New England
are to Lexington and Concord on the
west, to Salem on the north, and to Plymouth on the south.

INTRODUCTION

Somehow the thought of another book about Boston is like the thought of another book about Shakespeare. What more is there to say? Nothing and everything.

— David McCord, *About Boston,* 1948

WE UNDERSTAND POET AND ESSAYIST MCCORD'S QUANDARY as he undertook his book in 1948, for we had to ask the same question. There are shelves of books about Boston. What could we add to the eloquent insights of historians Samuel Eliot Morison and Walter Muir Whitehill? Or, for that matter, to the charming personal appreciation of David McCord?

In other words, why Boston? Why now?

We're under no illusion of standing in the company of those distinguished writers. But, like all great cities, Boston is not fixed in time. Despite a long and usually proud history, it remains a work in progress. We count ourselves fortunate to live in the city (OK, across the river in Cambridge) during a particularly exhilarating point in its evolution.

Boston is generous to the visitor, too, revealing its quirks and charms without apology, and we hope this book will serve you as a letter of introduction to the city as it enters the new millennium. We have taken as our goal to furnish a fresh look at Boston that acknowledges and celebrates the past, discloses and elucidates the present, and sketches some of the city's dreams for its future.

We're not talking pipe dreams here. Boston has constantly remade itself by re-ordering the very soil on which it stands, its street patterns, its architecture. Walk it, enjoy it. Look down on 17th-century streets and up to the glassy pinnacles of the newest skyscrapers. Wherever your gaze alights, you will see a city on the move: cleaning its harbor, making new green space, conjuring public plazas from windswept wastelands. It is even improving the now venerable Freedom Trail.

Yes, the Freedom Trail remains a key to Boston. No other city has so many sites directly related to the American Revolution—actual places where American colonists chose to be transfigured as American citizens. Like the Puritans a century and a half earlier, there was no going back. They would be free or die trying. Liberty was Boston's birthright and remains Boston's legacy.

Much of Boston's story since the Revolution has been a tale of how the people of the city have gone on to exercise their hard-won freedom. Cities by their nature

(previous pages) The Custom House glows after sunset in downtown Boston.

are democratic places. Their scale tends to level distinctions of class and wealth; moreover, they offer opportunity for industry and commerce. Boston is no different, which is one reason why it has been a magnet for talent and ambition almost from the beginning. But Boston's status as a center of learning and culture has also drawn the best and brightest from around North America and the rest of the world.

Visitors often comment that Boston physically resembles European cities. Geography posed some of the same constraints on us that fortifications imposed on those Old World centers. And, like them, we grew dramatically during that expansive century of 1790-1890, applying the same concepts of architecture and urban design. But as European as the cityscape might appear, our people come from all over the globe. Our internationalism is incarnate in the origins and traditions of our residents; it pervades our art and culture; it finds expression in our colleges and universities, where knowledge holds little respect for boundaries on a map.

So meet as many of us as you can. Taste our food and come to our festivals. Join us in our neighborhoods; unlike so many failed metropolises, Boston does not empty out at the end of the work day. See the Freedom Trail and the museums and the historic houses, but see the living city too.

Whenever you come, keep in mind that Boston is alive and alert in all seasons. And we do have seasons. We take complaining about the weather as a right as inalienable as life, liberty — and complaining about our sports teams, public transportation and traffic. The truth is, the extremity of each season is moderated by our proximity to the ocean. In winter, snow drapes the shoulders of Edward Everett Hale's statue in the Public Garden; skaters grace the Frog Pond; and more than a few storm drains clog up and flood the streets. We shrug: That's what boots are for. In the summer we moan when the humidity rises and the temperature flirts with 90 degrees; then we head to the banks of the river or to our beautiful reclaimed waterfront, or we don Ray-Bans and settle in with a cold one at a Newbury Street cafe. We don't quibble much with spring and fall. The city bursts suddenly into bloom at the end of April and it seems there could be no better place on earth — until autumn brings brilliant foliage, a crisp slant of light, and a high blue bowl of sky.

On those spectacular days, when the last beams of sunset illuminate the city on a hill that its founders planned, we are reminded of Charles Dickens's opinion, "Boston is what I would like the whole United States to be." And we are satisfied that more than a century later, Boston remains unique.

H I S T O R Y

It was impossible to beat the notion of liberty out of the people as it was rooted in them from their childhood.
— General Thomas Gage, Commander of British forces in North America

BOSTON'S BEGINNINGS WERE INAUSPICIOUS for a city that would come to celebrate its sense of place. Little more than a knob of glacial rubble and blue clay connected to the mainland by a narrow isthmus, the peninsula at the mouth of the Charles River was largely ignored by the native peoples of the area after they arrived 10,000 years ago at the end of the last North American glaciation. Recent excavations for a new sewage treatment plant on the harbor islands uncovered ancient shell middens of the so-called Paleo-Indians, indicating seasonal clambakes but no permanent habitation. It was a nice place to fish—but who'd want to live there?

By A.D. 1630, two Algonquian peoples dominated the coast of Massachusetts Bay: the Massachusetts, from whom the region took its name, and the Wampanoags, who occupied the bay's south shore and Cape Cod. They depended upon a mixed economy, growing squash, maize, and beans, and moving seasonally

The decoration on a fire engine from 1836 is a fanciful depiction of "Trimont"—the original site of the town of Boston—in 1630. (The Bostonian Society)

The Mayflower *sails into Cape Cod harbor.*

within tribal boundaries to fish, hunt, and gather. Neither people bothered with the peninsula at the mouth of the Charles River, a hilly piece of ground they called Shawmut, translating loosely as a "place of many waters." The nearest indigenous village lay on the mainland in what is now Jamaica Plain, and their numbers had been decimated in 1616-1617 by a still-undiagnosed epidemic.

Although other European explorers had sailed past the peninsula that would become Boston, the 1614 voyage of Captain John Smith (of Jamestown, Virginia, fame) alerted the English to the area's possibilities. His *Description of New England* both named the region and provided the first detailed map of its coastline.

"New" England sounded good to dissenters within the Church of England, who sought to escape religious persecution and what they perceived as England's social decadence. A band of Separatists, called Pilgrims for their 12-year exile in Holland, planted a ragtag colony on the south shore of Massachusetts Bay at Plimoth Plantation in 1620. As their leader William Bradford later wrote, they were to be "even as stepping-stones unto others."

The "others" were a group of more moderate Puritans. In 1629 several wealthy and influential Puritans met in Cambridge, England, and decided that their kind could flourish best by leaving the mother country and establishing a godly city in the wilderness of New England. They bought into the New England Company, which that year obtained a royal charter from Charles I and changed its name to the Massachusetts Bay Company. More importantly, the charter granted the company the right to govern the territory between the Mystic and Charles rivers. (The original merchants who formed the company were blithely unaware of the realities of New England. The first seal for their Massachusetts Bay Colony, reproduced in a modern State House window, depicted a Native American in a grass skirt voicing the plea [in Latin], "Come Over and Help Us.") The Puritans elected John Winthrop as their governor. Under his stewardship, the focus of the Massachusetts Bay Colony turned immediately from land profits to prayer.

Governor Winthrop led his people to their dearly purchased promised land on March 22, 1630, on a small fleet that sailed from Southampton with between 700 and 800 passengers. These Puritans sought a New World where they could make a civilization based on the virtues they prized as outward signs of God's favor: intellectual achievement, hard work, thrift, sobriety, and unerringly moral conduct. En route, Winthrop emphasized their holy task: "For we must consider that we shall be as a City upon a Hill. The eyes of all people are upon us."

For all their conviction of divine guidance, the Puritans did not easily find a hill upon which to erect the Lord's city. They landed first at a settlement in Salem, which was too crowded to support them. Winthrop and deputy governor Thomas Dudley each led parties to explore alternative sites but disagreed on the best spot. They compromised by joining a small settlement at Charlestown, a marshy peninsula at the confluence of the Mystic and Charles rivers. Over the summer, more ships arrived, swelling the Puritan ranks to more than 1,000. Disease swept through their squalid, unsanitary encampment, and the water supply was so taxed that undrinkable salt water seeped in. Family by family began to abandon the group to launch their own villages elsewhere.

Salvation arrived from across the harbor through William Blaxton, an Anglican clergyman turned hermit who had settled on the Shawmut Peninsula in 1624 because it had good water. Blaxton had been chaplain to a failed colony, and had chosen to remain behind when others returned to England. By October 1630, Winthrop and 150 others accepted Blaxton's invitation to resettle. They erected stick-and-mud huts on Town Cove (roughly the present corner of State and Congress streets) and built a meeting house for the First Church of Boston, which doubled as the seat of government that followed Winthrop across the harbor. The Englishmen had called the peninsula "Trimountaine" for its three peaks (a name that survives in Tremont Street), but once settled, they rechristened it Boston after the Lincolnshire hometown of one of their leaders.

Winthrop was both pragmatic and optimistic. He could foresee that the stony coast would yield little to the plow. Boston would have to make its living from the sea. As he and his charges huddled on the cold shore of New England that fall, bereft of all the comforts of their middle-class English lives, Winthrop ordered his first ship. *Blessing of the Bay* was launched on July 4, 1631, the first vessel of what would become a major seaport.

■ THE EVOLUTION OF CHARACTER: 1630-1730

From the outset, the Massachusetts Bay Colony was independent and planned to stay that way. The Puritan group decreed that only members who emigrated could own stock in the company, thereby averting meddling from armchair pioneers. And, in an unprecedented step to avoid royal interference, the company took its charter (which granted almost unlimited self government) to the New World.

The Puritans were not democrats, although the seeds of democracy lay in their reformist impulses. Asked their leading minister, John Cotton, "If the people be governors, who, then, shall be governed?" Authority rested with men of God, the

A fanciful rendition of Boston's Old Town House Square in the 1650s. (Library of Congress)

"Elect," who showed by their deportment and prosperity that they were the Lord's chosen. The charter provided for a governor, a deputy governor, and a General Court of Assistants elected by all the company's property-owning church members. In practice, this meant that Winthrop ruled as governor, advised in practical matters by the other wealthy Puritans and in all matters by the clergy, in particular the Reverend John Cotton.

Nonetheless, a spirit of independent thinking took root, and forms of democratic government evolved within the first few generations on American soil. By organizing religion on the congregational model, each church became a union separate unto itself. Once each congregation was approved, it managed its own affairs and elected its own pastor, who would teach his own particular strain of Puritan theology. These Boston Congregationalists—whose starkly furnished, simple churches would eventually dot the entire New England landscape—rejected central power in favor of local rule.

The settlers reformed government as they had reformed religion. In 1634, the company established a representative elected body to assume the day-to-day chores of the Assistants. By 1644, this arrangement had evolved into an elected bicameral colonial legislature, a model for American governance distinct from the British parliamentary form. The legislature, however, was still dominated by prosperous Puritans—an "aristocracy of saints." By Winthrop's death in 1649, Boston was a solid community of 3,000 souls with a nascent international commerce and a rule of law drawn from the Old Testament and, where it was consistent with Biblical teaching, English common law.

Like persecuted true believers of every age, the Puritans were determined to safeguard the purity of their mission and guarantee the triumph of their beliefs. While non-Puritans were permitted to dwell in Boston, they were not to practice heretical beliefs openly, and free thinking among the Elect was strongly discouraged. Anyone who publicly disagreed with dogma as enunciated by the Boston clergy was expelled: Roger Williams left to found Providence Plantation and Anne Hutchinson to found Portsmouth, both in what would become Rhode Island. Quaker Mary Dyer, who repeatedly returned from exile to bear witness to her faith, was hanged.

Puritan leaders governed Boston with little interference while fellow believer Oliver Cromwell presided over England. They developed a fishery that competed with England, as well as a native industry that minimized the need for English imports. After the Restoration in 1660, Massachusetts at first refused to recognize the authority of Charles II. Royal dissatisfaction with New England's perceived lack of obeisance and its demonstrably inadequate contributions to the state treasury ultimately led to the annulment of the Massachusetts Bay Colony charter in 1684, making Massachusetts a royal colony. The first royal governor, Sir Edmund Andros, arrived in December 1686 empowered to make law, assess taxes, and dispense justice. He was to be assisted by an appointed—not elected—council. Andros opened up freedom of worship and prepared New England for an expected attack by the French and Indians in Canada.

When word reached Boston in April 1689 that William and Mary had taken the English throne, Andros and members of his council were imprisoned and a Committee of Safety composed of the Puritan oligarchy took over governance. With Increase Mather pressing their case in England, the Puritans fought to regain their original charter but were forced to compromise. The 1691 charter made Massachusetts (including Plymouth and Maine) a royal colony with a royal governor. All forms of Protestant worship were to be permitted and local voting rights were to be vested in property ownership alone. But Massachusetts alone of all the royal colonies won the right to participate in the selection of its governor's council.

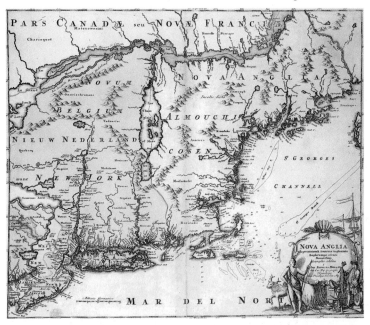

This map from 1720 shows English New England sandwiched between French Canada to the north and Dutch New York to the south and to the west.

As the official power of the clerical leadership faded at the end of the 17th century, a secular aristocracy of maritime traders quickly assumed political authority. Bostonians did not set aside their religious principles, but they successfully redirected their greatest overt energies into this world rather than the next. By the time Boston reached a population of 12,000 in the early 18th century, it had emerged as a major outpost in the British trading system. Blessed with few natural resources, Boston turned raw materials from elsewhere into finished goods and flourished on trade. Besides dominating American shipping, by mid-century Boston led the colonies in meat packing, leather finishing, hat making, hardware manufacture, coach building, and rum distillation. Boston merchants dominated the Triangle Trade, wherein African slaves were traded for West Indies sugar, which was distilled into rum and sold to England. New York and Philadelphia surpassed Boston's population in the 1760s, but by dint of its access to northern forests and teeming fishing banks, Boston continued to lead in shipbuilding and codfishing and would boast the largest merchant fleet in North America into the 1840s.

Not everything was rosy for the town (for it was still officially a town). Boston was deeply drawn into Britain's century of warfare with France, beginning in 1689 with the first of the French and Indian Wars, the last of which concluded in 1763. Boston was a staging ground for attacks on French Canada, a source of soldiers to fight the Indians, and a source of badly needed tax revenue. Massachusetts in general and Boston in particular bore the brunt of this English-French struggle for North American hegemony. But Boston's burden had strategic implications; by the time of the American Revolution, New England had a generation of soldiers who were familiar with British military practices—and knew the countryside far better than any Redcoat.

■ THE TAXPAYERS' REVOLT: 1730-1783

Much of Boston's sense of itself and its place in American history is drawn from the tumultuous events leading up to independence. Following the triumph over the French in 1763, Britain pursued a plan of imperial reorganization that soon roused a storm of protest in the colonies. In the next decade what began as a quarrel over taxes and trade regulation became a constitutional crisis: Who was to rule within the colonies—the British Parliament or the colonial assemblies? Boston emerged as center of opposition to Parliament's claims. Protests centered on the Old State House (which housed the colonial government), Faneuil Hall (where

THE BOSTONIANS PAYING THE EXCISE-MAN OR TARRING & FEATHERING

Copied on stone by D.C Johnston from a print published in London 1774 ___ Lith of Pendleton Boston 1830

In this English propaganda poster, American Rebels tar and feather the hapless Tax Man beneath the Liberty Tree as their fellows dump tea over the side of an English merchant ship. (Library of Congress)

(above) British troops open fire on a civilian mob in Paul Revere's classic illustration of the Boston Massacre. (Massachusetts Historical Society)

(right) Colonists dressed as Indians throw English tea overboard in the Boston Tea Party.

Boston Town Meeting gathered), and the Old South Church (which could accommodate the largest crowds). A now-familiar cast of characters arose as the chief leaders in the politics of protest: John Hancock, the city's richest merchant; Samuel Adams, its master politician; Joseph Warren, one of Boston's foremost doctors; and Paul Revere, a silversmith and jack-of-all-trades.

The quarrel soon turned violent. On March 5, 1770, a small squad of British soldiers in front of the State House was surrounded by a hostile crowd of colonials who began pelting the detachment with snowballs laden with rock and ice. The intimidated soldiers fired into the mob, killing five civilians and wounding others. Revere's engraving, "The Boston Massacre," and Joseph Warren's commemorative orations in the Old South Church kept the episode alive in patriot propaganda. After the Boston Tea Party of December 16, 1773, when a valuable consignment of British tea was dumped by Bostonians into the harbor to protest a tax on tea, the political quarrel was progressively transformed into a military conflict. Samuel Adams, writing to patriots in New York and Philadelphia, was sure that a break with England was inevitable: "The Dye is cast: The People have passed the River and cutt away the Bridge."

Britain angrily responded to the Tea Party by closing Boston's port to trade and by cutting back the power of both the Massachusetts Assembly and of Boston's town government. General Thomas Gage, commander of British forces in North America, was made governor of the colony. In response the Patriots withdrew

COLONIAL PORTRAIT GALLERY

John Winthrop
1588 - 1649

This London lawyer sailed on the *Arbella* with a group of Puritans to Massachusetts, where he became the first governor of the Massachusetts Bay Colony, as well as an enforcer of the Puritans' stringent moral code.

Samuel Adams
1722 - 1803

Born in the Massachusetts colony, tax collector Adams became an agitator in the Boston Tea Party. He later served twice as a delegate to the Continental Congress in Philadelphia, where he signed the Declaration of Independence.

John Hancock
1737 - 1793

As President of the First Continental Congress, Hancock oversaw the forming of a new government and army, as well as the writing of the Declaration of Independence, of which he became its most famous signator.

Paul Revere
1735 - 1818

A silversmith of French Huguenot heritage, Revere was a devoted patriot who became famous for his midnight ride to Lexington to warn Hancock, Adams, and other colonists of the Redcoats' imminent arrival.

from colonial government and established an illegal Provincial Congress, which met in various towns outside of Boston and took over the affairs of the colony under the direction of a Committee of Public Safety. A select group from the young and very able of the colony's militia was organized to defend the colony— the Minute Men, so called because they could be ready at a minute's notice.

The road to war was swift. The Crown declared Massachusetts in a state of rebellion and tightened its economic stranglehold by closing all New England ports and banning New England fishermen from the Grand Banks. Parliament bolstered the Boston garrison by 10,000 more troops. In April 1775, General Gage learned that Samuel Adams and John Hancock were in Lexington for a meeting and sent a detachment of 700 troops to arrest them and to seize a store of weapons and ammunition hidden in Concord.

After sunset on April 18, 1775, boats began ferrying British soldiers across the Charles River to Charlestown, where they would begin their march to Lexington. Dr. Joseph Warren, head of the Committee of Safety, received word and dispatched Paul Revere and William Dawes to alert the countryside and warn Adams and Hancock of the British plan. Meantime, Revere's friend Robert Newman placed lanterns in the steeple of Christ Church to signal the Redcoats' movements: one if they were marching to Boston Neck, two if they were crossing the Charles River to Cambridge (the "one if by land, two if by sea" recounted by Longfellow). When the British marched into Lexington near dawn, they were met by 77 Minute Men who had been up all night bolstering their courage at the tavern. There was a brief exchange of fire in which 10 Americans were killed, and the Redcoats marched on to Concord to make a house-to-house search for weapons. During the search, 400 colonial militiamen attacked a British unit of 90 soldiers at Concord Bridge, routing them in a brief skirmish ("the shot heard 'round the world"). A running battle back to Boston ensued, with militiamen sniping at the fleeing troops, aiming principally at officers; 73 British soldiers were killed, 200 wounded. (See "Patriots' Day" page 306.)

Within days 16,000 armed New England colonists descended on Boston, penning up the British on the peninsula. Gage sat tight and waited for reinforcements, which arrived in May under General William Howe. The Second Continental Congress met in Philadelphia, named the colonial forces the Continental Army, and placed them under the command of General George Washington, who was sent to Cambridge to take command.

Howe planned to break out of Boston by taking a series of heights around the city, beginning with Bunker Hill in Charlestown. The Committee of Safety learned of the plan and quickly had 1,200 men entrenched at Breed's Hill, which lies closer to the harbor and was often mistaken for Bunker Hill on Colonial-era maps. On the afternoon of June 17, Howe's forces struck. Holding fire until they could "see the whites of their eyes," the Americans mowed down the Redcoats. A second assault under cover of bombardment from Copp's Hill in the North End also failed. Howe called in 400 marines from Boston and made a third assault on the Americans, now almost out of ammunition, and took their position. The mis-named Battle of Bunker Hill was a Pyrrhic victory: British casualties were high, and the Americans took heart at being able to meet the British successfully in pitched battle.

Washington took over the Continental Army in Cambridge on July 2, but the siege dragged through the winter—until Washington implemented a plan to drive the British from Boston without engaging in bloody battle. Using British cannons captured at Fort Ticonderoga, he fortified Dorchester Heights on the South Boston peninsula under cover of bombardment of Boston from Somerville, East Cambridge, and Roxbury. When dawn broke on March 5, 1776, General Howe found his fleet of warships literally under the gun and accepted Washington's offer of peaceful retreat. On the morning of March 17, Howe boarded his soldiers on the fleet and set sail to Halifax. The date (which conveniently coincides with the most Irish of Boston's holidays) is celebrated by many in Boston as Evacuation Day.

(left) The Bunker Hill Monument commemorates an event which actually took place on nearby Breed's Hill. (Robert Holmes) The Massachusetts State Pine Tree Penny was designed and engraved by Paul Revere. Although it never went into circulation due to a copper shortage, the coin might well be considered America's first penny. (Massachusetts Historical Society)

Losing Boston was the first major setback to Britain's efforts to subjugate its rebellious colonies. But the city was saved only in a manner of speaking. The occupying army had ripped up homes and public buildings, including Old South Church, for firewood, and American bombardment had destroyed much of what the occupiers had not. The wharves were in ruins, the shipyards rotting, the streets clogged with rubble. The battlefronts soon shifted south, but Boston continued to provide soldiers and leaders to the war effort and the Continental government. (John Adams, Samuel Adams, and John Hancock played large roles in the events leading up to the Declaration of Independence.) And Boston's sailors did what they knew best: cut off from trade, the merchants turned privateers, mounting guns and filling their cargo holds with ammunition to harass British shipping. By the end of the Revolution, the prewar population of about 20,000 had fallen to 6,000.

■ ATHENS OF AMERICA: 1783-1860

Although much of the property of Boston lay in a shambles at the end of the Revolution, many property owners survived the passage from British subject to American voter with their power intact, even amplified. It was no coincidence that merchant and revolutionary John Hancock served as governor from 1788 to 1793.

Boston's merchants refitted their privateers for trade. With the British Empire market closed to them, Boston joined other Massachusetts ports to dominate the China trade. The same companies also began to evade Britain's Atlantic fleet to trade in the Baltic and the Mediterranean, and they rounded the Cape of Good Hope en route to the Indian subcontinent and the isles of the South Pacific. Boston and Charlestown shipyards contributed war vessels to the cause of this new commerce, in 1797 launching the USS *Constitution,* a frigate that earned her sobriquet "Old Ironsides" in 1803 battling the Barbary pirates off Tripoli.

The "codfish aristocracy" also remade the face of the city as no one had since the first settlers. Harrison Gray Otis and James Mason formed the Mount Vernon Proprietors and tore down the peaks of Beacon Hill to raise on its flanks domestic monuments to the new prosperity. Among their group was architect Charles Bulfinch, whose graceful adaptation of English country style to the new American city defined one of the most elegant eras of American architecture. As the real estate speculators developed Beacon Hill, they began to fill the marshy riverbanks at its foot to create even more land. Boston grew fatter still with the annexation of

Dorchester in 1804 and the filling of mudbanks to swell the Neck that joined Shawmut to the mainland, thereby creating much of South Boston.

Boston's reputation for patriotism was badly damaged during the War of 1812. Devoted to the Federalist party and hostile to the Jeffersonian Republicans, Bostonians opposed the war, which they referred to disdainfully as "Mr. Madison's War." Only the political skills of Harrison Gray Otis, builder of Beacon Hill, at a Federalist convention at Hartford in 1814 averted a New England threat of secession from the Union. When Madison brought his war to a satisfactory conclusion soon thereafter, Federalist Boston was embarrassed by its opposition to the war. But these descendants of the Puritans were a tough and resilient people and under the political leadership of Daniel Webster, Boston reestablished its reputation for devotion to the Union.

The War of 1812 changed Boston's economic base. Shut out of the Atlantic shipping lanes, Boston merchants invested their money in the new cotton mills being built along the fall line of New England rivers. Boston money built mills at Waltham up the Charles from Cambridge. In 1825, businessmen from Boston founded the textile town of Lowell, named after Francis Cabot Lowell, and two decades later, the town of Lawrence, named after Abbot Lawrence. By 1830 Boston's representatives in Washington were less interested in fostering overseas trade than in erecting tariff protection for textiles, a major source of New England wealth for the next century.

Daniel Webster

FLAT TOPS AND SHIFTING SHORES:
A TOPOGRAPHICAL HISTORY OF BOSTON

We say the cows laid out Boston. Well, there are worse surveyors.

— Ralph Waldo Emerson, "Wealth" in *Conduct of Life*

When the Puritans made their stand on the Shawmut peninsula, they chose a property that was the ultimate fixer-upper. After wintering over (most of them in tents and wigwams) on the fields around Town Cove, they set about renovating their scrappy 783 acres by cutting down every glacial hummock in sight to fill the marshy shores. Their peninsula floated in Massachusetts Bay like a bulbous buoy, tethered to the mainland by the slimmest of lines, an isthmus known as the Neck. After three and a half centuries of fussing and filling, the Neck has grown so thick that the seaward side of Shawmut is little more than a bulge on the coastline. Even after absorbing most of the surrounding towns, Boston remains only 46 square miles—smaller than the Denver airport. So we continue reinventing our topography, indulging what Walter Muir Whitehill, long-time director of the Boston Athenaeum, termed Boston's "perennial occupation of making room for itself."

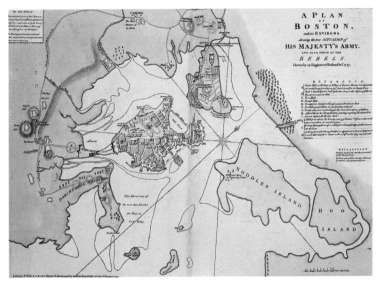

This map from the Revolutionary War illustrates Boston's pre-landfill dimensions, with the Shawmut Peninsula connected to the mainland by a thin thread of land.

The Taking Down of Beacon Hill, *by John Bufford, 1857-58.*
(Massachusetts Historical Society)

A 1634 tract designed to lure new settlers introduced Realtor-speak to the colony, making a fine silk purse from Winthrop's sow's ear of a site. Noted *New England Prospects,* "being a necke and bare of wood," Boston was therefore free from "the three great annoyances of Woolves, Rattle-snakes and Musketoes."

By 1645, the settlers had at least partially filled every marsh on the peninsula and enclosed a cove to create the 50-acre Mill Pond near the present North Station. By the 1660s, the town fathers had granted almost anyone who asked the right to build a wharf out from his shoreline house. The records are thick with documents granting permission to one captain or another "to wharfe before his owne ground adjoyninge to his dwelling house." In short order, mud deposited around the pilings (sometimes helped by a little judicious dumping of rubble) and Boston's shoreline ballooned. Once a wharf became dry land, another wharf went out into deeper water, inexorably swelling the peninsula out into the bay.

Still, much of the original shape of Shawmut survived through the American Revolution. The tidal mouth of the Charles River lapped at Mount Whoredom (rechristened Mount Vernon) and the Boston Common in 1775 when British soldiers boarded boats to be ferried to Charlestown for their fateful march to Lexington. State Street ran little more than a hundred yards downhill from the Old State House before it encountered the shore and beginnings of Long Wharf—"the great street running to the sea." Most of what is now Atlantic Avenue was part of the Atlantic Ocean. At high tide, Back Bay lived up to its name.

Boston did not await the invention of the steam shovel or the bulldozer to begin smoothing its interior irregularities. In the mid-1790s, the Mount Vernon Proprietors whacked fifty feet from the top of Mount Vernon to build up the banks of the Charles at the foot of this western peak of the Trimountaine, creating the Flats section of Beacon Hill. Carts of dirt slid down an inclined plane to fill the murky banks below. Harrison Gray Otis, one of the group's two leaders, wrote that the procedure "excited as much attention as Bonaparte's road over the Alps." It took a dozen years to lop sixty feet off Sentry Hill (behind the present State House) to fill the Mill Pond created by the first settlers. During the same period, part of Copp's Hill was taken down to create new land on the shores of the North End. And between 1804 and 1807, abutting landowners individually filled in the mudflats separating Dorchester Neck from Shawmut Peninsula, creating a large portion of modern South Boston.

As Whitehill observed, it was as if the real estate speculators of the 19th century took their text from Genesis 1.9: "Let the waters under the heaven be gathered together unto one place, and let the dry land appear: and it was so." Developers joined the city and state governments to turn tidal flats into house lots, filling up the bays on either side of the Neck. In all, they augmented the original 783 acres of Boston with another 450 acres of residential land.

The South End fill project began in 1850, concluding abruptly when the Panic of 1873 dumped many of the new house lots into bank hands. Back Bay fill began in 1859 with gravel brought by rail from Needham and progressed a block or two per decade well into the 1880s. For the first 13 years, workers moved at the astonishing pace of two house lots per day, as gravel-laden trains arrived every 45 minutes, thanks to the pioneering use of steam shovels at the Needham pits.

The widening of the Neck created three major avenues to augment the single road to Roxbury, which by mid-century was traversed by horse-drawn street cars. The electrification of the streetcar system in the 1880s suddenly expanded the city's practical limits. By this time, Boston's modern lines were drawn. No longer a peninsula, it annexed most adjoining towns—which, except for Brookline, were happy to link up with Boston's superior water and sewer systems. Further alterations of the face of Boston involved transportation. Although Boston installed the first American subway in 1898, the greatest changes lay in the conversion of streets to highways.

It's easy to tell new Boston from old by the straightness of the streets. Emerson to the contrary, cows did not lay out the original paths, but meandering humans on foot did. Straight streets virtually all date from after the Revolution as part of planned development. Boston grew to its modern physical limits before the automobile, so entire neighborhoods were destroyed to make room for highways. Frederick Law Olmsted's beautiful parkways were among the first roads appropriated for auto traffic, and the creation of Storrow Drive in the late 1930s walled the elegant Back Bay off from riverbank access. For the first time in history, East Boston was linked to the rest of the city via a tunnel in 1934 and the city's airport was constructed there on the former mudflats of the former Noddle Island.

Few projects, however, so altered the city as the construction of the Central Artery, the so-called "Highway in the Sky" when it opened in 1959. To build the interchange with Storrow Drive, the city demolished part of the West End, taking the rest of it in the late 1950s for urban renewal. By routing the Central Artery between the wharves and the financial district, Boston turned its back on the waterfront. Ironically, the six-lane highway was almost immediately obsolete—burdened with twice the number of vehicles for which it was designed.

Only 30 years later, Boston began the tedious process of dismantling the Central Artery and constructing a third tunnel to East Boston (a second one opened in 1961). Cost estimates change almost daily, but should come in somewhere around $14 billion—the gross national product of a fairly flush Third World country and the most expensive public highway project in the history of the United States. Digging the tunnel provided clay to cap the old landfill on Spectacle Island to create a 105-acre park. But the change Bostonians anticipate most eagerly is the final destruction of the rusting green supports of the old highway—slated for sometime before 2010. The project will move the present daily aboveground flow of 280,000 vehicles into underground tunnels, reopen 27 acres of green space, and reunite the business district with the waterfront.

By the time Boston adopted the city form of government in 1822, it was among the richest places in the young nation. About this time Boston invented the family trust fund, which protected family wealth from spendthrift scions. The result was to ensconce a class of Boston families whose names still remain prominent in Boston life: Cabot, Lodge, Lowell, Forbes, Cunningham, Appleton, Bacon, Russell, Coolidge, Parkman, Shaw, Codman, Boylston, Hunnewell. . . . These families, whom Dr. Oliver Wendell Holmes would dub the Boston Brahmins, intermarried in a complexity beyond unraveling. The city had become, as a later ditty put it, "good old Boston, / The home of the bean and the cod, / Where the Cabots talk only to the Lowells, / And the Lowells talk only to God."

As heirs to the Puritan concern for communal life, these new aristocrats turned portions of their economic resources to philanthropy. In the early 19th century they founded the Massachusetts General Hospital, now one of the world's foremost, and the Perkins School for the Blind, now located in Newton, west of Boston. The Boston Athenaeum, a private subscription library, also sprang up as

The elite of Boston step out for an evening of waltzing at the Copley Plaza Hotel.

A view of Faneuil Hall Marketplace in 1827. (The Bostonian Society)

the focus of the city's cultural life. Citing the interest of the city's poorer citizens, Boston's second mayor, Josiah Quincy, built a public market adjacent to Faneuil Hall and organized the city's first sanitary improvements.

Feeding into this spirit of civic humanitarian concern was a religious renewal as Unitarian preachers took over pulpit after pulpit in the old Congregational churches. Emphasizing the perfectability of man, Unitarianism encouraged wide-ranging social reforms. William Ellery Channing, the creed's foremost preacher in Boston, founded the Massachusetts Peace Society, dedicated to abolishing war. William Lloyd Garrison founded his newspaper, *The Liberator,* dedicated to abolishing slavery. Horace Mann agitated to improve public education and Dorothea Dix to improve conditions in prisons and mental asylums. Margaret Fuller launched the women's rights movement to the consternation of many men and the ridicule of the public press. "We are all a little wild here," wrote Ralph Waldo Emerson in 1840 to fellow philosopher Thomas Carlyle, "with numerous projects of social reform."

Emerson was the central figure in what critic Van Wyck Brooks called "the flowering of New England": the outburst of literary creativity that marked New

The just man shall be in eternal remembrance

Labored over Forty Years for the cause of Freedom.

William Lloyd Garrison

England at midcentury and that made Boston the nation's cultural capital for most of the half-century that followed. In one way or another, most of the major figures were associated with Boston: fiction writers Nathaniel Hawthorne, Louisa May Alcott and Herman Melville; poets Henry Wadsworth Longfellow and James Russell Lowell; essayists Emerson and Henry David Thoreau; and historians, including Francis Parkman. The publishing house Ticknor & Fields and the journal *The Atlantic Monthly* (established to be "free without being fanatical") spread Boston literature and thought across the English-speaking world. In 1852, the city established the first urban free public library on Boylston Street.

By midcentury Boston was in the grip of an American renaissance not only in thought and deed, but in design. The discovery of gold in California created the need to sail quickly from coast to coast around Cape Horn. The answer was the clipper, first built in New York in 1845, then in Boston in 1850. The largest and swiftest came from the East Boston boatyards of Donald McKay, whose ships could run 400 miles a day. They were the apogee of artful Yankee ingenuity. As historian Samuel Eliot Morison noted in his *Maritime History of Massachusetts,* "Never, in these United States, has the brain of man conceived, nor the hand of man fashioned, so perfect a thing as the clipper ship. In her, the long-suppressed artistic impulse of a practical, hard-worked race burst into flower."

But the clipper's narrow hold was suited only to premium cargoes, and she was a hard ship to handle—easily broken by conspiracy of wind and reef. Wrote Morison, "For a few brief moments of time they flashed their splendor around the world, then disappeared with the sudden completeness of the wild pigeon." The Panic of 1857 virtually closed down the clipper trade, and when the Civil War ended, the sturdier and larger Downeasters from Maine had supplanted the Boston clipper for speedy ocean runs. Moreover, American commerce became more intrastate as the new railroads replaced ships as primary carriers.

New York and Philadelphia were eclipsing Boston's significance as a national mercantile center, but prosperous Bostonians ignored their relative decline as the city became the economic and trade center of New England. Boston's cultural imperialism, which proclaimed it to be the Athens of America, was largely accepted throughout the nation. The confluence of money and talent in mid-19th-century Boston was expedited by the presence of Harvard College, founded by the Puritans in 1636 to educate ministers; it emerged as one of the world's great universities

(above) Shipbuilding in the dry docks of East Boston during peak of the clipper ship days.
(following pages) Boston Harbor *by Fitz Hugh Lane, ca. 1855-58. (Museum of Fine Arts)*

BOSTONIAN ENTHUSIASM

*B*ut practically, and in general, the people of Boston believed in the infinite capacity of human nature, and they knew "salvation's free," and "free for you and me."

As a direct result of this belief, and of the cosmopolitan habit which comes to people who send their ships all over the world, the leaders of this little community attempted everything on a generous scale. If they made a school for the blind, they made it for all the blind people in Massachusetts. They expected to succeed. They always had succeeded. Why should they not succeed? If, then, they opened a "House of Reformation," they really supposed that they should reform the boys and girls who were sent to it. Observe that here was a man who had bought skins in Nootka Sound and sold them in China, and brought home silks and teas where he carried away tin pans and jackknives. There was a man who had fastened his schooner to an iceberg off Labrador, and had sold the ice he cut in Calcutta or Havana. Now, that sort of men look at life in its possibilities with a different habit from that of the man who reads in the newspaper that stocks have fallen, who buys them promptly, and sells them the next week because the newspaper tells him that they have risen.

With this sense that all things are possible to him who believes, the little town became the headquarters for New England, and in a measure for the country, of every sort of enthusiasm, not to say of every sort of fanaticism.

—Edward Everett Hale, *James Russell Lowell and his Friends,* 1899

during the presidency of Charles William Eliot (1869-1909). Other important educational institutions sprouted like seed after a spring rain: Boston University in 1839, Tufts College in 1852, Massachusetts Institute of Technology in 1861, the New England Conservatory of Music in 1867—in all, more than 40 colleges and universities in or around Boston, which to this day possesses the largest concentration of higher education institutions in the United States.

Boston's population expanded as its wealth grew. The provincial town of 24,000 in 1800 had grown to a city of 61,000 thirty years later; by 1850, the population had soared to nearly 137,000.

■ BOSTON WITH A BROGUE

Those rising numbers reflected a dramatic shift in Boston demographics. Increasingly, the Athenian Yankees found themselves awash in a Hibernian sea. A trickle of Irish immigrants in the early 1800s turned to a steady flow in the 1830s, then a deluge when the Irish potato blight of 1845-52 struck. The resulting famine killed more than a million and led to the emigration of a million or more. Boston's harborside wards soon filled with impoverished Irish newcomers. In 1847 alone, 37,000 Irish entered Boston.

Nativist opposition to the Irish had led to the burning down of a Roman Catholic convent in Charlestown in 1834, and the coming of the famine Irish escalated nativism. The secretive American Party—an anti-immigrant and anti-Catholic national political organization—took root. (It was popularly termed the Know Nothing Party because its members, when questioned about anti-immigrant activities, would reply, "I know nothing.") The party's open agenda was to check the flow of immigration and the political influence of immigrants. Although it briefly controlled Massachusetts politics, the American Party soon faded as the urgent issues that led to the Civil War took over public attention.

Boston and its satellite manufacturing cities profited from the war. So did the Irish. Their service in the war, particularly as infantrymen in the Massachusetts Ninth regiment—the Irish regiment organized by Colonel Thomas Cass—won the admiration of former critics. Boston's noble side was also expressed by the 54th Massachusetts regiment, the first African-American regiment organized by any state, led by youthful Brahmin Colonel Robert Gould Shaw. With the easing of anti-Catholic hostility, Harvard in 1861 conferred an honorary degree upon the Catholic leader, Bishop John B. Fitzpatrick; two years later the Jesuits founded Boston College.

The great labors of building post–Civil War Boston meant that the old "No Irish Need Apply" signs had to come down. Irish workers filled in the flats of the Back Bay and laid out the streets, block by block, up from the Public Garden to Massachusetts Avenue. Boston was booming, annexing Roxbury in 1867 and Dorchester two years later. In short order, Charlestown and West Roxbury (which included both Jamaica Plain and Roslindale) joined Boston. In 1912, Hyde Park was annexed. Brookline and other towns resisted annexation. As Boston expanded to take nearby communities into its fold, Irish contractors built the streets, sewers, and water systems—vaulting themselves into the middle class in the process.

Meanwhile new immigrants from southern and eastern Europe entered the city. Italians and Eastern European Jews took over the North End from the Irish. The Italians settled along Hanover Street, while Salem Street and Phillips on the North Slope of Beacon Hill became the Jewish community. The North End Irish moved across the Charles River bridge to join the long-established Irish community in Charlestown; others moved to swell the already large Irish population in South Boston. Upwardly mobile Irish were drawn to Dorchester. By the century's end Boston's population had risen to 670,000, with the Irish outnumbering any other immigrant group.

In *The Last Hurrah,* Edwin O'Connor's protagonist sums up the Yankee culture shock:

> A hundred years ago the loyal sons and daughters of the first white inhabitants went to bed one lovely evening, and by the time they woke up and rubbed their eyes, the charming old city was swollen to three times its size. The savages had arrived. Not the Indians; far worse. It was the Irish. They had arrived and they wanted in. Even worse than that, they got in.

The Irish have arrived.

And they got in rather quickly. In less than three decades from Know Nothing days, the Irish had established an alliance with old-line Yankees in the Democratic party and had elevated a number of their kind to positions of influence and respect. Irish-born Hugh O'Brien served four terms as mayor, beginning in 1885. Patrick Collins served in the Congress and succeeded Webster as the city's favorite orator.

The Yankees were hardly in eclipse. Many fled the city to the suburbs, but many more congregated in the elegant new environs of Back Bay where they constructed institutions designed to champion arts and culture. The Museum of Fine Arts was founded, given a grand Back Bay home, and then, later, its monumental site in the Fenway. Henry Lee Higginson founded the Boston Symphony. The great monument of H. H. Richardson's Trinity Church on Copley Square was matched, a generation later, by Charles Follen McKim's palace of the people, the Boston Public Library. Isabella Stewart Gardner, something of a bellwether of taste, turned to collecting art (and sometimes artists) and built her own palace in the Fenway to display her acquisitions.

John Singer Sargent's portrait of Isabella Stewart Gardner was considered scandalously revealing by Boston bluebloods. (Isabella Stewart Gardner Museum)

■ NEIGHBORHOOD REIGN

When Patrick Collins died while mayor in 1905, a new generation of Irish politicians came forward. Born in Boston, they broke with the Irish-Yankee alliance to win office on the power of the Irish vote. John F. Fitzgerald, grandfather of John F. Kennedy, succeeded Collins as the first of the new breed. He was soon pushed aside by James Michael Curley, who was elected mayor in 1914 and would dominate city politics for the following 30 years.

Brilliant, arrogant, and self-taught, Curley took delight in tweaking Brahmin Boston and lambasting his perceived enemies. What Boston needed, he said, was "men and the mothers of men, not gabbing spinsters and dog-raising matrons in federation assembled." He also called the old "ward heelers"—that is, those in the local political machine who could force their voting districts to heel, or obey—a "collection of chowderheads," and stripped them of their power so he could control the patronage system himself. Curley also succeeded in delivering benefits to his immigrant constituents, most of them on the outer neighborhoods of the city. He enlarged City Hospital, built recreational sites such as the L Street Baths in South Boston, paved streets, widened roads, and extended the subway system. His highway project to connect the western suburbs with the business district, Storrow Drive, cut Yankee Back Bay off from the pleasures of the Charles River.

Mayor James M. Curley (second from left) ascends the steps of the State House with an imposing-looking entourage. (Underwood Photo Archives)

Edward Kennedy, scion of Massachusetts' most famous political family.

Curley wasn't always mayor—the state legislature made it impossible for him to succeed himself, so over the years he also served in the U.S. Congress and did one term as governor of Massachusetts. But whoever sat in the mayor's chair did so under Curley's shadow. So popular was Curley that he won his final election in 1945 while under indictment from a Federal grand jury for mail fraud. Convicted and jailed, he returned triumphantly to run the city when Harry Truman commuted his sentence.

Curley had presided over a city in decline. The port of Boston was stagnating. From the 1920s onward, the textile industry, so important to Boston's health, was migrating to the South in pursuit of cheap labor. The shoe and leather industry would soon migrate westward. More of the middle- and upper-class Yankees decamped from the city to remote suburbs. Boston's role as cultural arbiter to the nation had long since been ceded to New York, with its vast publishing industry. The Great Depression accelerated the processes of decay. The census of 1940 recorded, for the first time since the Revolutionary War, a population decline.

The sideshow of Curley's cult of personality diverted attention from the institutionalization of Irish-American political power. Through the Democratic ranks came a new breed of national politicians. They included men like John McCormack and Thomas P. "Tip" O'Neill, who would both serve as Speaker of the House, and the line of descendants of "Honey Fitz" on one side and former ambassador/ financier Joseph Kennedy on the other: John, Robert, and Edward Kennedy.

HISTORY

■ BOSTON REBUILT: 1950-2010

The mid-19th-century Brahmins so secure in their optimistic prosperity would have been shocked to see the Hub in 1945 described by the *Boston Globe* as "a hopeless backwater, a tumbled-down has-been among cities." But like many American cities at the end of World War II, Boston was losing its population and jobs to the suburbs. In 1949, John Hynes (who had served as temporary mayor during Curley's incarceration) thrashed Curley in a political upset. "Whispering Johnny" Hynes was an effective, business-like mayor who managed to engage the Yankee financiers on State Street while quietly winning the middle class and blue-collar base of Curley's traditional support. Hynes's agenda was to rebuild Boston by mustering both the political support of the ethnic neighborhoods and the trust of the Yankee financiers on State Street. In 1957, he established the Boston Redevelopment Authority (BRA) as the agent of change.

The BRA's second large project, "redevelopment" of the West End, was a political and social disaster: the wholesale destruction of an old, immigrant neighborhood to build isolated islands of office buildings, parking garages, and upscale housing. In 1960 Hynes's successor, John Collins, brought in ace urban planner Edward Logue to oversee further redevelopment. Logue stayed seven years, during which Government Center replaced seedy Scollay Square and the Prudential Center replaced the rail yards of Back Bay. The successful public projects galvanized the private development community as well, and the 1960s and '70s saw the Christian Science Center rise in Back Bay, Tufts Medical Center expand in Chinatown, and the beginning of a wave of skyscrapers in the Financial District. Under Collins and his successor, Kevin White, redevelopment ultimately lifted the face of 11 percent of Boston, including the old Quincy Market district in a project that became the prototype of similar historic preservation/restoration projects throughout the country.

At the same time, the technical and scientific institutions of Boston higher education were reinventing an economic base for the region: computing. The founding of Wang Laboratories and Digital Equipment Corporation along the circumferential highways helped jumpstart Boston's economy. The intellectual model for Boston became Archimedes instead of Pericles, and after a protracted wait-and-see stance, the money managers hopped on board the high-tech express.

The years running up to the American Bicentennial gave Boston the chance to showcase its economic and physical transformation. With the Freedom Trail and the shining new Faneuil Hall Marketplace, Boston became one of the most popular tourist destinations in the United States. But the buoyant bubble was soon burst by nightly news coverage of explosive racial politics that focused, ironically enough, on two of the city's most prized Revolutionary sites: Bunker Hill in Charlestown and Dorchester Heights. Boston, like most Northern cities, had assumed that the 1954 Supreme Court decision outlawing school segregation applied principally in the South. But Judge W. Arthur Garrity, Jr., found that "unconstitutional segregation" existed in the Boston school system and ordered a busing plan to bring about integration.

Integration by busing flowed smoothly in most of Boston in September 1975, but the largely Irish neighborhoods isolated on the peninsulas of South Boston and Charlestown erupted in protest at the loss of local autonomy. Scenes of white protesters attacking school buses glowed from the nation's television screens. Among the more moderate opponents of "forced busing" was a young South Boston politician and former professional athlete, Raymond Flynn.

Ironically, Flynn and his African-American opponent in the 1983 mayoral election, Melvin King, helped heal the racial rift in the city during their campaign. Once elected (with nearly the entire white vote) Flynn made an effort to open the doors of city government to all Bostonians.

The booming economy of the 1980s saw the rise of a virtual battalion of skyscrapers in the Financial District, wholesale conversions of apartment buildings into condominiums, and a stanching of the outward flow of professionals to the suburbs. In a reversal of recent tradition, an ethnically mixed middle class began to cast its lot with urban life.

Under Thomas Menino, the first non-Irish mayor in four generations, Boston has re-envisioned its public areas as places to celebrate the city. With the cleanup of Boston Harbor completed, parks and other waterfront embellishments are beginning to surround the downtown wharves. Southwest Corridor Park provides a green link to close the circle of Frederick Law Olmsted's Emerald Necklace, and Olmsted's Charles River Playground is the keystone of a new park that connects the Charles River embankments to the Harbor. Even City Hall Plaza is under scrutiny for redevelopment. Most notable of all, the Central Artery is under reconstruction, with the elevated highway slated to fall by 2010. In its place will stand yet another broad, green park that will at last reunite downtown Boston with its deepest and most enduring roots, the waterfront and vital harbor.

HISTORY TIMELINE

1630   Puritans, led by Governor John Winthrop, arrive in Massachusetts and settle Boston as their "City on a Hill."

1632   First law against smoking in public established.

1635   Boston Latin School, America's first public school, opens.

1636   Harvard College is founded in Cambridge as the "seminary in Newtowne." In 1638, John Harvard's library and half his fortune are willed to the school and it is renamed in his honor.

1656   First New World environmental law passed, prohibiting butchers from dumping "beast entrails" into Boston Harbor.

1680   "Paul Revere" house built; purchased a year later by merchant Robert Howard.

1686   As Massachusetts Bay Colony's charter is revoked, Sir Edmund Andros arrives in Boston as the first Royal Governor of New England.

       First commercial bank in the colonies opens in Boston.

1690   America's first newspaper is published in Boston (and banned).

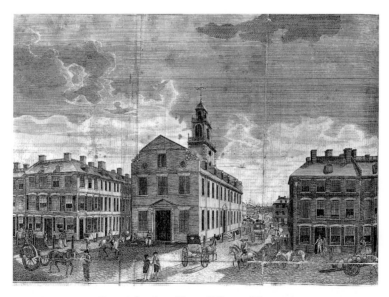

Boston's first State House. (Library of Congress)

(opposite) The Minute Man statue on Lexington's battle green was sculpted by Daniel Chester French, who also sculpted the seated Lincoln at Washington's Lincoln Memorial. (Robert Holmes)

1711   The State House (now known as the Old State House) is built.

1716   Boston Light, oldest lighthouse in United States, is erected in Boston Harbor.

1765   Stamp Act is imposed; riots occur in Boston and other cities. Sons of Liberty form to defend colonists' rights.

       America's first chocolate factory is built in Dorchester.

1767   Townshend Acts lead to colonial boycott of British goods.

1768   British troops land in Boston to maintain order.

1770   Nervous soldiers on patrol fire into crowd throwing snowballs; five colonists are killed, several wounded in Boston Massacre.

1773   Patriots dressed as Indians dump three shiploads of tea into harbor to protest tax; event becomes known as Boston Tea Party.

1774   Patriots form the Minute Men.

1775   Battles of Lexington and Concord begin the Revolution. Colonists lose Battle of Bunker Hill but keep British penned up on Shawmut Peninsula. George Washington arrives at Cambridge to take command of the Continental Army.

1776   Boston evacuated by British.

1790   *Columbia,* the first American ship to circumnavigate the globe, begins journey from Boston.

1790s Beacon Hill development begins.

1795   Paul Revere organizes America's first "labor union."

1808   The Exchange Coffee House, America's first hotel, opens.

1822   Boston incorporates as a city.

1830s Horace Mann establishes public school system.

1842   Charles Dickens visits Boston, cites it as his favorite American city.

1845   Irish potato famine sends flood of refugees to Boston.

1850   South End fill project begins.

1851   Donald McKay's China clipper, the *Flying Cloud,* makes record run from Boston to San Francisco.

1852   Boston Public Library is founded; its motto is "Free to All."

1857   Back Bay fill begins.

1861	Elizabeth Peabody founds first kindergarten in the United States.
1865	Massachusetts Institute of Technology opens.
1876	Alexander Graham Bell invents the telephone.
1879	Mary Baker Eddy charters Church of Christ, Scientist.
1882	John L. Sullivan becomes first American world heavyweight champion boxer.
1896	Fannie Farmer's *The Boston Cooking School Cook Book* is published.
1897	First running of Boston Marathon takes place.
1898	Tremont Street subway, first underground subway in America, opens.
1901	"King" Camp Gillette invents the safety razor.
1907	Albert Champion invents the spark plug in the South End's Cyclorama.
1908	William Filene invents the Automatic Markdown Basement.
1912	Fenway Park opens.
1914	James Michael Curley becomes mayor of Boston for the first time.
1918	Boston Red Sox win the World Series. In 1920 they incur the "Curse of the Bambino" by selling Babe Ruth to the New York Yankees and never win World Series again.
1947	Logan International Airport opens on site of old Boston Municipal Airport.
1949	John Hynes ends Curley era by winning mayoral race.
1958	Freedom Trail path of red brick and paint is laid out.
1959	Central Artery ("The Highway in the Sky") opens, cutting off downtown Boston from the waterfront.
1975	Court-mandated school integration sparks anti-busing riots.
1976	Faneuil Hall Marketplace opens, establishing prototype for festival marketplaces.
1985	Court-mandated cleanup of Boston Harbor begins.
1990	Third Harbor Tunnel/Central Artery Project begins. Tunnel opens to commercial traffic only in 1995 as Ted Williams Tunnel.
1996	Central Artery Project cost estimate passes $14 billion, making it the most expensive public works project in American history.

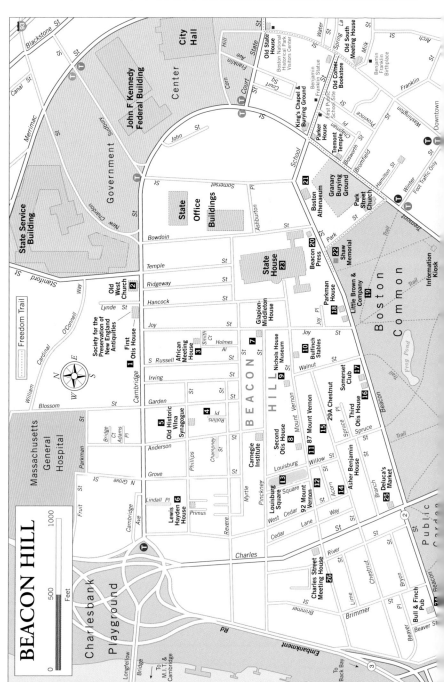

BEACON HILL

BEACON HILL

State Service Building

Government Center

John F Kennedy Federal Building

City Hall

State Office Buildings

State House

Massachusetts General Hospital

Charlesbank Playground

BEACON HILL

Boston Common

Public Garden

Old State House
Boston National Historical Park Visitors Center

Old South Meeting House

Benjamin Franklin Birthplace

King's Chapel & Burying Ground

Benjamin Franklin Statue
First Public School Site
Old Corner Bookstore

Parker House

Tremont Temple

Granary Burying Ground

Park Street Church

Boston Athenaeum

Shaw Memorial

Information Kiosk

Beacon Press [20]

Shaw Memorial [22]

Parkman House [18]

Little Brown & Company [19]

Nichols House Museum [9]

Bulfinch Stables [10]

Somerset Club [17]

Third Otis House [16]

29A Chestnut [15]

87 Mount Vernon [11]

Second Otis House [8]

Asher Benjamin House [14]

Deluca's Market [25]

92 Mount Vernon [12]

13 Louisburg Square

Lewis Hayden House [6]

Old Historic Vilna Synagogue [5]

4 Rollins Pl

African Meeting House [3]

First Otis House [1]

Old West Church [2]

Society for the Preservation of New England Antiquities

Carnegie Institute

Glapion-Middleton House [7]

Charles Street Meeting House [26]

Bull & Finch Pub

Freedom Trail

Feet
0   500   1000

B E A C O N H I L L
& F R E E D O M T R A I L O V E R V I E W

Boston State House is the hub of the solar system.
—Oliver Wendell Holmes, *Autocrat of the Breakfast Table*

EVEN THOUGH 60 FEET WERE LOPPED OFF ITS TOP in the 1790s, Beacon Hill is still literally and figuratively the loftiest perch in downtown Boston. Historians point to the orderly rows of handsome brick townhouses as Boston's best collection of Federal architecture, while preservationists cherish the treacherous brick sidewalks, the gaslights, and the strict regulations that govern even minuscule exterior changes. Bounded by Boston Common on the sunny side, Charles Street and the "flat side of the hill" at its base, and Cambridge Street on the back side, Beacon Hill is the hump that rises at the heart of the city.

The leafy south slope, built almost entirely in the first half of the 19th century, is the area most people mean when they speak of Beacon Hill: it has been Boston's most prestigious neighborhood since John Adams turned over the presidency to Thomas Jefferson. Yet even the less aristocratic north slope—what poet Robert Lowell described as "unbuttoned"—has acquired cachet in recent decades. Its classic narrow brick walk-ups bring a healthy price on the real estate market from Bostonians eager to gain a foothold on the hill.

Beacon Hill was long the home of the Boston Brahmins, a class defined in 1860 by Oliver Wendell Holmes as that "harmless, inoffensive, untitled aristocracy" with their "houses by Bulfinch, their monopoly on Beacon Street, their ancestral portraits and Chinese porcelains, humanitarianism, Unitarian faith in the march of the mind, Yankee shrewdness, and New England exclusiveness." Brahmin numbers have dwindled since, and today they are joined on Beacon Hill by a wide range of people of varying class, ancestry, and occupation—many of them drawn by the charm of the neighborhood, which remains largely as it was built: a chiefly residential preserve dotted with private courtyards, private streets, even a private square.

Small as Beacon Hill may be, it still requires a full day to see. Three museums and the State House penetrate the otherwise smooth façade of the neighborhood. There's even a for-real, everyday shopping street, where old-fashioned markets, a friendly drugstore, and a hardware store persist among the purveyors of brie, vintage port, and antiques. You have no choice but to take the hills at a leisurely pace, pondering the neighborhood's perverse pride in having preserved those frost-heaved brick sidewalks.

■ BEACON HILL WALKING TOUR

1 First Harrison Gray Otis House
Located at 141 Cambridge Street, this house is one of the few surviving historical remnants of the razed West End. Now separated from Beacon Hill proper by a busy four-lane street, it is nonetheless the birthplace of the Hill. Otis was a visionary real estate developer and lawyer-politician who plotted the revamping of the Hill from farmland into residences.

Descended from both British bureaucrats and firebrand patriots, Otis had the pedigree to fill the sudden void left by the ouster of the Tory aristocrats at the end of the American Revolution. To demonstrate his worthiness, he commissioned Charles Bulfinch to design the Cambridge Street showcase house, which the Otises occupied in 1796. Over the next decade Bulfinch would create an architectural style that defines Federal-era Boston, while Otis would become an orator and politician of considerable talent: Otis presided over the Hartford Convention in 1814-15 that ultimately kept New England from seceding from the Union.

The Society for the Preservation of New England Antiquities rescued this first of Otis's houses in 1916 (it had fallen on hard times, serving as a ladies' Turkish bath in the 1830s, then a patent medicine shop, and finally a boarding house) and now uses it for its headquarters and opens it for tours. The SPNEA used to present the house in a "Williamsburg Colonial" style—the term preservation professionals use to describe the plain, even drab style affected in that Colonial Virginia settlement. But following chemical and art historical detective work, curators returned the house to the bright, even gaudy, style favored by the Otises, reinstalling such indicators of upper-class taste as wallpaper bordered with illustrated scenes of ancient Pompeii, and a profusion of lithographs in the hallway. The scholarly house tour demands a certain fascination with life during the Colonial and early Federal eras, but it's worth the time to examine how Boston's first elite

The first home of Harrison Gray Otis, at 141 Cambridge, is one of the few survivors of the razed West End. (Robert Holmes)

Ridgeway Lane meets Cambridge Street in Beacon Hill. (James Marshall)

of the American era lived. Although the Otises would build two more Bulfinch mansions on Beacon Hill in their decade-long ascension to preeminence, this is the only one open to the public.

2 **Old West Church**
On Cambridge Street, practically next door to the Otis House, is Old West Church. In 1775 occupying British troops razed the 1737 wood-frame church that once stood on this site; the British feared that revolutionary sympathizers were using the church steeple to signal Continental troops in Cambridge. The current red-brick structure, designed by Bulfinch protégé Asher Benjamin, was erected in 1806. Old West houses a superb Fisk tracker-action pipe organ and often hosts organ concerts.

To the west of the church, **Joy Street** is the only street that crosses the steep side of Beacon Hill from the plebeian north slope to the patrician south. Like the surrounding narrow streets, Joy is lined with skinny four- and five-story tenements built in the late 19th century to replace the original ignoble wooden houses mostly destroyed by fire. Wave after wave of immigration has washed up on the north slope, each ethnic group settling briefly before moving on.

3 **African Meeting House**
About halfway up Joy Street on the right is Smith Court, site of the African Meeting House, the oldest standing black church in

America and the primary location of the Museum of Afro-American History. The first ethnic enclave of this part of Beacon Hill was African American. The waterfront slave market opened in Boston in 1638, but by the time Massachusetts became the first state to outlaw slavery in 1783, the city had a large free black population, often immigrants from the West Indies.

This community constructed the African Meeting House in 1806, adapting the façade design from Asher Benjamin to create a site grand enough to rival white churches and serve as a social, economic, and religious center of African-American society. The meetinghouse basement housed the first black school in Boston (later absorbed into the **Abiel Smith School** next door, which closed in 1855 when integration was mandated by the Massachusetts General Court). In 1832, the influential New England Anti-Slavery Society was founded in this "obscure schoolhouse," as William Lloyd Garrison called it.

The meetinghouse, along with much of the surrounding neighborhood, was an important stopover for slaves on their way to Canada in flight from southern bondage. Not only would many householders willingly conceal a fugitive, but the rabbit warren of alleys and mews meant no slave-catcher was ever successful on Beacon Hill.

Holmes Alley, at the end of Smith Court, is typical of the "streets" of the north slope in the 17th and 18th centuries—barely wide

Smith Court, in the heart of Beacon Hill. (Robert Holmes)

THE OUTER RIM OF THE HUB

*I*n 1924 people still lived in cities. Late that summer, we bought the 91 Revere Street house, looking out on an unbuttoned part of Beacon Hill bounded by the North End slums, though reassuringly only four blocks away from my Grandfather Winslow's brown pillared house at 18 Chestnut Street. In the decades preceding and following the First World War, old Yankee families had upset expectation by regaining this section of the Hill from the vanguards of the lace-curtain Irish. This was bracing news for my parents in that topsy-turvy era when the Republican Party and what were called "people of the right sort" were no longer dominant in city elections. Still, even in the palmy, laissez-faire '20s, Revere Street refused to be a straightforward, immutable residential fact. From one end to the other, houses kept being sanded down, repainted, or abandoned to the flaking of decay. Houses, changing hands, changed their language and nationality. A few doors to our south the householders spoke "Beacon Hill British" or the flat *nay nay* of the Boston Brahmin. The parents of the children a few doors north spoke mostly in Italian.

My mother felt a horrified giddiness about the adventure of our address. She once said, "We are barely perched on the outer rim of the hub of decency." We were less than fifty yards from Louisburg Square, the cynosure of old historic Boston's plain-spoken, cold roast elite—the Hub of the Hub of the Universe. Fifty yards!

—Robert Lowell, *Life Studies*, 1956

enough to accommodate a burly man's shoulders. A fugitive could easily escape down this dark and narrow path. The alley is a private way, but because it is part of the Black Heritage Trail (a National Park Service route), abutters permit visitors.

The top of Holmes Alley emerges onto **Myrtle Street,** site of one of the 18th-century rope factories, or "ropewalks," that produced cordage for Boston's merchant fleet. These very long, thin buildings, where the hemp was twisted and tarred, burned frequently, since both hemp and tar are highly flammable. As a result, little remains of the pre-1800 north slope. A quick jog down Garden Street to Revere Street provides a peek at the most unusual cul de sac on Beacon Hill, Rollins Place.

⁴ Rollins Place

Two-story brick Greek Revival homes from 1843 line the place, but the charming white two-story wooden portico at the end is an illusion—a false front masking a 20-foot fall to Phillips Street below.

Phillips Street lies a block farther down Garden and has a number of interesting buildings.

5 Old Historic Vilna Synagogue

Located at 14 Phillips Street, this synagogue was built in 1919 for the Lithuanian congregation founded around 1900 in the adjacent West End.

6 Lewis Hayden House

Number 66 is perhaps the most historically compelling house on Phillips Street. A former fugitive slave, Hayden opened his home to other fugitives as well as to abolitionists. He kept two kegs of gunpowder in the basement, and swore he'd rather blow up the building than let a slavecatcher in.

Along **Pinckney Street,** two streets above Phillips, stretches the border between Beacon Hill's north and south slopes. Pinckney Street, was historically a dividing line between rich and poor, white and black. African American John J. Smith crossed the color line to buy a south slope house at 86 Pinckney in 1878. Already a civic leader and member of the Massachusetts House of Representatives, Smith was an early crusader for civil rights. Today's color line is green, with houses above Pinckney selling for more than twice as much as those below.

7 Glapion-Middleton House

Back uphill, the modest 1791 wooden house at the corner of Joy and Pinckney (now divided into two homes, numbers 5 and 7 on Pinckney) is one of the oldest houses still standing on the Hill. It was built by Lewis Glapion, a mulatto barber, and George Middleton, the black Revolutionary War colonel who led the company of African-American soldiers known as the Bucks of America.

Mount Vernon, Chestnut, and Beacon Streets on the south slope are the golden portion of Beacon Hill and the district where Charles Bulfinch did his most inspired architecture. The "best" families of Boston have lived here since the Mount Vernon Proprietors, the real estate syndicate organized by Harry Otis and fellow lawyer/politician Jonathan Mason, bought the property in the 1790s from the agent of painter John Singleton Copley at $1,000 per acre. (Tory Copley had decamped to England in 1774, and his agent had little bargaining power; Copley always claimed he was cheated on the price.) Henry James called the stretch of Mount Vernon between the Massachusetts State House and Louisburg Square "the most civilized street in America."

8 Second Otis Home

Harry Otis's second home survives as a private residence at **85 Mount Vernon,** complete with grand carriage turnaround on land steep enough to recall the peaks smoothed out elsewhere. Jonathan Mason owned perhaps the more prime property closer to the State House. His mansion is long gone, but the more modest houses he built for his daughters at **55, 57,** and **59 Mount Vernon** still stand. They sit back from the street by at least 20 feet, the result of a gentlemen's agreement among the Mount Vernon Proprietors, who had intended their development to consist entirely of freestanding, landscaped homes. The economic slump brought on by President Jefferson's 1807 embargo on trade put an end to such finery, leading to the more thrifty practice of building connecting townhouses with shared walls.

9 Nichols House Museum

The Otis "daughter house" at **55 Mount Vernon Street** was built in 1805. Like its sisters, it faced downhill toward Daddy's manse, although it is the only one of the three to maintain that orientation. It is not Bulfinch's best work, and some of the home was oddly "modernized" in 1830: the entrance was transformed from Federal style into a poor excuse for Greek Revival, and the front hall was truncated to make room for a staircase. Nonetheless, it does have the

distinction of being the only Beacon Hill home you can "visit without a letter of introduction"—the intent of its last private owner, Rose Standish Nichols, when she created the house museum in her 1960 will.

The Nichols family acquired the house in 1885, when Rose was 13, and she spent her life there as a Beacon Hill paradigm. Possessing a little family money (her father was a doctor) and either no prospects or interest in marriage, she invented a genteel career as a landscape designer, became a prominent social and political activist, and created Boston's own version of an artists' salon. Nichols kept her home furnished with a very eclectic mix of family heirlooms and of items collected on her own travels. As resident curator William Pear explains: "She was of the opinion that an excellent

Ornate grillwork adorns a home on Mount Vernon Street. (James Marshall)

piece of any era went with an excellent piece from any other—as long as it wasn't Victorian."

10 Bulfinch Stables

The unusually low structures at 50 Mount Vernon are known as the Bulfinch Stables. Now more prized as human rather than equine domiciles, they went with the houses that Hepzibah Swan built for her daughters on Chestnut Street. She drew the property deed to prohibit alterations of the structure above a height of 13 feet, presumably to preserve the view between Chestnut and Mount Vernon. James Swan, a member of the Proprietors, was forever off in France picking up heirlooms from ex-nobility at a sou to the franc, leaving Hepzibah to run their business deals for more than 20 years.

11 87 Mount Vernon

Charles Bulfinch lost his family fortune in the 1790s with an ill-planned development, only recouping sufficiently in the early 1800s to build his own house at 87 Mount Vernon. But his creditors caught up before he moved in; he sold the house to escape their clutches. Fortunately for Bulfinch, friends in high places found him a city job, where he established the first building safety and sanitation codes in Boston. Later, President Monroe rescued him from bureaucratic life by installing him in Washington as the final architect of the U.S. Capitol.

12 92 Mount Vernon Street

The window on the top of 92 Mount Vernon Street marks the studio where sculptor Anne Whitney (1821–1915) labored for two decades. Her public work in Boston includes the statue of Samuel Adams outside of Faneuil Hall and the heroic statue of Leif Eriksson on the Commonwealth Mall.

13 Louisburg Square

Between Mount Vernon and Pinckney Streets runs the Greek Revival block of Louisburg Square, developed after 1830 and arguably the most prestigious address in Boston. Visitors often find Louisburg Square less awe-inspiring than most Bostonians do. Yet real estate here trades in seven figures for narrow little buildings on an ill-paved square that girdles a tiny patch of greenery surrounded by a high iron fence with locked gates. Even the pedestrian statues of Aristedes and Columbus at each end of the "park" originally arrived as ship's ballast from Italy. The buildings are fine examples of restrained Greek Revival, but they're hardly the best on Beacon Hill, let alone in Boston.

The appeal, perhaps, is ownership. Louisburg Square is the last private square in Boston—those on-street parking spaces for the Jags and Mercedes are all deeded. About two-thirds of the buildings on Louisburg Square are divided into apartments; the others remain as sumptuous private quarters. Physician and blockbuster author Robin Cook, who spent more than $2 million renovating his Louisburg Square building, described the façades to the *Boston Globe* as "modest, like the old Italian palaces, but once you get inside, it's a completely different world." The roster of past

BALANCED SQUARE

*A*s Brady turned and examined each quarter of Louisburg Square he felt an enormous and inexplicable relief, as if he were seeing something for which he had been desperately searching. The harmony of construction, purpose, use, history was what moved him. This was a world in which all conflicts—architectural, cultural, esthetic—had been resolved in the perfect tension of the classic. Brady saw it as an image of his own hope for himself; the conflicts set loose by loss and loneliness and betrayal and even, once, murder, can be, if not resolved, held in an order and simplicity like what he beheld. That hope in the human capacity for balancing polarities and thus banishing chaos is what built cities in the first place. Brady, once a farmer who knew the curse of rustic loneliness, understood why the city itself was the greatest achievement of culture, and Louisburg Square was having its effect on him because it was the polished, exquisite gem of his city. Nothing in London or Edinburgh or Dublin or Rome or Paris would surpass it for simple ordered beauty. Louisburg Square was an example of what Anglo-Saxon culture at its best could achieve, and Brady, for the first time in years, felt absolutely at home. He was part of what wanted such a place. He was part, he insisted to himself, of what had produced it.

—James Carroll, *Mortal Friends,* 1978

and present inhabitants is a provincial who's who—Louisa May and Bronson Alcott, William Dean Howells, senators Edward Kennedy and John Kerry, Boston Celtics owner Don Gaston. The Society of St. Margaret, an Episcopal order of nursing nuns, occupied **13, 17,** and **19 Louisburg Square** for more than a century, vacating in 1992 because the posh address seemed a poor fit with a vow of poverty. Most recently these spare quarters were expensively renovated by Senator Kerry and Teresa Heinz. The American tradition of Christmas Eve caroling supposedly began on Louisburg Square in the late 19th century.

West Cedar Street almost transects Beacon Hill, running from the Cambridge Street side of Charles Street Circle through as far as **Chestnut Street**—stopping one block shy of Beacon.

14 Asher Benjamin Home

Asher Benjamin, architect of almost everything of note in this area not designed by Bulfinch, built his own home at **9 West Cedar.** Better at business than his mentor, he had the pleasure of living in the house he built.

Little **Acorn Street**, probably the most heavily photographed way on Beacon Hill because it still has the original cobblestones, parallels Mount Vernon and Chestnut. (Stumble up the street and you'll quickly see why brick was considered an improvement.)

15 **29A Chestnut Street**
Residents of Chestnut Street hail it as superior to the showier Mount Vernon, and they have a point: the modest scale and mid-19th-century wrought-iron ornamentation create an air of restrained gentility. The oldest house built by the Mount Vernon Proprietors stands at 29A Chestnut Street. Its purple window panes are prized badges of antiquity, dating from an 1820 shipment of manganese-contaminated glass from Hamburg. Many householders later installed faux purple panes, but connoisseurs can spot the real thing by the undulating colors in the glass. Actor Edwin Booth was living here when his brother, John Wilkes, assassinated President Lincoln. Edwin canceled his last performance of *The Iron Chest* (a murder mystery, ironically) and skipped town to avoid publicity.

Beacon Street is linked to Chestnut Street by tiny and exclusive **Spruce Street**. At the Beacon Street corner stands a plaque commemorating William Blaxton, the eccentric who invited Winthrop's band over from Charlestown to get Boston started. The plaque marks the northeast corner of the parcel he reserved when he sold the property that was designated Boston Common.

16 **Third Otis Home**
As the prime location overlooking Boston Common, Beacon Street boasts the grandest houses on the hill. Number **45 Beacon Street** is one of the finest examples of Bulfinch domestic architecture. It now houses the American Meteorological Society, but it was built in 1805 as Harry and Sally Otis's final home in their journey across Beacon Hill. Most of its glories lie hidden: the 11 bed chambers, for example, and the elliptical room behind the front parlor where doors and walls both curve— engulfed by the attachment of the house next door where the walls curve inward. Something of a gourmet, Otis was often sighted trundling over Beacon Hill to Quincy Market with a basket on his arm.

17 **Somerset Club**
Numbers **42–43 Beacon Street** house the Somerset Club. Populist mayor James Michael Curley would lead his supporters on election night victory marches to the Legislature, pausing at the Somerset to sound a raspberry to Boston's Anglo elite.

18 **Parkman House**
Rather more democratic use is made of the Parkman House at **33 Beacon Street**— thanks, in part, to a highly sensationalized murder. In November 1849, the socially prominent Dr. George Parkman, donor of the land for Harvard Medical School (now Massachusetts General Hospital), was allegedly murdered by Harvard professor and fellow socialite Dr. John Webster, who had evidently borrowed money from Parkman.

(opposite) Because of its picturesque homes and cobblestone pavement, Acorn Street is probably the most photographed street on Beacon Hill. (Robert Holmes)

The resulting scandal shook Brahmin Boston, not only because, as Harvard president Jared Sparks testified, "[Harvard] professors do not often commit murder," but also because the judge in the case, Lemuel Shaw, was related to Parkman and sent the accused to the gallows. The murdered man's son, George Francis Parkman, retreated with his sister and mother to 33 Beacon, and George Francis lived here in seclusion until his death in 1908. In his will he donated the house to the city, which has renovated it as a conference and reception center.

19 Little, Brown and Company

Beacon Hill writers have always had their Beacon Hill publishers. Number **34 Beacon Street** was long the headquarters of Little, Brown and Company, publisher of *Fannie Farmer's Boston Cooking School Cookbook,* the western histories of Francis Parkman

(same family as the Parkman House donor), the maritime histories of Samuel Eliot Morison, Peter Bartlett's *Familiar Quotations,* and so on.

20 Beacon Press

The world headquarters of the Unitarian Universalist Association and its distinguished publishing arm, Beacon Press, occupy **25 Beacon Street**.

21 Boston Athenaeum

At **10 1/2 Beacon Street** is the Boston Athenaeum, incorporated in 1807 as if to prove Boston's self-perception as the Athens of America. In effect, it was (and is) a private library and art gallery, the last of its 1,049 shares having been issued in the 1850s. The Athenaeum houses the books from the libraries of George Washington and Henry Knox (Knox was a bookseller

The Shaw Memorial honors abolitionist Robert Gould Shaw and the members of the 54th Massachusetts Regiment under his command during the Civil War.

who became famous in the Revolutionary War, when he transported cannons across Massachusetts), as well as theological volumes originally supplied to King's Chapel by William III. On a lighter note, the library boasts one of the finest collections of detective fiction in the country. The Athenaeum also helped establish Boston as a fine art center. Its 1827 sale of Thomas Jefferson's paintings rescued his impoverished heirs, and an 1831 purchase of unfinished portraits by Gilbert Stuart of George and Martha Washington likewise saved the Widow Stuart from the poorhouse. (The Stuart paintings became part of the nuclear collection for the Museum of Fine Arts.) The brownstone building may not be a standout, but the Athenaeum does permit visitors to the genteel Brahmin world of its first two floors.

22 Shaw Memorial

The ostensible subject of one of Robert Lowell's best poems, "For the Union Dead," also stands on Beacon Street at the corner of Park across from the State House. The Shaw Memorial, a bas relief by Augustus Saint-Gaudens (uncle of Rose Nichols, by the way), honors Robert Gould Shaw, an abolitionist of "gentle birth and breeding," and the soldiers of the 54th Massachusetts Regiment of the Union Army chronicled in the film *Glory.* Choosing to lead the all-black 54th over the prestigious 2nd Massachusetts, the 25-year-old Shaw commented, "I feel convinced I shall never regret having taken this step... for while I was undecided I felt ashamed of myself, as if I were cowardly." Scion of a wealthy Boston family, Shaw died with a quarter of

Sgt. Henry Stewart of the 54th Massachusetts Regiment was killed on Morris Island, South Carolina, months after this portrait was taken in 1863. (Massachusetts Historical Society)

his men in the mud outside Fort Wagner in the harbor of Charleston, South Carolina. The memorial was commissioned in 1883 and dedicated in 1897, but the names of the black soldiers who fought at Fort Wagner were not added until 1982.

23 State House

The crowning glory of Beacon Hill is the State House, a building much altered and even more imitated and still, from a Bostonian standpoint, the Center of the Universe, or at least the Hub of the Hub. The golden dome atop this Bulfinch-designed building is the marker point for Massachusetts mapmakers: a highway sign that reads "Boston 23 miles" means that the sign lies 23 miles from the State House dome.

The famous Sacred Cod hangs over the House of Representative at the State House in honor of what was once an important industry in Massachusetts.

The State House stands on what used to be the pasture of John Hancock, he of the grandiose signature on the Declaration of Independence. Its cornerstone was laid on the Fourth of July, 1795, by Samuel Adams and Paul Revere, the latter in his capacity as Grand Master of the Masons. It was completed in January 1798, and Revere came back in 1802 to cover the dome with copper sheathing to stop the leaks in the roof. Not until 1861 did gilding begin, and by 1872 it was covered with 23-carat gold leaf, which was renewed most recently in 1969. During World War II the gleaming dome was hidden from the enemy under a coat of black paint.

The original Bulfinch design is only a small portion of the existing building, which acquired a yellow-brick extension between 1889 and 1895 and white marble wings in 1917. The power of great architecture shows; Bulfinch's portion triumphs over the mediocrity imposed by lesser talents. It served as a model for modifications to the U.S. Capitol building in Washington and influenced about half the state capitols in the country.

Visitors do not use the central front entrance to the building; those doors are opened only for a departing governor to leave the building at the end of his term, to receive a Massachusetts regimental flag returning from war, or for official visits by the President of the United States.

Inside is a civic equivalent of Westminster Cathedral: soaring spaces and artwork relate the mythic history of Massachusetts. Guided tours are available on weekdays. The walls of **Nurses' Hall** are covered with murals of Paul Revere on horseback, the Boston Tea Party, and James Otis orating against the Writs of Assistance. Murals in the **Hall of Flags** depict the Mayflower Pilgrims sighting land, John Eliot preaching to the Natives, and the Battle of Concord Bridge. The main attraction, however, is the rotating exhibition of the flags of Massachusetts regiments carried to battle from the Civil War through Vietnam. The **Sacred Cod,** perhaps the most famous public art in the building, has hung above the gallery in the House of Representatives since 1784 as a symbol of the importance of the fishing industry (now extremely depressed) to the early state economy. The House will not convene without the pine carving; indeed, when staff of the *Harvard Lampoon* kidnapped the revered fish on April 26, 1933, business was halted for days until the pranksters called to inform the furious legislators that their icon lay hidden in a State House closet.

The grounds around the State House are dotted with sculpture. Below the central colonnade are statues of Daniel Webster, educator Horace Mann, Civil War General Joseph Hooker, and John F. Kennedy. Rather less assuming are figures of religious martyrs Anne Hutchinson, banished in 1638 for heresy, and Mary Dyer, twice banished and finally hanged in 1660 on Boston Common for her Quaker beliefs. Behind the State House stands a mighty golden eagle, a memorial to the American Revolution designed by Bulfinch and first

erected on Sentry Hill years before the State House was built. When the hill was flattened, the statue was re-installed atop a column that legend says is the same height as the original hill.

The remains of Beacon Hill's third peak, Pemberton, lie behind the State House. Once a warren where ladies of the evening plied their trade, the district now houses lawyers' offices and state office buildings.

Prestige compensates for lack of altitude on the "flat side" of Beacon Hill: Charles Street and the streets below it that flow down to the river. Between 1802 and 1805, Otis and his associates cut down the peaks of Beacon Hill and slid the dirt on a gravity railroad to the bottom of the hill to stabilize Charles Street (originally the tidal shore) and create land below it to sell. Neither blessed with the good fortune of the first-born like the south slope nor cursed with an air of illegitimacy like the north, the Flats has managed to evolve its own cachet.

24 Bull & Finch Pub

One of Boston's chief tourist attractions also lies on the Flats: the Bull & Finch Pub at the Hampshire House, 84 Beacon Street. The model for the "Cheers" pub in the television show by the same name, the one-time neighborhood bar has devolved into Boston's tourism answer to Graceland.

Over the years, the Charles Street area has become the haven of more than two dozen antiques stores as well as the shops supplying the modest but discerning lifestyle affected on Beacon Hill.

25 DeLuca's Market

DeLuca's Market at 11 Charles long predates the emergence of "gourmet" grocers; Julia Childs' butcher, **Savenor's,** stands at the other end of Charles (Number 160) after a fire in its original Cambridge location forced it to move. In between is a growing selection of good, small restaurants.

26 Charles Street Meeting House

Charles Street Meeting House, built at Charles and Mount Vernon Streets in 1807 from Asher Benjamin's design, originally stood on this site on the banks of the Charles River, a convenient place for a congregation of Baptists who needed a handy spot for immersion. The meetinghouse was purchased in 1876 by the African Methodist Episcopal Church, which used it until the congregation moved to Roxbury in 1939. Today the building has commercial uses.

Longfellow Bridge at the end of Charles Street was named for Henry Wadsworth Longfellow, who used to walk across its predecessor from Cambridge when he was courting his wife. Nicknamed the "pepperpot bridge" for the shape of its towers, the design was freely adapted from a bridge in St. Petersburg, Russia.

(above) An 1855 view of Beacon Street looking towards Charles Street. (opposite) The belfry of the Charles Street Meeting House is visible in this view down Charles Street. (James Marshall)

From Charles Street it is prudent to cross the traffic intersection via the overhead walkway through the Charles/MGH Red Line station to reach **Massachusetts General Hospital**. Not much to look at, "Mass General" is one of the great research and teaching hospitals in the world. Ask for directions at the front desk to the **Bulfinch Pavilion and Ether Dome**. The 1817 portico was Bulfinch's last Boston design. The Ether Dome acquired its name because Dr. John Collins Warren first demonstrated the use of ether as an anesthetic here in 1846, when he operated on the jaw of a patient who'd been given ether by dentist (and anesthesiologist) Thomas Green Morton.

The famous permanent sleeper in the dome, however, is a mummy that arrived in 1823.

A different set of stairs at the end of Charles leads instead over Storrow Drive to the Charles River Esplanade, a grassy park along the river basin and site of the July 4 fireworks and concert. The **Hatch Memorial Shell** hosts the Boston Pops Orchestra for that blowout and any number of other performers for warm-weather concerts, which are often free. In many respects, the summer Esplanade experience defines what Bostonians admire about their city: an oasis of civility and culture on green land at the water's edge.

The Red Line crosses Longfellow Bridge (above), connecting Cambridge to Beacon Hill. Classes and research in anesthesiology are still conducted in the Ether Dome at Massachusetts General Hospital (right). (both photos by Robert Holmes)

■ FREEDOM TRAIL OVERVIEW

Past and present converge on the Freedom Trail, a 2.5-mile path marked with red paint and bricks that links 16 sites representing the early history of America. About 4 million visitors a year walk at least some portion of the Trail, and well they might. It forms a perfect introduction to the central core of Boston where the city and the nation began. No other city can boast—and we do boast—so many sites directly related to the American Revolution and yet still firmly anchored in the present.

Boston recognized its responsibility to history from the outset. Private efforts began as early as 1818 to save some sites from demolition. Many historic buildings became museums: Old South Meeting House in 1876, the Old State House in 1882 and the Paul Revere House in 1908. The USS *Constitution* ("Old Ironsides") was rescued several times: in 1830 thanks to a poem by Oliver Wendell Holmes, in 1897 through the lobbying of Congress by Rep. John F. Fitzgerald, and in 1925 by American schoolchildren donating their pennies.

But the city continued to grow up around these Revolutionary sites; in 1951 Bob Winn of Old North Church observed that visitors had a hard time finding them. The late William Schofield, editorial writer of the Brahmin broadsheet *Boston Herald Traveler,* picked up on Winn's theme and suggested in March that Boston should "connect the dots" and create what he called a "Puritan Path" or a "Loop of Liberty." Mayor John Hynes knew effective promotion when he saw it and the city placed plywood signs at significant spots in Downtown and the North End. By June 1951, the "Freedom Trail," as it came to be called, was signed, sealed, and delivered. Within two years 40,000 people a year were making the rounds.

The now-familiar red path appeared in 1958. In 1974 the National Park Service established the Boston National Historic Park, which includes the Freedom Trail sites. Finally, in 1988 the red pathway was extended to include sites in Charlestown: Old Ironsides and Bunker Hill Monument.

Because the Trail represents a Colonial city embedded in the midst of a vital, modern city, the transit is not always as fastidious as it would be in a sanitized theme-park version of history. The Freedom Trail is a walk through three and a half centuries of Boston, warts and all. In 1998, however, improved signage was posted all along the route.

Not all of the Trail resembles the skyscraper-lined path through the Financial District to the stately forum of Faneuil Hall. The need to duck under the Expressway and traipse through a parking lot to get to the Paul Revere House leaves many

Trail walkers back at the raw bar of Ye Olde Union Oyster House. The loss is theirs; that awkward transition opens into the 17th-century streets of the North End. Walkers also stop at Copp's Hill, gazing across the water at the USS *Constitution* from afar. They miss the oldest part of the living waterfront where recreational fishermen pull striped bass from the mouth of the Charles River, and the piers and pilings knock with tie-ups for small working boats and little recreational vessels.

True enough, the Freedom Trail is a history lesson of sorts, but history didn't end with the Revolution. Follow the red path to meet the men and women of Boston who continue to translate a powerful dream of freedom into a working city.

Rather than extract historical sites from their modern contexts, we have chosen to detail the specific sites of the Freedom Trail in their respective topographical chapters. But for the visitor who'd like a concise tour of the Freedom Trail, following is a list of sites with basic information.

■ FREEDOM TRAIL SITES

Sites are listed in order of their location on the Freedom Trail, beginning with the State House on Beacon Hill and heading north. Please refer to the map on page 78.

■ BEACON HILL
State House. *pages 69-71*
Built 1795-98; open weekdays.
Beacon and Park Sts.; 617-727-3676.

■ DOWNTOWN & MARKET DISTRICT
Boston Common. *pages 79-83*
Bounded by Park, Tremont, Boylston, and Charles Sts.

Park Street Church. *page 85*
Built in 1809; open Tues.-Sat. summer only, Sunday services year-round.
Tremont and Park Sts.; 617-523-3383.

Granary Burying Ground. *page 85*
Laid out in 1660; open daily.
Tremont near Park Street Church; 617-635-7385.

King's Chapel. *page 92*
Built in 1748-1754; call for hours.
58 Tremont St.; 617-523-1749.

King's Chapel Burying Ground. *page 92*
Oldest part laid out in 1630; open daily.
617-635-7385.

First Public School Site/ Benjamin Franklin Statue. *page 92*
Erected in 1856. 45 School St.

Old Corner Bookstore (Boston Globe Store). *page 93*
Built in 1712; open daily. 285 Washington St. (at School); 617-367-4000.

Old South Meeting House. *pages 93-94*
Built in 1729; open daily. 310 Washington St. (at Milk); 617-482-6439.

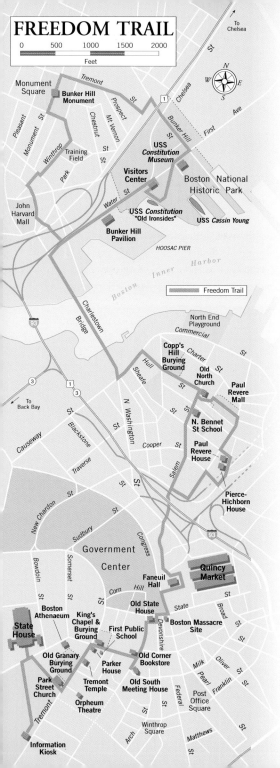

FREEDOM TRAIL

0	500	1000	1500	2000

Feet

Monument Square

Bunker Hill Monument

Tremont St

Prospect St

Chestnut St

Mt Vernon St

Winthrop St

Training Field

Park St

Pleasant St

Monument St

John Harvard Mall

Water St

Visitors Center

USS *Constitution* Museum

USS *Constitution* "Old Ironsides"

USS *Cassin Young*

Bunker Hill Pavilion

HOOSAC PIER

Boston National Historic Park

Boston Inner Harbor

Chelsea St

To Chelsea

Bunker Hill Ave

First St

Freedom Trail

Charlestown Bridge

93

North End Playground

Commercial St

Copp's Hill Burying Ground

Charter St

Old North Church

Paul Revere Mall

Hull St

Sheafe St

Salem St

N. Bennet St School

Paul Revere House

Pierce-Hichborn House

To Back Bay

3

1

3

N Washington St

Blackstone St

Cooper St

Traverse St

Causeway St

New Chardon St

Sudbury St

Government Center

Bowdoin St

Somerset St

Congress St

Faneuil Hall

Quincy Market

Old State House

State

Broad St

Corn Hill

Boston Athenaeum

King's Chapel & Burying Ground

First Public School

Boston Massacre Site

Devonshire St

State House

Old Granary Burying Ground

Parker House

Old Corner Bookstore

Milk St

Oliver St

Pearl St

Franklin St

Park Street Church

Tremont Temple

Old South Meeting House

Post Office Square

Orpheum Theatre

Tremont St

Federal St

Winthrop Square

Arch St

Matthews St

Information Kiosk

■ **DOWNTOWN & MARKET DISTRICT** *(cont'd)*

Old State House. *pages 95-96*
Built in 1713; open daily.
206 Washington St.;
617-720-3290.

Boston Massacre Site. *page 96*
Congress and State Sts.

Faneuil Hall. *page 101*
Built in 1742; open daily.
Dock Square; 617-242-5642.

■ **NORTH END & CHARLESTOWN**

Paul Revere House. *page 110*
Built in 1677; open daily.
19 North Square; 617-523-2338.

Old North Church. *page 117*
Built in 1723; call for hours.
193 Salem St.; 617-523-6676.

Copp's Hill Burying Ground.
page 118
Oldest part laid out in 1660.
Hull and Snowhill Sts.;
617-635-7385.

Bunker Hill Monument.
pages 124-25
Erected in 1825; open daily.
Charlestown; 617-242-5641.

USS *Constitution.* *pages 193-95*
Launched in 1797; open daily.
Charlestown Navy Yard;
617-242-5670.

D O W N T O W N &
M A R K E T   D I S T R I C T

*Crossing a bare common, in snow puddles at twilight, under a clouded sky,
without having in my thoughts any occurrence of special good fortune, I have
enjoyed a perfect exhilaration.*

—Ralph Waldo Emerson, *Nature,* 1836

FORGET SUBURBIA. BOSTON'S DOWNTOWN ARGUES FOR an old city center where
history shakes hands with possibility. Other urban downtowns may become empty
stage sets after hours, but Boston's pulses as a center of power, money, pleasure,
and ingenuity. Yet feisty Samuel Adams and crafty John Hancock could still navigate the twisting alleys between counting house and alehouse. Most downtown
streets were in place by 1708, and only a few changed names after independence
to honor someone other than an English king. Soaring glass boxes of Reagan-era
corporate hubris may cast long shadows where chandleries and tailor shops once
stood, but much of the Colonial- and Federal-era city persists as the skeleton on
which modern Boston commerce hangs.

■ BOSTON COMMON   *map page 80, A-4/5*

The best way to arrive in Boston's green heart is by subway. Arising from the Sty-
gian dark of **Park Street Station,** a National Historic Landmark, travelers emerge
into the bright light of Brimstone Corner at Boston's crossroads of humanity: the
Common, an ancient ground that belongs simultaneously to No One and Everyone.

Bounded today by Tremont, Boylston, Charles, Beacon, and Park Streets, the
pentagonal park is the 48-acre parcel sold to the town in 1634 by William Blaxton
(later known as Blackstone), the pre-Puritan settler who lost title to the rest of the
peninsula when, in a fit of generosity, he invited John Winthrop's band to join him
on Shawmut. (These early luminaries are celebrated by **The Founders Monument**
inside the Beacon Street wall.) The town used it as a militia drill field and common
pasture for two centuries. Each Bostonian was limited to grazing 70 milk cattle

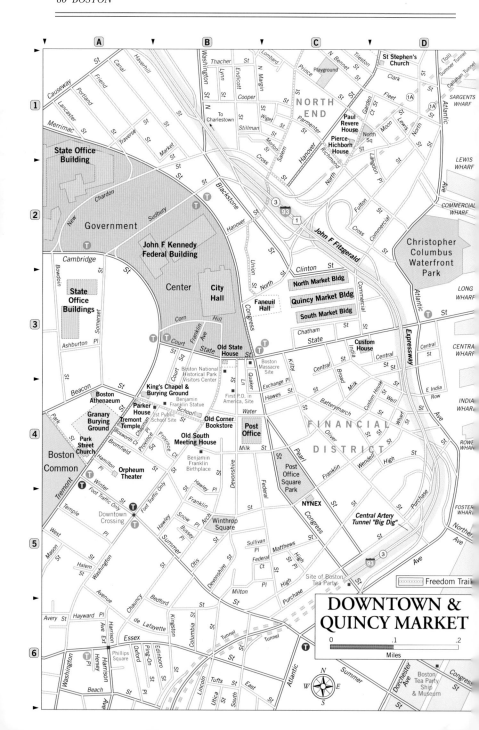

DOWNTOWN &
QUINCY MARKET

there until the 1820s; livestock were evicted altogether in 1830. But the Common has always been more than pasturage. It has housed stocks, pillories, and gallows as well as a jail and a poorhouse. Here Puritans hanged Quakers for heresy. Here too, Martin Luther King, Jr., spoke before a vast crowd, and Pope John Paul II celebrated Mass.

From their Boston Common encampments British soldiers boarded boats to march on Lexington and Concord and to assault Bunker Hill. And to this sod many of them returned in perpetuity. The **Central Burying Ground** on the Boylston Street side holds many such remains, as well as the grave of painter Gilbert Stuart, whose portrait of George Washington you probably have—reproduced in green—in your wallet. The northeast corner of the grounds contains the jumbled bones of about 1,000 dead disturbed by excavations in the 1890s to create America's first subway.

Generations have skated on the **Frog Pond.** (Native Edgar Allan Poe once disparaged Boston as "Frogpondium.") Children still slide the slopes in winter, and boys and girls of summer play fiercely competitive baseball on its fields. Dogwalkers and diplomats, panhandlers and gospel-talkers, Sufi whirlers and saxophone soloists, and lovers (always lovers) stroll the Common paths, though most sensible

Smokers' Circle, on Boston Common. (Library of Congress)

residents stick to the perimeter after dark.

The Common is the turf Boston has always used most and sometimes best. From the Common hillsides rang Samuel Adams' angry voice, whipping the crowds to fury over royal excesses. And even today, the city grants more than 200 permits a year for outdoor fairs, marches for hunger and other causes, and assemblies where the First Amendment is exercised to the ragged limits of the United States Constitution.

The Tremont Street side of Boston Common houses the Visitors Center (maps, flyers, restrooms) and two subway stops (Park Street for both Red and Green lines, Boylston for Green).

NEWS ITEM: "July 7, 1917 BOSTON Soldiers and Sailors tearing to shreds one of the flags carried by Socialists in the anti-war demonstration held in Boston.

At this spot along the line 8,000 watched the uniformed men and cheered their action. An attempt by Boston Socialists and more extreme radicals to parade in the Boston Common and hold an anti-war meeting there was thwarted by a riot which involved over 10,000 persons and was led by uniformed men of the army, navy, and National Guard. The parade's ranks were shattered, their flags and banners torn from their hands, their meeting banned by the police, and their headquarters wrecked and the literature found there heaped in a pile and burned. Such was the treatment accorded to the group of dissenters who by their actions create a false impression abroad and indirectly aid the enemy."

(Underwood Photo Archives, San Francisco)

(left) As in all city parks, pigeons of Boston Common rule the roost.

COMMON MACHINERY

*P*receded by the beadle, and attended by an irregular procession of stern-browed men and unkindly-visaged women, Hester Prynne set forth towards the place appointed for her punishment. A crowd of eager and curious schoolboys, understanding little of the matter in hand, except that it gave them a half-holiday, ran before her progress, turning their heads continually to stare into her face, and at the winking baby in her arms, and at the ignominious letter on her breast. It was no great distance, in those days, from the prison-door to the market-place. Measured by the prisoner's experience, however, it might be reckoned a journey of some length; for, haughty as her demeanour was, she perchance underwent an agony from every footstep of those that thronged to see her, as if her heart had been flung into the street for them all to spurn and trample upon. In our nature, however, there is a provision, alike marvellous and merciful, that the sufferer should never know the intensity of what he endures by its present torture, but chiefly by the pang that rankles after it. With almost a serene deportment, therefore, Hester Prynne passed through this portion of her ordeal, and came to a sort of scaffold, at the western extremity of the marketplace. It stood nearly beneath the eaves of Boston's earliest church, and appeared to be a fixture there.

In fact, this scaffold constituted a portion of a penal machine, which now, for two or three generations past, has been merely historical and traditionary among us, but was held, in the old time, to be as effectual an agent in the promotion of good citizenship, as ever was the guillotine among the terrorists of France. It was, in short, the platform of the pillory; and above it rose the framework of that instrument of discipline, so fashioned as to confine the human head in its tight grasp, and thus hold it up to the public gaze. The very ideal of ignominy was embodied and made manifest in this contrivance of wood and iron. There can be no outrage, methinks, against our common nature,—whatever be the delinquencies of the individual,—no outrage more flagrant than to forbid the culprit to hide his face for shame; as it was the essence of this punishment to do. In Hester Prynne's instance however, as not unfrequently in other cases, her sentence bore, that she should stand a certain time upon the platform, but without undergoing that gripe about the neck and confinement of the head, the proneness to which was the most devilish characteristic of this ugly engine. Knowing well her part, she ascended a flight of wooden steps, and was thus displayed to the surrounding multitude, at about the height of a man's shoulders above the street.

—Nathaniel Hawthorne, *The Scarlet Letter,* 1850

■ COLONIAL CORE OF THE CITY

The streets surrounding the Common—Park, Tremont, Charles, Boylston, Beacon—are lined with some of Boston's most famous historic buildings and sites. The Freedom Trail begins on the Common's southeast corner. (See essay, "Freedom Trail," pages 76-78)

Park Street Church

map page 80, A-4

Henry James called the 1809 Park Street Church, across from the subway kiosks at the corner of Park and Tremont, "the most interesting mass of bricks and mortar in America." The influence of its pulpit cannot be overestimated. Heir to the Puritan legacy, Park Street Church sent Congregational missionaries in the wake of Yankee traders, proselytizing the entire Pacific from an 1819 mission in Hawaii. Here William Lloyd Garrison gave his first speech against slavery and Katherine Lee Bates's proposed national anthem, "America," debuted. Ill-informed trolley drivers suggest that preachers' zeal gave Brimstone Corner—the intersection of Park and Tremont—its name, but the term refers to the stores of gunpowder stashed in the church basement during the War of 1812.

Granary Burying Ground

map page 80, A-4

The Granary Burying Ground next door dates from 1660. Its illustrious dead include Paul Revere, Samuel Adams, John Hancock, Benjamin Franklin's parents, Peter Faneuil, and victims of the Boston Massacre. Although most believe otherwise, Elizabeth Foster Goose (Boston's candidate for Mother Goose) is not buried here—but her husband Isaac's first wife, Mary, is. The orderly arrangement of headstones is a nod to modern groundskeepers and rarely, if ever, do the markers indicate the actual resting spot of the person in question. John Hancock may not be here at all: graverobbers cut off his signing hand the night he was interred in 1793, and during 19th-century construction, some claim, the rest of his remains were snatched. Although the cemetery's heroes date more from the Colonial era than any other, Paul Revere enjoyed such long life that the cemetery was almost too full for him to join his comrades-in-arms when he died in 1818.

Orpheum Theatre

map page 80, A-4

Hamilton Place, across Tremont from Park Street Church, deadends at the 1852 Orpheum Theatre. The former Old Music Hall was the birthplace of the New England Conservatory and site of the Boston Symphony Orchestra's 1881 maiden concert. In 1915 the Orpheum became Boston's first cinema, but has since reverted to its original role as a concert hall, mostly for pop and rock acts.

PARK STREET UNDER

Public transit began early in Boston: in 1631, when a colonial charter authorized ferry service among Boston's peninsulas. Trolleys began rolling on city tracks in 1846; electric trolleys superseded the horse-drawn system in 1889. But the big excitement came September 1, 1897, when more than 100,000 people ponied up a nickel each to ride the Tremont Street Subway, a 0.6-mile strip modeled on the subterranean trolley tunnels of Glasgow, Paris, London, and Budapest. Boston's subway — the first in North America — was created to alleviate the traffic hazards of electric surface trolleys (which still foul up traffic in outlying parts of the city).

The original Park Street Station was at the level of today's Green Line, with the Red Line's "Park Street Under" added in 1912. Two of the original "headhouses" (castigated as "mausoleums" in 1897) are still in use and were named National Historic Landmarks in 1964. Now known as the Massachusetts Bay Transportation Authority (MBTA), the system comprises 64 miles of subway and trolley lines (on the Green, Red, Orange, and Blue lines) and more than 1,000 route miles, including commuter rail and buses. Most Bostonians call it the "T," which is how stops are marked on signs and maps.

Lilli Ann Killen Rosenberg's 1978 mosaic mural near the Park Street entrance on the Green Line level marks the spot where the system excavation began in 1895; braces between the panels are the original tunnel supports. Red Line riders especially benefitted from a 1980s modernization program that incorporated art into each

station as it was built or renovated. At Alewife, *End of the Red Line* (1985) by Alejandro and Moira Sina makes a pun with a series of red neon tubes hanging at the terminus of the northbound track. At Porter Square, Mags Harries's *Glove Cycle* (1985) scatters life-sized cast bronze gloves throughout the station as if dropped by commuters. At Kendall Square, Paul Matisse's *The Kendall Band* (1987) consists of three audiokinetic sculptures (harmoniously in key) for waiting riders to play. Another Mags Harries piece, *Fossil* (1982), moves around. She sculpted a handprint into a standard aluminum pole inside Red Line Car 1506—as if a rider had held it so long that the metal softened. "You can never go to find it," Harries says. "It finds you." (Shades of "poor old Charlie.")

Itinerant musicians have long used subway entrances to play for change, and in the 1970s the MBTA began officially inviting them inside at Park Street, and eventually throughout the system. (Some cynics commented that the T figured it was cheaper to entertain waiting patrons than improve service.) More formally, South Station is often a venue for lunchtime concerts.

The grandest station of all is South Station, which recaptured its Neoclassical Revival splendor in a 1989 renovation. Dedicated on New Year's Eve 1898, during the heyday of rail transport, South Station was the busiest passenger station in America. Today it serves commuter trains from the south, Amtrak's Northeast Corridor trains and the T's Red Line. Its shops, restaurants and services are as popular with area office workers as with travelers.

Tremont Temple

map page 80, A-4

The path up Tremont Street passes Tremont Temple at Number 88, the first racially integrated church in America.

Parker House

map page 80, A-4

The Parker House, on the corner of School and Tremont, was Boston's first grand hotel and now the oldest continuously operating hotel in America. In the mid-19th century, it was home to virtually every visiting luminary and the preferred dining spot for many Bostonians. (Exhibit cases in the lobby both commemorate some of the more illustrious visitors and some of the more memorable special dinners.) The Saturday Club—a monthly gathering of intellectuals such as Ralph Waldo Emerson, poet and *Atlantic Monthly* editor James Russell Lowell, Henry Wadsworth Longfellow, and visitors such as Charles Dickens and Samuel Clemens—gave the establishment a literary luster it has never quite lost. Famous guests were sometimes matched by famous staff: Malcolm X was a waiter, Ho Chi Minh a kitchen worker. When the hotel was built, the combination of lodging and fine dining was a novelty, although the hotel's enduring contributions to cuisine are unassuming if oft-imitated: the Parker House roll and Boston cream pie.

The Park Street Church (left) was described by Henry James as the "most interesting mass of bricks and mortar in America." Next door, the Granary Burying Ground (above) dates from 1660, and holds the remains of such Revolutionary War luminaries as Paul Revere, Samuel Adams, John Hancock, and the victims of the Boston Massacre. (photo at left by Robert Holmes)

DOWNTOWN &
MARKET DISTRICT

King's Chapel and Burying Ground

map page 80, A-4

On an opposing corner of Tremont and School stands King's Chapel and Boston's first cemetery, known now as King's Chapel Burying Ground. The chapel, founded in 1686, was the first Anglican church in Puritan Boston to serve the British officers dispatched to the city by the king. No Puritan would sell land to the crown, so the governor appropriated a corner of the cemetery. The present stone building was constructed between 1749 and 1754 from a design by Peter Harrison, who also designed Christ Church in Cambridge. Its projected steeple was never built. To avoid disrupting Anglican services, the "new" building was built around an older one, which was then dismantled and thrown out through the windows. When the British evacuated Boston in 1776, more than half the Anglican pew-holders followed them to Nova Scotia. In 1787, King's Chapel became the first Unitarian Church in America under its first post-Revolution minister, the Rev. James Freeman. The church still has the original box pews, including a special pew to the right of the main entrance reserved for condemned prisoners to hear a final sermon before going to the gallows. The bell, cast in 1816 by Paul Revere, was used to toll the deaths of major figures, including Revere himself two years after he completed the bell. King's Chapel is still active in Boston life; under director and composer Daniel Pinkham, the chapel sponsors 60 concerts per year.

The 1631 Burying Ground, which may hold 10 to 20 burials for every stone, holds the remains of Governors John Winthrop and John Endicott. In the center is a cluster of notable graves: William Dawes (who spread the alarm with Revere on April 18, 1775), Mary Chilton (the first Pilgrim to touch Plimoth Rock), William Paddy (a historical unknown whose 1658 stone is possibly the oldest still extant in Boston), and the long-suffering Elizabeth Pain (who inspired Hawthorne's *Scarlet Letter* character Hester Prynne). The diabolical-looking octagonal metal cage has nothing to do with burials; it's a vent shaft for the subway.

Site of Boston Latin School

A few steps down School Street, a hopscotch-like mosaic in the pavement marks the 1635 site of Boston Latin School, the first public school in the nation. (The "exam school"—that is, a public secondary school that selects its students based on an entrance exam—remains Boston's most prestigious public high school.)

Ben Franklin statue

map page 80, B-4

A statue of Boston Latin's most famous dropout, Benjamin Franklin, stands nearby in the courtyard of **Old City Hall** the florid French Second Empire structure from 1865 that now houses private offices and the restaurant and cafe of Maison Robert. A bronze likeness of Josiah Quincy, Boston's second mayor and the man responsible for Quincy Market, shares the setting.

Old Corner Bookstore

map page 80, B-4

The corners of School and Washington Streets include both the maudlin **Irish Famine Memorial** and the Old Corner Bookstore, built around 1718 for apothecary Thomas Crease. The building's apogée of influence was 1845–65, when it housed the offices of Ticknor & Fields, publisher of Emerson, Longfellow, Hawthorne, Harriet Beecher Stowe, and *The Atlantic Monthly.* From its presses rolled the works of what critic Van Wyck Brooks called the "Flowering of New England": *Walden, The Scarlet Letter, Hiawatha,* and the broadside "Battle Hymn of the Republic." (William Dean Howells observed at the time that in Boston "to be a poet was not only to be good society, but almost to be good family.")

Old South Meeting House

map page 80, B-4

Here, at the corner of Washington and Milk, is the second building of the second oldest church in Boston. The first meeting-house of South Church was built here on Governor John Winthrop's garden in 1670; Benjamin Franklin, who was born on near-by Milk Street, was baptized in the old structure in 1705. After serving its parish for 60 years, the oak and cedar building was pulled down in 1727. In 1729, Joshua Blanchard completed work on the new church,

Both Boston Latin and Boston English schools moved into this Montgomery Street building shortly after its construction in 1877. Designed by George A. Clough, the structure was the largest in the world to be used as a public school. (Boston Public Library)

DOWNTOWN & MARKET DISTRICT

Benjamin Franklin was baptized in the first meeting house of Old South Church. Today, a lookalike leads tours around the area. (Robert Holmes)

As Colonial Boston's largest meeting hall, Old South hosted the town meeting that launched the Boston Tea Party and other "subversive" acts. Perhaps as retribution, the British Army used its cavernous interior as a riding school from 1775 to '76; they even added insult to injury by installing an officers' bar in the former place of worship. It took Americans nearly five years to repair the damage done by General "Gentleman Johnny" Burgoyne's cavalry. The congregation moved to Copley Square in 1875 and Old South was nearly demolished in 1876, but a group of concerned Bostonians, Julia Ward Howe and Ralph Waldo Emerson among them, saved the meetinghouse through their own fundraising efforts and turned it into a monument and museum—an early victory for the city's nascent historic preservation movement. It was, according to Walter Muir Whitehill, longtime director of the Boston Athenaeum and himself an ardent preservationist, "the first instance in Boston where respect for the historical and architectural heritage of the city triumphed over considerations of profit, expediency, laziness and vulgar convenience."

whose red brick and slender wooden spire were modeled on the style of Christopher Wren's country churches. Phillis Wheatley, who came to Boston as a slave and became the first African-American poet, worshipped in the new building.

The Old State House *by James Brown Marston, 1801. (Massachusetts Historical Society)*

Old State House

map page 80, B-3

Although dwarfed by looming office towers, the Old State House, Boston's oldest surviving public building, commands the top of State Street as it did when it was erected in 1713. (The original view from the building, which stretched clear to the Atlantic, is preserved in Robert Salmon's colossal 1829 painting, *View of Boston from Pemberton Hill,* hanging in the lobby of One Boston Place across Washington Street from the back entrance.) Whitehill noted in *Boston: A Topographical History* that public life centered on the State House, where the street leading to the harbor (now designated "the Walk to the Sea") met the main road across the Neck to the mainland.

Located on the site of a 17th-century outdoor market (and of Puritan stocks and pillories), the Old State House was preceded by the Town House, the seat of Royal government and the Courts of Justice for the colony from 1657 until the Great Fire of 1711. Two years later, the red-brick State House (called the Town House until 1775) was completed, and by the mid-18th century, the first floor was serving as a merchants' exchange, while government operated in the rooms upstairs.

Meanwhile, the Town House was fast becoming a hotbed of rebellious activity. James Otis, Jr. made his famous eight-hour speech against the Writs of Assistance on the second floor in 1761. A cobblestone circle on the front plaza—destined for

makeover in the coming years—marks the site of the Boston Massacre. The Declaration of Independence was read from the balcony on July 18, 1776; later that evening the fanciful-looking lion and unicorn carvings, symbols of the Crown, were torn from the roof. (Modern replicas are in place now.) And when Massachusetts became a state, its first governor—John Hancock—was inaugurated here.

Following the completion of the new State House on Beacon Hill, however, the castoff served variously as a firehouse, a newspaper office, and even a city hall. In 1881, the recently organized Bostonian Society came to the rescue, restoring the Old State House and turning it into a museum of Boston and Revolutionary War history—of which it is its own greatest artifact. The building, which also serves as the entry and exit for the "State" stop on the Orange and Blue subway lines, was fully renovated in 1991 and '92. Sharing a plaza with the Old State House is the Downtown Visitors Center of the Boston National Historic Park, which has a floor of its own exhibits and extensive tourist services.

■ FINANCIAL DISTRICT

Boston is not New York (for which Bostonians give daily thanks), but Boston money managers do control an inordinate proportion of the world's wealth. Boston invented the mutual fund in 1925 (Fidelity Investments is based at 21-35 Congress St.) as a capstone to inventing venture capital in the 1790s. The city's financiers helped entrepreneurs open trade with the Far East, and later funded the development of railroads, the telephone, and more recently, the minicomputer industry. Start-ups still come here looking for capital. Meanwhile, in the early 19th century Boston bankers created the "spendthrift family trust," which was meant to protect family wealth from ne'er-do-well members. Today, in an age of global economy, entire Financial District offices do little more than invest and grow the fortunes of single families. Puritan theology held that wealth was one of the signs of God's favor. Boston businesspeople still believe it.

The Financial District is a logical expansion of the primitive mercantile exchange that began in the Old State House. Money men began to line King's Street between the exchange and Long Wharf, becoming increasingly ensconced after the Revolution, when King became State Street. Although bank consolidations have demanded new towers to celebrate the conquest of financial kingdoms, financial institutions still dominate State Street and have inched over to cast their shadows on Post Office Square, named for the magnificent 1929-31 Art Deco post office.

Two employees of the Federal Reserve Bank hold one million dollars in cash. Their faces are hidden, as those who work here are required to protect their identities.

Post Office Square Park

map page 80, C-4/5

This open space was nearly lost to another glass office spire but the need to preserve parking (it had been topped with a plug-ugly parking garage) prevailed. When an innovative seven-level underground garage was built in 1990, the ground level became a fabulously successful pocket park. The glass and lattice gazebos break the normally fierce winds of skyscraper canyons, creating a beguiling place to sit to watch the office workers and contemplate the competing aesthetics of 20th-century architecture.

New England Telephone building

The monumental Art Moderne New England Telephone building anchors the Franklin Street end of the open space. (Now a Verizon building, 185 Franklin has a wonderful heroic-worker mural of the telephone industry in the lobby as well as a display of the first and oldest telephone and the world's first telephone exchange. It is open to visitors around the clock by asking the security guards.) The lobby of the oddly bulging bank building across Congress Street contains immense paintings of maritime scenes by N. C. Wyeth.

An institution of another sort, the ice cream shop and grille known as **Brigham's of Boston** (founded 1914) occupies 50 Congress Street.

■ GOVERNMENT CENTER   *map page 80, A&B-1,2,3*

No part of Boston so clearly embodies the social engineering of city planning as Government Center, an 11-acre mass of stone and brick and concrete between Cambridge and Congress Streets that links downtown with the Market District.

Scollay Square

Some Bostonians will never forgive Government Center for displacing Scollay Square, one of the livelier, if seedier sections of the city's first three centuries. Literally known in every port of the world as a sailor's paradise, Scollay's neon mass of bars, flophouses, tattoo parlors, shooting galleries, and strip joints ill-suited the ambitions of post–World War II Boston, so red lights yielded to gray eminences. (The name survives in the **Scollay Square Farmers Market** on Monday and Wednesday afternoons from July to October.)

City Hall Plaza

When the cluster of local, state, and federal office buildings opened in 1968, it marked Boston's emergence from a generation and a half of economic Dark Ages—the first major new buildings in the city in 30 years. I. M. Pei and Associates, creators of the overall City Hall Plaza design, modeled it on an Italian piazza, but as finally built, Government Center lacks the triumphant inevitability of its models.

A view down State Street in the 1920s. The Old State House is visible at the end of the street. (Underwood Photo Archives, San Francisco)

City Hall

map page 80, B-3

Although City Hall itself was warmly embraced by many Bostonians at first, the ensuing three decades have seen the plaza of 1.8 million bricks and its eclectic collection of modern architecture suffer a barrage of insults. Perhaps Bostonians are simply more fond of the warm Neoclassicism of Bulfinch's State House than of Government Center's overbearing Brutalist style, no matter how technically impressive. The current mayor calls City Hall "ugly." But, as former mayor John Collins (under whose administration the contracts were awarded) observed as recently as 1993, the squat gray fortress of City Hall isn't as grim as some say. "A few light bulbs and some soap and water would help," Collins grumbled to a reporter.

Sears Crescent

Perhaps City Hall suffers on the Cambridge Street side from the contrast between its gray concrete slabs and the more artful lines of the Sears Crescent's curving bow and the white granite **Sears Block.** Attached to the latter is the beloved **Steaming Kettle**—a massive animated advertisement commissioned by the Oriental Tea Company in 1873 to coppersmiths Hicks and Badger. The kettle holds 227 gallons, two quarts, one pint, and three gills and produces nearly as much hot air as the elected denizens of adjacent City Hall.

Teenagers from City Year, a public service group, end their morning meeting at Government Center with a handshake.

A statue of Samuel Adams guards the front of Faneuil Hall. (James Marshall)

■ THE MARKET DISTRICT

Although the area across Congress Street from City Hall is historically part of the North End, a highway cut it off nearly a half century ago. As a result, Faneuil Hall Marketplace—the mid-1970s development that unified Faneuil Hall and Quincy Market—has evolved into the closest to a theme park that Boston can boast, complete with a signature grasshopper icon modeled on the Faneuil Hall weathervane.

Faneuil Hall

map page 80, B/C-3

Faneuil Hall, a.k.a. "the Cradle of Liberty," was Huguenot merchant Peter Faneuil's 1742 gift to the city as an auditorium and public food market. Until that time, food was sold door to door from pushcarts; Faneuil Hall revolutionized the distribution system. It played another "revolutionary" role as well. A sequence of Town Meetings in 1763 made Faneuil Hall the focal point of Revolutionary rhetoric—and cemented a local tradition of outspokenness. Here William Lloyd Garrison often spoke against slavery, and in 1903 Susan B. Anthony addressed the New England Woman Suffrage Association. John F. Kennedy launched his first campaign for Congress in the venerable second-floor hall, which is still made available by the city for public meetings and artistic events.

Faneuil's original structure burned in 1761 and was rebuilt. In 1805, it was enlarged to double its size under the oversight of Charles Bulfinch. The 1992 renovation added an elevator (south entrance). The top floor houses the Ancient and Honorable Artillery Company of Massachusetts (chartered in 1638) with a meeting hall, library, and museum of military history. Because ground floor merchants have always paid rent, Faneuil Hall may be the only self-supporting monument in the country.

Quincy Market

map page 80, C-3

Quincy Market (named for the mayor who supported the creation of a mercantile center on Dock Square) was designed by Alexander Parris at the height of the Greek Revival fad. From its 1827 opening, the 535-foot granite market served as the produce, meat, and fish market center of the city. A vestige of that market era survives in the colorful open-air produce market at nearby Haymarket. In the 1960s, the New York Times described Quincy Market as a "dingy, historic, and conspicuously empty stage." It survived, in part, because no developer wanted to foot the tax bill for the six-acre site.

But architect Benjamin Thompson saw it differently and proposed revitalizing the markets with food stalls, cafes, restaurants, shops, and pushcarts—all operated by local merchants. So successful was Thompson's vision as realized by the mall developers, the Rouse Company, that it was quickly imitated at Baltimore's waterfront, New

For centuries, merchants have rented the first floor of Faneuil Hall, as this engraving from the early 19th century shows. (Library of Congress)

The outdoor park between Quincy Market Building on left and the north Market Building on the right is lined with shops and restaurants, including the venerable Durgin Park restaurant. Fanueil Hall is visible in the background. (James Marshall)

York's South Street Seaport, New Orleans' Riverwalk, and elsewhere. It is hard to recall that at the time nothing like it existed in North America; Thompson drew his inspiration from similar operations in Helsinki and Copenhagen.

Faneuil Hall Marketplace has suffered, perhaps, from excess success since its opening in August 1976. Thompson envisioned it principally as a resource for citydwellers, but some of the character he envisioned has faded as signs get ever larger and less tasteful and national chains displace locally owned shops. Thompson has remarked of the Marketplace in particular (and American pop culture in general) that "the proliferation of T-shirts threatens to build the image of an underwear factory." The architecture, however, endures as a perfect blend of the modern Thompson with the stolidly Federal Parris. (Note the granite pillars of Quincy Market cut from single great pieces of rock. It was the perfection of the technology for quarrying and cutting such large stones that sparked Boston's granite style.) The public spaces between buildings throb with activity throughout the year, with the plazas at each end forming impromptu theaters for street performers. The original market building is a giant food court.

Durgin Park Restaurant
map page 80, C-3

One grand survivor from the old North Market building days is Durgin Park Restaurant, "established before you were born." It excels at plain Yankee food—scrod, baked beans, Indian pudding—at plain prices on plain tables.

Blackstone Block
map page 80, B-2/3

The adjacent Blackstone Block is chiefly notable as Boston's oldest commercial block. The oldest building, 41 Union Street, dates from before 1714. On the second story of the same building were the presses of *The Massachusetts Spy*, the newspaper of the Whig patriots from 1771 to 1775. In 1798 the three-story townhouse was home to tailor James Amblard; overhead lived the Duke of Chartres, who eked out a meager living teaching French to Boston businessmen before later assuming the French throne as Louis Philippe. In 1826, the first oyster business opened in the building and the original bar is still in use at the Union Oyster House.

Directly in front on Union Street are the six glass towers of the **New England Holocaust Memorial,** unveiled in October 1995. The somber, etched glass of the towers evokes the grim smokestacks of the Nazi crematoriums. The site was chosen because its proximity to the Freedom Trail provided high visibility in a historical district.

And directly across from Faneuil Hall stands the symbol of the greatest modern defeat of Boston preservationists: McDonald's. Over outcries of desecration, the company traded such concessions as foregoing its trademark arches to install a lucrative franchise next to the heaviest foot traffic in town. Although the fast-food giant has proven a good neighbor, Boston preservationists are still smarting that they failed where Harvard Square, so far, has succeeded.

This view of the Boston skyline reveals its jammed freeways—to be relieved, hopefully, by the highway project known as the "Big Dig."

A Harpers Weekly *from the 1880s illustrates Boston street characters in these "City Sketches." Around this time, the North End was attracting a great number of the city's new immigrants.*

N O R T H   E N D
&   C H A R L E S T O W N

The fact that Boston's past touches us daily is the most modern thing about the city.
— Benjamin Thompson, architect, 1975

PARTIAL ISOLATION HAS ALWAYS BEEN the North End's lot, perhaps accounting for the district's tendency to develop deeply etched character lines. The area was settled the spring after the Puritans landed in Boston, and remains the oldest continuously occupied neighborhood in the city. Although many Revolutionary War shrines dot the neighborhood, the North End fell out of favor with established families after independence, becoming the first home to successive waves of immigrants.

■ ITALIAN TRADITIONS

Today the neighborhood is in transition from its 20th-century identity as a Sicilian and southern Italian enclave to 21st-century gentrification. Italian traditions die hard; although no new waves of immigration have renewed the North End's population, many families refuse to follow their cousins to the suburbs and the religious and social clubs provide a continuity that can make the streets more Neapolitan than Yankee.

The North End never seems more Italian than during the religious festivals that begin in June and peak on August weekends. Although some observers see the festivals as the final gasps of a culture on the verge of assimilation, these events prove that there is a lot of spirit left in the old neighborhood. Religious society members hoist a sedan with their patron saint's image up to their shoulders, then wend and weave through the neighborhood to the accompaniment of small marching bands and the inevitable entourage of photographers. All along the narrow streets people lean from their windows to greet the procession. Confetti rains down and households vie to outdo each other with their contributions of dollar bills—and often larger denominations—to be pinned to the saint's train for charity. The street theater leads invariably to the 1899 doors of **St. Leonard's** at the corner of Prince and Hanover, the first Italian Catholic church in Boston. The pious file in for Mass, while a larger group segues into more secular revelry.

Beneath the red, white, and green bunting that envelops the neighborhood,

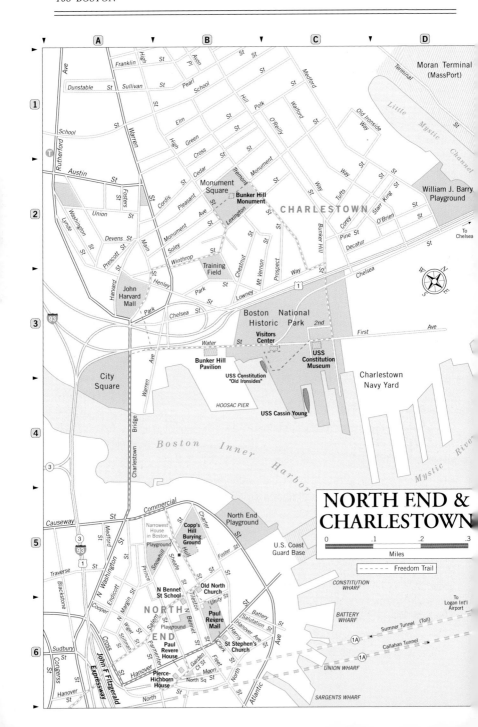

NORTH END & CHARLESTOWN

visitors and North Enders alike celebrate everything Italian—music, food, and *la dolce vita*. The incense of the fair is garlic and the vendors' stalls bear signs that read like a grandmother's cajoling, *Mangia, mangia!*

The North End's village ambience results, in part, from the close streets almost unaltered from their 17th-century layout. Although arterial Hanover Street was widened in 1870 and peripheral Commercial Street is even broader, the interior of the North End remains a rabbit warren of winding ways that suddenly open into small courts and squares (which are never truly square in Boston). Most of these quaintly named streets, which predate the 1708 effort to standardize Boston place names, are lined with 19th-century tenements—many now transformed into luxury condominiums. New residents are defined more by income than by ethnicity.

■ NORTH SQUARE

The house at 19 North Square was already 90 years old when upwardly mobile Huguenot silversmith Paul Revere moved to this neighborhood of wealthy Tories in 1770. At the head of the triangular square stood North Meeting House, the

Italians in the North End pose with the Madonna del Soccorso at a festival held every year to raise funds for the fishermen's club.

Second Church of Boston, where the powerful Puritan divines Increase, Cotton, and Samuel Mather preached their stern creed. Two of the city's grandest homes stood on the square: a 26-room Georgian built by merchant William Clark in 1711 and a mansion ca. 1700 occupied by Royal Governor Thomas Hutchinson until a mob angered by the Stamp Act damaged it in 1765. ("The hellish crew fell on my home with the rage of devils," Hutchinson reported.) Tory riches and royal reign would not outlast the Revolution. British soldiers tore down North Meeting House for firewood during the siege of Boston and the mansions were razed when the streets were widened in 1834.

Revere's house outlasted them all.

Paul Revere House
map page 108, B-6

The Paul Revere House, now a museum and Freedom Trail stop, is the only 17th-century dwelling in Boston still standing on its original site. It was built in 1677 and purchased in 1681 by merchant Robert Howard. During a 1906-08 restoration the building was returned to Howard's period by removing, among other things, the third story that Revere had needed for his growing family. (Revere sired 16 children by two wives over 30 years, though never more than eight dwelled with him at any one time. His mother also lived with the family for several years.)

Spacious and modern when it was built, the Revere House now seems archaic and awkward, but it's a good example of late medieval domestic architecture in early Boston. The steeply pitched roof with its prominent second-story overhang, the diamond-paned casement windows, and the massive fireplaces are typical of late Elizabethan architectural style—a style long out of fashion in England, but still used in modified form for generations in the colonies. Three of the rooms are shown in the decor of Revere's time, a fourth as Howard might have furnished it. Some of Revere's personal belongings, including a silver pitcher he made, are among the furnishings.

But there are tales here more compelling than the architecture. With Redcoats garrisoned all around him, Revere crept from this house to nearby taverns for clandestine meetings of the Sons of Liberty and to the harbor for the Boston Tea Party. The night of April 18, 1775, he snuck from these quarters to row over to Charlestown to begin his famous ride—one of the few overblown tales about an otherwise exceptional man. One of three messengers, Revere managed to warn Adams and Hancock in Lexington of the approaching British troops—as did William Dawes, who met up with Revere after his own ride through Cambridge. Revere was captured and released en route to Concord, losing his steed to the British as spoils of war.

Pierce-Hichborn House

map page 108, B-6

The Paul Revere Memorial Association runs the Revere House and the nearby early Georgian-style Pierce-Hichborn House, built by glazier Moses Pierce in 1708 and occupied later by Revere's cousin Nathaniel Hichborn. While not neglecting the fascinating career of Revere, the association's interpretive programs emphasize domestic life in the North End over the centuries,

sometimes gleefully explaining more than you might want to know (for example, that the lot behind the Revere house enclosed both privy and well).

The Revere and Pierce-Hichborn houses survived because they were adapted to tenement dwellings on the upper floors and small shops at ground level. During the 1800s, the Revere House served as the site of a candy store, an Italian bank, a cigar factory, and a Jewish produce market.

The Revere House was once the site of an Italian bank and a cigar factory. (Bostonian Society)

Paul Revere left North Square in 1800, just before the area's most serious decline. By the early 1800s, North Street (then called Anne Street) was famously rowdy; it was known for the "nymphs of Anne Street" until reformers swept through and tidied things up in 1850.

By this date, North Square and much of the North End was solidly Irish, for the potato famines had hastened the diaspora and Boston was a choice destination. Boston's first Irish-American mayor, John F. "Honey Fitz" Fitzgerald, was born nearby on Ferry Street (now obliterated by the Callahan Tunnel). His darling daughter, Rose (mother of President John Fitzgerald Kennedy), was born at 4 Garden, a spot she later described as "a modest flat in an eight-family dwelling." Even after the Irish had moved on, Honey Fitz kept a house at 8 Unity Street as a "voting residence" and fondly and frequently spoke of the old neighborhood as "the dear old North End." Hence, North Enders for some years were known as "Dearos."

(above and opposite) North Square, a neighborhood of wealthy Tories when Paul Revere lived there, has since been home to Jewish, Irish, and Italian immigrant communities. (photo opposite by James Marshall)

NORTH END &
CHARLESTOWN

■ HANOVER STREET   *map page 108, A/B-6*

The social and commercial heart of the North End beats purposefully on Hanover Street, the main street that stretches less than a mile from the expressway to Constitution Wharf. Since the earliest days of the colony, Hanover has been the link from the North End wharves and shipyards to the downtown commercial market district. And so it remains, despite a gaping lacuna imposed by the John F. Fitzgerald Expressway, a.k.a. the Central Artery.

The street scene on Hanover is friendly and easygoing. Old men with cigars sit on benches in the sun. Women push baby strollers, while the men cluster on street corners to berate the Boston Red Sox or argue in animated Italian about the European soccer matches showing in the bars. Streetside chatter is the daily coin of North End life, but celebrations and tête-à-têtes usually occur over a plate of pasta, a bottle of wine, or a demitasse of espresso. Hanover is home to the city's greatest concentration of Italian caffès and trattorias, along with a handful of full-fledged restaurants. These dining spots, breeding ground of Boston's hottest young chefs, attract more outsiders than neighborhood residents.

The North End has long been known for its lively street markets.

Oranges with an attitude.

Much of Hanover's history is relegated to oral tradition because many of the sites of its early mercantile history have been lost. In 1836, 14-year-old Eben Jordan arrived from Danville, Maine, with $1.25 in his pocket; five years later he opened a dry goods shop at 168 Hanover (his first sale was a bundle of firewood) that would later grow into the Jordan Marsh department stores—a Boston fixture now absorbed into Macy's.

Symbolizing the deep ethnic and political divisions in Boston in the 1920s is **Langone's Funeral Home** at 383 Hanover. In 1920, Italian-born anarchists Nicola Sacco (a shoemaker) and Bartolomeo Vanzetti (a fish peddler) were charged with murdering the paymaster and the guard at a shoe factory and making off with a $16,000 payroll. Found guilty by a jury in 1921, perhaps more for their ethnicity and politics than the evidence, the men remained imprisoned through six years of motions and failed appeals before being electrocuted on August 23, 1927. Langone's laid them out that night, and a huge funeral cortege stretched the length of Hanover Street.

St. Stephen's Church
map page 116, B-6

St. Stephen's Church, the former New North Meeting House, is the only survivor of Boston's five Bulfinch churches. Erected in 1714, it was completely redesigned by Charles Bulfinch between 1802 and 1804 into a masterpiece of balance and clarity that seems the archetype of an American house of worship. The first of Paul Revere's church bells (of some 959 bells he eventually cast) hangs in its belfry. Like many Congregational churches in Boston, it became Unitarian in 1813, but its faith-of-our-fathers days were numbered. As early as 1822, minister Francis Parkman, father of the historian, was complaining that it had become "ungenteel . . . to attend worship in the North End."

In 1862, the Roman Catholic archdiocese bought the building, removed the weathervane, constructed a spire above the cupola, and dedicated it to St. Stephen. The church was moved back 16 feet and raised more than six feet when Hanover Street was widened in 1870. Bostonians have a sentimental attachment to St. Stephen's, for it was Rose Kennedy's parish church. (She was baptized here on July 23, 1890, and was buried from here on January 24, 1995.) By 1964, the dilapidated structure was considered for destruction, but Richard Cardinal Cushing, Archbishop of Boston, stepped in with funds for a complete restoration to the Bulfinch era, including lowering the church back to ground level. *401 Hanover.*

Paul Revere Mall
map page 116, B-6

Across from St. Stephen's the North End suddenly opens up into the Paul Revere Mall (known in the neighborhood as "the Prado") that connects Hanover and Salem Streets, the transition between what had once been the Italian North End and its contemporary Jewish quarter. Constructed in 1933—partly to remove the densely packed wooden frame structures that could have served as tinder to threaten the churches at either end—the pedestrian mall has a look of permanence. An equestrian statue of you-know-who, modeled in 1885 but not cast and installed until 1940, dominates the Hanover Street end. Bronze plaques along the enclosing brick walls tell brief tales of people and events in the North End. The Prado is also a North End social center: old men hunker over tables playing cards and checkers, small children scurry about while their grandmothers look on, teenagers strike poses. The walkway, which narrows as it climbs, is also the most direct approach to Christ Church, Episcopal, better known as "Old North Church" in popular lore and Longfellow's stanzas:

One, if by land, and two, if by sea
And I on the opposite shore will be,
Ready to ride and spread the alarm
Through every Middlesex village and farm,
For the country folk to be up and to arm.

■ SALEM STREET AND COPP'S HILL   *map page 108, A/B-5/6*

Old North Church
map page 108, B-5

Old North Church—today known as Christ Church—built in 1723 after the style of Sir Christopher Wren is Boston's oldest surviving church. The first bell-ringers of its 1744 peal of eight bells were seven neighborhood boys, among them teenager Paul Revere, who in 1750 signed a contract "once a week in Evenings To Ring the Bells for two hours Each Time." Twenty-five years later he convinced sexton Robert Newman to hang two lanterns in the belfry to alert patriots that British troops were on their way to Lexington by "sea," i.e., in rowboats from the Common to Cambridge. Newman's descendants still reenact his part in the annual Patriot's Day festivities (see page 306). General William Gage, commander of British forces in North America, later watched the Battle of Bunker Hill from the bell tower, (now accessible on some tours). Some history buffs argue that the lanterns were hung from the now destroyed Old North Meeting House on North Square, known in 1775 as "Old North." But Christ Church stands on higher ground and its 191-foot steeple has always been the city's tallest.

The interior of the building is classic, lovely and restrained: a model of box pews, brass chandeliers and airy light. Among its more ornate decorations are four trumpeting cherubim in the upper gallery, donated in 1746 by Captain Thomas James Gruchy. Gruchy, at the helm of his privateer vessel *The Queen of Hungary,* "liberated" them from a French ship en route to a Catholic church in Quebec. (It's never been proven but was widely alleged in Gruchy's time that he dug a tunnel between his house on Salem and Charter streets and the nearby wharves to facilitate his lucrative smuggling activities.) A small museum gift shop next door to the church displays such artifacts as a musket from the Battle of Lexington and Concord and a vial of tea from the Boston Tea Party.

44 Hull Street
map page 108, B-5

Christ Church fronts on Salem Street, another of the original North End streets. Directly across from the entrance is Hull Street, where, legend has it, the 10-foot-wide, narrowest house in Boston at 44 Hull was built simply to spite the neighbors by blocking their light and view. Note the old parking garage on the left going down Hull Street. On January 17, 1950, nine men broke into the garage, then headquarters of the Brinks Armored Car Company, and stole more than $1 million in cash. Only a small fraction was ever recovered.

Copp's Hill Burial Ground

map page 108, B-5

At the corner of Hull and Snowhill streets is Boston's second-oldest cemetery, Copp's Hill Burial Ground, where an estimated 10,000 Bostonians were interred beginning in 1660. (Grace Berry's 1625 tombstone and remains were moved from Plymouth by her husband.) It lay between white and black Boston; the area west of the burial ground was Boston's first African-American community, known in colonial times as "New Guinea." The famous and obscure lie side by side: one modest crypt holds the mortal remains of preacher-politicians Increase, Cotton, and Samuel Mather, while the stone on Captain Thomas Lake's plot notes that he was "perfidiously slain by ye Indians in 1676." A broken column marks the grave of Prince Hall, soldier in the Revolution, early leader of Boston's African-American community and head of the Black Masons. Patriot Daniel Malcolm's tombstone, chipped by British musketballs, reflects that he asked to be buried "in a stone grave 10 feet deep" to be safe from British bullets. Also interred at Copp's Hill is George Worthlake, first keeper of Boston Light, who drowned off the Light with his family in November 1718.

(above and opposite) Built in 1723, Old North Church, also known as Christ Church, is the city's oldest surviving place of worship. (photo opposite by Robert Holmes)

Because it towers above the surrounding streets, the burial ground is more bright than melancholy, its lofty heights affording a sweeping view across the harbor to the Bunker Hill Monument and the USS *Constitution* ("Old Ironsides"), which was built just below the Copp's Hill bluff. During the Battle of Bunker Hill, British cannon leveled Charlestown from these heights. Before the Revolution, the hill was often used for public hangings because many citizens could surround it to witness the spectacle.

Copp's Hill Terrace
map page 108, B-5

The Terrace, just off Salem Street across from the burial ground is where the Great Molasses Flood occurred in 1919. A 2.5-million gallon molasses tank burst and the ensuing sticky wave killed 21 as it swept away houses and people. The molasses smell, old-timers say, lingered for decades after.

Salem Street
map page 108, A/B-5/6

It's easy to follow the molasses trail back downhill along Salem Street, once the East-

Before the Great Molasses Flood of 1919, other disasters wreaked havoc in the city. The worst fire to break out in Boston occurred in 1872, when most of downtown was destroyed. (Boston Public Library)

ern European, mostly Jewish section of the North End. (Or, follow the Freedom Trail's red line down Hull to Commercial Street to reach the Charlestown Bridge.) Today Salem Street is demonstrably Italian, with some of the neighborhood's best butchers and grocers.

North Bennet Street School

map page 108, B-6

This school was established in 1881 by educator/social worker Pauline Agassiz Shaw to teach jobs skills to immigrants. Now it's considered a leader in preserving vanishing handcrafts. *Salem St. at 39 North Bennet.*

■ CHARLESTOWN *map page 108, top, center*

Charlestown, occupying its own peninsula just across the harbor from the North End, predates the rest of Boston by a year. But few traces of the early town remain because cannon and conflagration destroyed the community during the Revolution. Rebuilt in the early 19th century, Charlestown officially joined an expanding Boston in October 1873.

Like the North End, Charlestown is a community in transition. The blue-collar Irish population, who go under the rubric of "Townies," may soon be outnumbered by young (and not so young) professionals. The area's housing stock is better designed for spacious urban living than the compact former tenements of the North End, and the real estate market has restored a near-Victorian decorum to many of these handsome bow-fronted streets.

The **Charlestown Bridge** dates from 1899 (and looks it); it is a successor to a 1786 span which had replaced the ferry service that was a money-making franchise operated exclusively by Harvard College. The bridge connects the area of the North End once largely used for ropemaking to City Square, an open area that was a highway-ridden wasteland until 1995. Excavations here for the Artery/Tunnel project uncovered what may be the remains of the Great House built by John Winthrop in 1630 before he opted to move across the Charles River to the Shawmut Peninsula.

City Square sits at the base of **Town Hill,** where the first community settled in 1629 when ten families and their servants came from Salem. Near the top of the hill was the pallisaded fort they erected in 1630; the site now contains John Harvard Mall, named in honor of the "sometimes minister of God's word" who lived nearby. The walled green space features several bronze plaques relating local history. One proclaims "this low mound of earth the memorial of a mighty nation." The "first public worship of God" by Winthrop's Puritans took place here "under a great oak"—the birth of the First Church of Boston.

But Harvard gets the last word, even though he only lived fourteen months in Charlestown before succumbing to consumption. A monument in the center of the mall explains that when he died in 1638, Harvard left half his estate and all his books to the fledgling college in Cambridge established two years earlier. His gift of 800 pounds and 300 books moved the powers-that-were to name the school for him. The tradition has continued; Harvard today possesses the largest endowment of any university in the United States.

The arching street above the mall (Harvard Street) is a mini-catalog of row-house styles from the 19th century. At the corner with Main Street stands a rare split stone building dating from about 1800. At the corner of Main and Pleasant Streets, the **Warren Tavern** was one of the first buildings erected after the British burned Charlestown. The establishment was named in honor of Dr. Joseph Warren, president of the Provincial Congress in 1774 and a general in the Massachusetts Army. Despite his rank, he volunteered to serve as a simple soldier under Colonel William Prescott at the Battle of Bunker Hill and was killed.

(above) In a genetics lab in Charlestown's Massachusetts General East, Dr. Rudi Tanzi displays a radiograph showing DNA sequencing. This lab has been instrumental in locating genes that contain defects such as Lou Gehrig's disease and Huntington's disease.

(opposite) Softball games are often played under Charlestown's huge Tobin Bridge.

■ BUNKER HILL *map page 108, B-2*

The Bunker Hill Monument, which stands atop Breed's Hill, memorializes the Revolutionary War battle of June 17, 1775. The American colonials lost this first pitched battle of the war, but inflicted heavy casualties while halting the breakout of the British from their siege position inside Boston. The valiant stand of the American troops boosted morale and gave birth to a great deal of inflated rhetoric over the ensuing decades. Notes an inscription at the **Massachusetts Gate** to the monument, "Colonel William Prescott of Massachusetts led the Colonial forces here on Breed's Hill. His commanding figure and strong will inspired the farmer soldiers to the greatness of the day." Indeed, the fighting statue of Prescott still appears inspiring.

The first monument to the battle, a Tuscan pillar, was erected in 1794 by the local Masonic Lodge to honor Dr. Warren. In 1823, the Bunker Hill Monument Association was created to raise money for a grander monument and to complete the battlefield purchase begun by Warren's heirs. The granite obelisk was built according to the plans and under the direction of Solomon Willard. The Marquis de Lafayette laid the cornerstone in 1825 during his farewell tour of America. Forty elderly veterans of the battle attended and Daniel Webster was the day's speaker. Construction costs grew and the association had to sell most of the battlefield to raise cash. In 1840 the "mothers and daughters of Boston" held a fair at Quincy Market that raised $30,035 toward the project. Finally, in 1843, Daniel Webster again gave an oration at the completion of the 221-foot monument; amazingly, 13 veterans from the 1775 battle attended.

Bunker Hill Monument
map page 108, B-2
The Bunker Hill Monument was the first monument built by public subscription and among the first touted as a tourist attraction. It also popularized the obelisk style, inspiring other shafts around America. Bunker Hill maintained its status as the tallest monument in the country until 1885, when the erection of the Washington Monument surpassed the Charlestown inspiration. Bunker Hill has no elevator; 294 steps spiral to the top. Townies remain proud of the monument and of the events that transpired in Charlestown more than two centuries ago, turning out in droves for the annual Bunker Hill Day parade in June.

Located in Boston National Historical Park; T:#93 bus from Haymarket (Green Line), MBTA water shuttle from Long Wharf; information 617-242-5641.

Monument Square and Winthrop Square

map page 108, B-2

Surrounding the Monument is Monument Square, some of Charlestown's most prized real estate. One corner of the square leads down to Winthrop Square, also known as Training Field. It was set aside in 1632 as a drill ground for local militia; troops left here for battle in 1775, 1812, and 1860. Plaques at the uphill side list the American casualties of the Battle of Bunker Hill. The chunky Victory with soldier and sailor honors the men who fought "for the preservation of the Union."

Bunker Hill Pavilion   *map page 108, B-3*

At the bottom of the hill is Main Street, which ends at Constitution Avenue. Along the waterfront is the Bunker Hill Pavilion, with a multimedia show about the battle, and the Charlestown Navy Yard. *Adjacent to Charlestown Navy Yard; 617-241-7575. (Also see page 195.)*

USS *Constitution*   *map page 108, B-3*

America's oldest fighting ship, also known as Old Ironsides, is moored at Drydock #1 in Charlestown. *(See pages 193-195.)*

A RAGGED TROOP ON BUNKER HILL

*E*very street and alley, every park and pier had its own ragged troop which hung on the corner, played football, baseball, and streethockey, and defended its turf against all comers. The Wildcats hung at the corner of Frothingham and Lincoln Streets, the Bearcats at Walker and Russell Streets, the Falcons outside the Edwards School, the Cobras on Elm Street, the Jokers in Hayes Square, the Highlanders on High Street, the Crusaders at the Training Field. Each had its distinctive football jersey (on which members wore their street addresses), its own legends and traditions.

The Highlanders, for example, took their identity from the Bunker Hill Monument, which towered over their hangout at the top of Monument Avenue. On weekends and summer afternoons, they gathered there to wait for out-of-town tourists visiting the revolutionary battleground. When one approached, an eager boy would step forward and launch his spiel, learned by rote from other Highlanders:

"The Monument is 221 feet high, has 294 winding stairs and no elevators. They say the quickest way up is to walk, the quickest way down is to fall. The Monument is fifteen feet square. Its cornerstone was laid in 1825 by Daniel Webster. The statue you see in the foreground is that of Colonel William Prescott standing in the same position as when he gave that brave and famous command, 'Don't fire till you see the whites of their eyes.' The British made three attempts to gain the hill . . ." And so forth. An engaging raconteur could parlay this patter into a fifty-cent tip.

—J. Anthony Lukas, *Common Ground,* 1986

CULTURAL DISTRICT,
THEATER DISTRICT,
& CHINATOWN

0   .1   .2   .3
Miles

CULTURAL DISTRICT

*I have just returned from Boston. It is the only sane thing to do
if you find yourself up there.*
—Fred Allen, Letter to Groucho Marx, 1953

CITY HALL'S DREAM TO HARNESS THE DEVELOPMENT boom of the 1980s to engineer a "Midtown Cultural District" bespoke the heady thinking of the time. The new business and entertainment area was to have swept away the Combat Zone, tidied up Chinatown and magically transformed the blocks along Tremont Street from the Common to the Massachusetts Turnpike into Boston's equivalent of London's West End.

For any number of reasons, it didn't happen.

But, unplanned and unbidden, an arts and entertainment district did begin to emerge on its own terms, even spreading from the modest confines of the tenacious old Theater District into parts of the South End and, by way of artists desperate for studio and gallery space, into a former manufacturing area. This self-seeded cultural district may lack the integration and modernity of the city's plans, but it compensates with a sometimes gritty vitality and, in some places, a hospitality to artistic expression far more adventurous than the predictable glitz of Broadway road shows. Although the Combat Zone, Boston's adult entertainment district only a block away, manages to hang on by a G-string, the once-dark legitimate theaters are lit again and a covey of bars and restaurants has alighted to serve their patrons.

■ THE THEATER DISTRICT

Boston has had a long and sometimes distinguished stage tradition, and just as long a history of opposition to the very idea of theater. During the height of America's struggle over defining obscenity in the 1920s, H. L. Mencken defined a Puritan as a person terrified by the "haunting fear that someone, somewhere may be happy." Speculation about their motivations aside, Boston Puritans did ban plays altogether, setting the tone of moral objection to stage shows that kept theater out of Boston until 1792.

But by the mid-1800s, Boston stages prospered with farces and melodramas and the occasional bit of Shakespeare. By the 1860s, Edwin Booth was Boston's star attraction. In 1878, religious leaders formed the Watch and Ward Society, an organization that screened books and plays for moral content and organized boycotts against the ones they found indecent or blasphemous. But righteous scourges could not dampen Boston's exploding theatrical scene. In the 1880s, B. F. Keith organized stage variety shows on Washington Street as "wholesome" entertainment. In 1894, he opened his B. F. Keith Theater as a showcase for a transformed style of variety that he christened "vaudeville." Within a decade, competitors at the Howard Athenaeum, once principally an opera hall, had added "living pictures" to the mix—comely ladies attired in skin-tight costumes. Before long, the costumes began to come off and burlesque was born.

In 1905, the city licensing division took it upon itself to deny performances that didn't meet the office's code. Among the prohibitions were women "appearing on the stage in legs bare," "all forms of muscle dancing" and—most importantly for later clashes between art and law—"portrayal of a moral pervert or sex degenerate." As the designation "Banned in Boston" became a surefire marketing ploy, the "Athens of America" was reduced to a national joke. Even former mayor John F. Fitzgerald groused that the 1929 ban on Eugene O'Neill's *Strange Interlude* was "more like the action of a hick town than a metropolitan city." The producers moved the show to Quincy, where it played to packed houses of Bostonians.

Despite the licensing board's strictures, by the 1920s Boston was thriving as a tryout town. With rising production costs (including demands of the new actors' union for rehearsal fees) and the advent of powerful and influential New York critics, producers found it prudent to polish a new play in the provinces before taking it to Broadway. Avid audiences and good train connections made Boston and Philadelphia obligatory stops for Broadway-bound productions. Tennessee Williams's first two plays died in Boston in the 1940s, and his third, starring Jessica Tandy and (in small print) the unknown Marlon Brando, spent two weeks in rewrites at the Wilbur before emerging on Broadway as *A Streetcar Named Desire*. Through the late 1940s and 1950s, Boston became the place to perfect big-budget shows. The terribly flawed *Away We Go* arrived in 1943 at the Shubert, spent weeks in rewrites, and left on the New York train as *Oklahoma!*

Amazingly enough, Edward Albee rewrote *Who's Afraid of Virginia Woolf?* for its 1962 Boston performances—not to improve it but to appease the censors—removing all the profanity and quite possibly rendering the play unintelligible. For many years thereafter, Albee refused to have his plays produced in Boston.

In 1965, the American Civil Liberties Union finally took the city to court, exposing the censorship pact between City Hall and the Boston theater managers. But the city found other ways to harass shows, closing *Hair* for four weeks in 1970 over alleged desecration of the American flag. Changing mores took the teeth out of the censor's bite and the city finally gave up its moral patrol of the theater in 1975, when *Equus* was produced as the first play in Boston with "full freedom of expression."

Despite the heel-nipping censors, Boston's theater district once included as many as 40 active venues from Washington Street near Downtown Crossing to the present district along Boylston and Tremont Streets. Three theaters on Washington Street near Downtown Crossing recently made the list of "America's Most Endangered Places" prepared by the National Trust for Historic Preservation: The Paramount, the Opera House, and the Modern stand as sad reminders of a much larger theater district.

As the dean of Boston theater critics, Elliot Norton, observed, "Theaters always tend to hang together, for comfort, for reassurance, and protection. They hang, and they huddle; at least they do in Boston." Today's huddling group along Tremont and Boylston Streets—though only a handful of the sumptuous theaters from Boston's heyday—nonetheless represents the most architecturally eminent group of early theaters in America. They carry on Boston's commercial theater tradition, while new plays and "art" productions are found in the nonprofit theaters scattered throughout the city, notably at Harvard and Boston University.

■ HISTORIC THEATERS

The eldest of the survivors, the 1,700-seat **Colonial Theatre** (106 Boylston Street), was built in 1900, and its lavish gilt and fresco interior was completely restored in 1995. The Colonial, which was lit much of 1996 with Donny Osmond in *Joseph and the Amazing Technicolor Dreamcoat,* has always favored spectacle. It debuted with *Ben-Hur,* complete with chariots drawn by horses on treadmills. The extravaganza proved very popular later in New York, and the Colonial became a prime location to doctor shows bound for the Big Apple. Florenz Ziegfeld launched his *Follies* here in 1927 and returned yearly to polish each edition. Several Rodgers and Hammerstein musicals also visited the Colonial for pre-Broadway rewrites, and the tryout tradition continues today.

DOWNTOWN CROSSING AND FILENE'S BASEMENT

Generations of Bostonians have trekked to Downtown Crossing at the juncture of Summer, Winter, and Washington streets to buy their Easter outfits or marvel at the animated Christmas windows, and to scoop up the best bargains in the city. The pedestrian mall along Washington Street (closed to all but delivery traffic since 1978) evolved around the department store anchors of Filene's and Jordan Marsh—a prototype on which suburban malls were constructed. In warm weather, pushcarts line the streets and the broad mall between the two large stores turns into a midday concert stage. But with a proliferation of chain stores and the absorption of its anchors into larger corporations, Downtown Crossing has come to resemble a suburban mall imitating Downtown Crossing.

Some aspects remain unique. The subterranean levels of Filene's hold a separate corporate descendant of the original Filene's Basement, pioneer (since 1908) of the "automatic markdown." Each item is tagged with a date of arrival and a sale price. Automatic discounts begin at 25 percent after two weeks, 50 percent after three weeks, 75 percent after four weeks. After five weeks, remaining goods are donated to charity. Many Bostonians, from Beacon Hill matrons to gum-snapping Townies, attire themselves from head to foot from "The Basement." Wading through tables of newly arrived closeouts from Barneys and Saks is Boston's idea of blood sport, and most shoppers try clothes on in the aisles rather than bother with changing rooms that slow the ambitious consumer.

The craziest days are the annual sales of wedding gowns and fur coats. On those days, a savvy customer will run through the aisles, grabbing the prettiest dresses she can find, in any size. Then she'll have bargaining power. For example, a size 6 bride-to-be grabs a size 10 designer original gown, then approaches a larger woman who's trying on a charming dress that—magically—turns out to be too small. Result? Win-win, thanks to the simplest form of bartering.

The longtime rival of Filene's was Jordan Marsh—now called Macy's, a Manhattanish name that obscures the initial partnership founded January 20, 1851, between Eben Dyer Jordan and Benjamin L. Marsh. Bostonians take change hard. As the *Boston Globe* observed in a January 1996 editorial, "Macy's replacing Jordan Marsh? . . . It's like hearing that Durgin Park is becoming Sardi's. Or that Fenway will be called 'Yankee Stadium North.' Or that frappes will be renamed egg creams. Or milkshakes. . . . But for a long time, maybe forever, some folks will still shop at 'Jahden's.' (Rhymes with 'Boston Gahden.') After all, they still call Government Center Scollay Square."

Bargain hunters crowd the aisles of Filene's Basement on Wedding Gown Day.

The Colonial anchors **Piano Row** (Boylston Street between Tremont and Charles Streets), once the corporate headquarters of the firms that made Boston America's center of piano building and music publishing in the 19th and early 20th centuries. The Beaux-Arts **Steinert Hall** (162 Boylston) houses both piano showrooms and a small concert hall no longer in use. The companies of E.A. Starck, Vose & Sons, and the redoubtable Wurlitzer Company, which also built most of the grand organs for Boston's theaters, have either died or moved to greener pastures, but their buildings live on. In 1860, when Piano Row was an open field, students of Mr. Dixwell's Private School organized the first known game of football where Boylston Place now stands. This alley-cum-courtyard is the entrance to the private Tavern Club and a nightclub as well as a quick shortcut through the block to the Transportation Building.

The Little Building at the corner of Boylston and Tremont Streets was converted in 1995 into a dormitory for Emerson College, known for its strong performing arts programs. Emerson students have enlivened the street life on this corner of the Common, helping to keep the nearby Combat Zone at bay. The college also acquired the old Majestic Theatre at 219 Tremont Street, completely rehabilitated the rococo interior, and restored this 800-seat 1903 gem to its original opulence. Having once hosted such performers as Ethel Merman, Lena Horne, W. C. Fields, and Harry Houdini, the Majestic was converted to a movie theater in 1956 and reached its nadir in the 1970s as a venue for horror films. The **Emerson Majestic Theatre**, as it's now known, mostly hosts major nonprofit dance, opera, and theatrical events, as well as Emerson student productions.

The 1914 **Wilbur Theatre** (246 Tremont St.) is one of the more intimate commercial theaters, seating about 1,200 in its most economical configuration. A deep balcony makes it seem even smaller; the steep rake of the upper-balcony seats may also account for the oft-repeated description of the Wilbur as "Beacon Hill in theater dress." Thornton Wilder's *Our Town* debuted here in 1938.

The Renaissance Revival palace next door at 268 Tremont Street was called the Metropolitan when it was built in 1925 as an opulent variety show and movie theater then seating more than 4,000 people (now reduced to about 3,700). Initial construction cost $8 million, and the restoration, completed in 1992, cost $10 million. Now called the **Wang Center for the Performing Arts** in honor of patron An Wang, it's the principal venue for headliners like Pavarotti and Baryshnikov, Broadway megashows (such as Andrew Lloyd Webber's supermusicals), and the larger productions of the Boston Ballet. The theater was modeled on the Paris Opera House, while the Grand Lobby (as seen in the film *The Witches of Eastwick*) was based on the design of Versailles.

At midcentury, the New York-based Shubert family owned seven theaters in Boston. To settle a federal antitrust suit, they divested themselves of all but the prestigious **Shubert Theatre** (265 Tremont St.) across from the Wang Center. Now used for productions that will not fill the cavernous Wang space, this 1,600-seat theater built in 1910 has a venerable history as the pre-Broadway home of *South Pacific, Camelot,* and Richard Burton's *Hamlet.*

No new theaters have been built in Boston in recent decades, but in 1976 the **Charles Playhouse** at 76 Warrenton Street was carved out of an 1838 church designed by Asher Benjamin. The resulting black box theater functions as the most casual and modern space in the district.

■ COMBAT ZONE

When construction of Government Center displaced the burlesque houses and showbars of Scollay Square in the 1960s, the city designated Washington Street between Essex and Kneeland Streets as an "adult entertainment zone." For inexplicable reasons, it soon acquired the nickname of the Combat Zone, a colorful designation that sticks to this day. Despite regular forecasts of the district's demise, the Combat Zone's prurient flame continues to flicker with a desultory strip bar, peep shows, and the standard urban porn vendors. Some of Boston's most down-and-out homeless people also congregate in the Combat Zone. Although this short stretch of Washington Street creates a mildly sinister barrier between the Theater District and Chinatown, adult entertainment is loosening its grip. The theater at the corner of Washington and Kneeland, for example, opened as a nickelodeon in 1907, became a legitimate theater in 1925, and was transformed into the X-rated Pussycat in 1976. It has been a sedate McDonald's since the late '80s.

Even the plastic insects and joy buzzers of Jack's Joke Shop (the oldest active joke shop in America, established in 1922) have felt safe enough to edge down Boylston toward the Combat Zone. And the state has placed the Registry of Motor Vehicles in a former strip-show building on the **site of the Liberty Tree,** an oak planted in 1646 where the Sons of Liberty often met until Tories and Redcoats cut it down in 1775. This corner of Essex and Washington Streets, marked by two plaques, was a block from the shoreline of South Cove, from which the patriots embarked in Indian garb for the Boston Tea Party.

■ CHINATOWN

The land of Chinatown and the Leather District is—no great surprise—fill, created in two phases in the early 19th century. As a combination harbor and rail depot, South Cove quickly became the squalid neighborhood of new immigrants, as Beacon Hill's north slope had been in Colonial days. Only the Chinese stayed, putting their stamp on this compact district of Beach, Oxford, Tyler, and Hudson Streets.

Although Chinese first came to Boston during 18th-century trade with the Far East, large-scale immigration didn't begin until the 1870s, when 200 Chinese were brought in by ship as strikebreakers to a Lawrence, Massachusetts, shoe factory. Once the strike was broken, the mill owners abandoned the Chinese, many of whom moved to Boston and settled in tents in a strip they called Ping-On Alley. They were soon joined by laborers who had come east after working on the transcontinental railroads. Alexander Graham Bell's central office was nearby, and as the Bell Telephone Company grew, many of the Chinese laborers laid the lines.

The Chinese Exclusion Act of 1882 kept the growth of the Chinese community slow, but by 1931 Chinatown had about 1,200 inhabitants and the neighborhood grew even faster when various immigration laws were repealed in the 1940s. In the 1960s, ethnic Chinese followed the pattern of previous Boston immigrant groups, with the young moving out to the suburbs and older people or those with the most entrenched community investments staying behind. At the same time, Chinatown became a magnet to Southeast Asian refugees and immigrants. While the old Chinese family and merchant associations still run Chinatown, a growing number of businesses display Vietnamese, Cambodian, and Thai scripts in their windows next to Chinese characters.

Visitors from cities with more substantial Chinatowns often find Boston's compact district a disappointment. But the streets of residential rowhouses do hold a variety of restaurants, grocery stores, and gift and martial arts shops at street level. A few outward stamps of ethnic identification, perhaps more for tourists than residents, are the red-pagoda phonebooths and a large dragon gate.

During the 1940s and '50s, when Broadway tryouts kept the Theater District lit almost every night, Chinatown restaurants flourished. After some years of decline, the restaurant activity is again on the upswing. Older restaurants, like the New Shanghai on Hudson Street (the district's oldest), fill with Chinese families visiting from the suburbs over dim sum. A profusion of Vietnamese and other Asian cuisines, as well as the rise of a generation of innovative young Chinese chefs, have made Chinatown a top dining spot for Boston foodies and especially for other Boston chefs.

Scenes from Boston's Chinatown.

Important landmarks in Chinatown include the **Chinese Merchants Association Building** (20 Hudson Street), a 1951 symbol of neighborhood pride and political power, and the **mural at 34 Oak Street** that recalls the area's history as a garment district. The **Old Quincy School** at 90 Tyler Street, built in 1847, was a radical innovation in American education. It was the first public school with graded classrooms and the first with an individual desk for each student and was a leader in de-emphasizing corporal punishment and including drawing and music in the curriculum. Until 1976, the building also served as a night school for waves of immigrants to learn the English language and "the American way."

■ LEATHER DISTRICT

The so-called Leather District, which stands just across Atlantic Avenue from South Station, used to be contiguous with Chinatown and was, into the 1940s, an industrial center for the manufacture of leather goods and clothing and the machinery to make both. Then came the Expressway, which took much of the land and left the remainder as a three-block traffic island wedged between Atlantic Avenue and expressway interchanges. So who moves into areas no one else wants? Artists. Lincoln, Utica, and South Streets are slowly gaining studios and galleries to complement the software companies already in residence, and some fine eateries and bars are following. Perhaps the strongest hint of future direction in the Leather District is **Do While Studios,** a collaborative group working at the interface of high art and binary code.

■ BAY VILLAGE

Bay Village, too, is another artifact of 19th-century Boston orphaned and isolated by highway construction. The bittersweet claim to fame of this charming neighborhood of picturesque brick rowhouses is that Edgar Allan Poe was born here in 1809 at 62 Carver Street, a building demolished in the 1960s. (Poe left as a babe in arms. Throughout his life, Poe loathed Boston; the city's powerful literary elite reciprocated in kind.) The original inhabitants of the neighborhood—circumscribed by Tremont, Charles, Stuart, and Arlington Streets—were artisans. The last remnant of this tradition is the **Haynes Flute and Piccolo Company** at 12 Piedmont Street. During Prohibition, the narrow little streets were flooded with speakeasies. One architectural landmark of note is the Park Plaza Castle, formally the First Corps of Cadets Armory, which frequently serves as a convention and exhibition hall.

CULTURAL DISTRICT

■ SOUTH END

Composed of more than 500 acres, the South End—roughly Berkeley Street to Massachusetts Avenue and the Southwest Corridor to Harrison Avenue—is the largest National Historic District in the nation. To Bostonians, however, it's always been the wrong side of the tracks—literally the wrong side of the railroad tracks laid along the Neck. South End fill began in 1834, a generation before Back Bay, and the area was developed in an English style of Georgian Revival bowfront row-houses surrounding small parks on self-contained blocks. At the end of each small cluster were broad avenues—Harrison, Washington, and Tremont Streets and Shawmut Avenue—designed less for visual appeal than speedy transit.

Faced with a choice between the closed blocks of the South End and the open French model of Back Bay, prominent Bostonians chose the latter, leaving the South End to absorb the human flood of 19th-century immigration. They came in waves—the Irish, the Eastern Europeans (including the Lithuanian family of art historian Bernard Berenson), the Greeks, the Syrians (among them the family of inspirational writer Kahlil Gibran). They all came and, for the most part, went. In the early 20th century, the newcomers were African Americans who built a vibrant

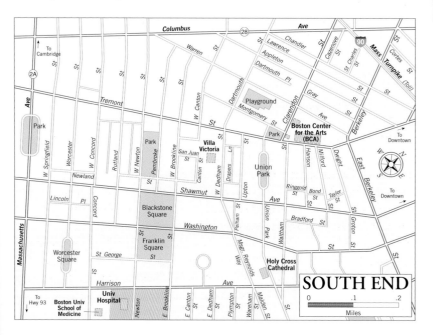

SOUTH END

SOUTH END IN TRANSITION

*T*he *Gay News* was located on a South End street that was "in transition." In some cities, that expression is an unfortunate euphemism for a racial evolution. In Boston, however, the expression is used to reflect a building-by-building renovation. The South End (not to be confused with the heavily Irish South Boston, where I grew up) is predominantly narrow streets, some with imitation gas lamps. The architecture is three- and four-story attached brick townhouses, many with beautiful bowfront windows. The population is a mixture of upper middle class, young professionals, gays, blacks, Greeks, Cubans, and a dozen other racial or ethnic minorities. The major condominium developers moved from Back Bay and Beacon Hill to the waterfront, somewhat leap-frogging the South End because of its streetside drug trade and derelicts that are somehow never brought under control. Accordingly, each block is torn between gentrification and degeneration.

—J. F. Healy, *Blunt Darts*, 1984

Tremont Street and the area around the BCA are today the center of a lively neighborhood on the rise. (James Marshall)

Jazz Age culture and black political organization before the middle class moved on to neighboring Roxbury. Since World War II, the immigrants have been Caribbean, principally from Puerto Rico.

But this district of handsome row houses, pocket parks, and broad avenues is a neighborhood very much in transition as a tide of gentrification gradually washes over boarded-up shells, revealing their handsome lines. Contrasts abound in the South End. A gay community dominates some streets, while others buzz with the polyglot patois of the islands. On one isolated corner stands the Pine Street Inn, the city's largest shelter for the homeless, located in a Victorian building based on the Palazzo Vecchio in Florence, Italy. Closer to the Back Bay there's a dynamic street life of performing arts and chic bistros.

■ TREMONT STREET

The main street of the newly resurgent South End is Tremont Street, which enters the neighborhood after skirting Bay Village en route from the Theater District. **The Boston Center for the Arts** (BCA), the centerpiece of the South End's lively arts district, occupies the four-acre parcel bordered by Tremont, Clarendon, and Berkeley Streets and Warren Avenue. Slowly redeveloped since 1970, the cluster of buildings includes the Boston Ballet Building, which houses the Boston Ballet's educational programs, rehearsal studios, and administrative offices. (The ballet generally performs in the nearby Wang Center.) Also part of the BCA, the Tremont Estates Building at the corner of Tremont and Clarendon was an organ company in the late 1860s when the South End's factories were the national center of piano and organ manufacturing. This building later became the factory for the "Velvet Grip," the original garter for silk stockings. Today it houses artists' studios and rehearsal spaces (the largest concentration in New England), a visual arts gallery, and a popular restaurant, Hamersley's Bistro.

The BCA's most unusual building is the circular, domed **Cyclorama**, which opened in 1884 to exhibit the 50-foot by 400-foot painting, *The Battle of Gettysburg*, by Paul Dominique Philoppoteaux. Cycloramas were immensely popular entertainments at the time, and for the next few years, Boston's was no exception. The 2.9-ton canvas was removed in 1889 to tour and spent several decades in storage before the National Park Service acquired it in 1942, installing it in a new building at Gettysburg National Historic Park in 1962.

CULTURAL DISTRICT

The domed Cyclorama housed a 400-foot-long painting of the Battle of Gettysburg, and served at different times as a flower market, a sparkplug factory, and a roller skating rink.

The Cyclorama itself fell to other uses, including serving as home to a bazaar that featured a carousel, roller skating, and bicycle riding. In the mid-1890s, the Cyclorama hosted several boxing matches, including at least one featuring the Boston Strong Boy, John L. Sullivan, a South End resident who went down in history as the "Last of the Bare-Fisted Sluggers."

Over the years the Cyclorama also served as a factory (Albert Champion invented the spark plug here in 1907), and from 1923 through the '60s, it was the home of the city's wholesale floral market. Since the late 1980s, the BCA has stepped up renovations on the structure, adding wheelchair access to all levels of the building and developing three theater spaces of varying sizes beneath the Cyclorama. These theaters host a wide variety of performances throughout the year. The often avant-garde theater, dance, and performance art by independent companies has helped cement the BCA's reputation as Boston's center of artistic innovation.

■ UNION PARK & ENVIRONS

The section of the South End within hailing distance of the BCA is one of the liveliest parts of the city. Its chic restaurants, bars, and cafés enjoy a hip and discriminating clientele. Moreover, businesses are beginning to recolonize the neighborhood as an atmosphere of permanence replaces the air of urban homesteading.

A few blocks past the BCA, Union Park was laid out in 1851 in the fashion of a London residential park, exemplifying the original vision for the South End as a quarter full of park-centered blocks. Finally realized and polished a century and a half later, Union Park is the showpiece to which others still aspire.

But gentrification has only spread so far. Just a block removed from Union Park is the thoroughfare of Washington Street, where the removal of the elevated transit system in the 1980s has left the street with that naked, astonished look of a man who's just shaved off his beard. The end closest to the city core is anchored by the gray mass of **Holy Cross Cathedral,** notable for its size (as large as Westminster Abbey) and its role in ministering to waves of immigrants since the mid-19th century. In 1998, Holy Cross completed a $1 million restoration of its gilt interior.

CULTURAL
DISTRICT

Union Park was laid out in 1851 in the fashion of a London residential park.
(James Marshall)

Its original Irish gone, Holy Cross now serves a large Puerto Rican population centered on Villa Victoria. In the late 1960s and early '70s, Puerto Rican tenants fought back against urban renewal plans and negotiated the development of this 10-acre planned community defined by Tremont, West Dedham, and West Newton Streets and Shawmut Avenue. Inquilinos Boricuas en Accion, the organization that emerged from that struggle, still functions as a community service agency and frequently sponsors Hispanic arts and cultural events at the Jorge Hernandez Cultural Center.

Faces of Boston: (opposite, above) a large Puerto Rican community populates Villa Victoria; (opposite, below) a cantina in Jamaica Plain, also home to a large Latino community; (this page below) flower markets dot the city, adding color to the landscape.

B A C K   B A Y

The main entrance to the Boston Public Library used to face Copley Square across
Dartmouth Street. . . . It felt like a library and looked like a library, and even
when I was going in there to look up Duke Snider's lifetime batting average,
I used to feel like a scholar.

— Robert B. Parker, *Looking for Rachel Wallace*, 1980

BACK BAY WAS BLESSED BY THE ALCHEMY of civic will. By transmuting 450 acres of
mud and slime into prime real estate, Boston escaped from its cramped colonial
quarters to reinvent itself as a cosmopolitan urban center. The now-fabled Back
Bay neighborhood was, in the 1850s, "nothing less than a cesspool" by the admis-
sion of the Boston City Council. Actually, it was an estuary on the Charles River
where the tides of the Atlantic Ocean twice daily uncovered pungent mud flats
rank with sewage and stagnant water trapped by a mill dam across the mouth of
the basin.

At the State House, where the aroma wafted with regularity, the Legislature
voted the most ambitious public works project in America to that time: filling in
the basin to create (more or less) dry land. The immense project began in 1859,
and thanks to the newfangled steam shovel, first used at gravel pits in West Needham, and the steam locomotive, which allowed 35 cars of gravel to arrive every 45
minutes, a largely Irish group of laborers filled two house lots per day for about 13
years. Work continued sporadically and at a slower pace for the next 30-odd years.

Architects and house-builders followed close behind, building from the Public
Garden to the Fens in an encyclopedia of Victorian architectural styles and tastes.
They were remaking the landscape in what *Boston Globe* architecture critic Robert
Campbell has called "bold American assertions of private wealth and initiative"
that still manage to "gather into an image of community."

But Back Bay is more than fine Victorian townhouses. Upwards of a third of
the "New Land," as it was called, was set aside for public use under architect
Arthur Gilman's gridlike plan of arrow-straight avenues crossed at regular intervals
by residential streets, named alphabetically in ascending order from the Public
Garden. The ensuing model of order and proportion is one of the few sections of
Boston that outsiders can navigate without a map. Today, Newbury and Boylston

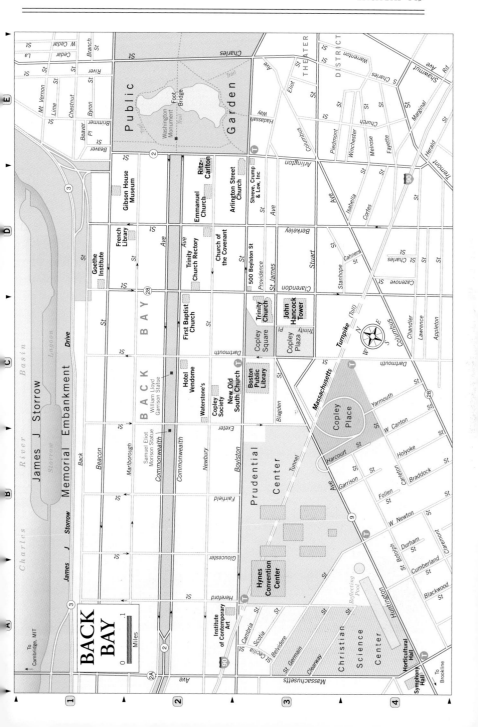

BACK BAY

0 Miles .1

To Cambridge, MIT

Charles River Basin

James J Storrow Memorial Embankment Drive

James J Storrow

Lagoon Storrow

Public Garden

Washington Monument Foot Trail Bridge

Goethe Institute

French Library

Gibson House Museum

Ritz-Carlton

Emmanuel Church

Trinity Church Rectory

Church of the Covenant

Arlington Street Church

Shreve, Crump & Low, Inc

500 Boylston St

BACK BAY

First Baptist Church

Hotel Vendome

William Lloyd Garrison Statue

Samuel Eliot Morison Statue

Waterstone's

Copley Society

New Old South Church

Boston Public Library

Trinity Church

Copley Square

Copley Plaza

John Hancock Tower

Turnpike (Toll)

Massachusetts

Copley Place

Prudential Center

Tunnel

Hynes Convention Center

Institute of Contemporary Art

Christian Science Center

Reflecting Pool

Horticultural Hall

Symphony Hall

THEATER DISTRICT

Shawmut Ave

To Brookline

Streets have emerged as streets of trade as much as of domiciles. They are upscale commercial straits where the glitterati sip espresso in outdoor cafes to rest up from hopping between boutiques, where hard-charging new money cloaks itself in stately architecture to quietly conquer new worlds, where art galleries command top prices for newly enthroned talent, and where everyone else goes to ogle each other and try to separate the *vero* Armani from the *faux* Chanel.

■ THE PUBLIC GARDEN   *map page 145, E-1/2*

If the Common is Boston's family rec room, then the adjacent Public Garden is the city's formal parlor. The nation's first public botanical garden, the 24-acre greenland serves today as a graceful gateway between downtown jumblement and Back Bay decorum. The original tidal mudflats were filled in before the rest of Back Bay, and the city twice tried to sell off the plot and twice succumbed to public pressure to keep it. An 1859 design competition led to the adoption of the English-style garden scheme of George F. Meacham, a young Boston landscape architect. By

The Swan Boats have long been a well-known feature of the Public Garden.

1861, the three-acre lagoon surrounded by weeping willows had been added. The Garden's plan exemplifies the Victorian penchant for indirection: all its paths meander around the water's edge.

Bounded by a cast-iron fence on Charles, Beacon, Arlington, and Boylston Streets, the Garden's formality has worn better than the casual Common. Thousands of people daily enjoy the 57 **formal flower beds** (America's first imported tulips were planted here in 1837), grand specimen trees and odd dots of public sculpture. The most commanding is Thomas Ball's **equestrian statue of George Washington,** the most peculiar a monument marking the first successful use of ether as an anaesthetic (at Massachusetts General Hospital). But Nancy Schon's 1987 *Make Way for Ducklings* sculpture, memorializing Robert McCloskey's children's book by the same name, wins all popularity contests. Expect crowds of camera-toting parents near the corner of Charles and Beacon Streets. Contrary to popular fiction, the **span over the lagoon** is not the world's smallest suspension bridge; it may be small, but it's not really suspended.

The 15-minute **Swan Boat cruises** have been a Boston tradition since 1877, when Roger Paget put in elaborate foot-pedaled boats inspired by sets from Wagner's opera *Lohengrin*. His family still operates the concession, and Bostonians as well as visitors regularly indulge in this giddiest of Victoriana.

■ RESIDENTIAL BACK BAY

Although all of Back Bay was once devoted to housing, only Commonwealth Avenue and Marlborough and Beacon Streets have persisted as predominantly residential. Following a decline from the Depression into the 1960s, they rebounded during the condo conversion boom of the 1970s.

In the early years of the landfill project, some of the more entrenched Beacon Hill families looked askance at the idea of living on "made land." But fashion eclipsed tradition, and by the 1870s Back Bay had become an irresistable tabula rasa on which to write one's social standing in brownstone and mortar.

Indeed, the understanding in Victorian Boston was that old wealth built on Beacon Street, especially on the water side, while less wealthy older families occupied shady Marlborough. Commonwealth was inhabited by the *nouveaux riches* (with *les plus riches* claiming the sunny side). Newbury and Boylston were left to social climbers and economic also-rans.

■ COMMONWEALTH AVENUE   *map page 145, A to E-2*

Stately Commonwealth Avenue was the centerpiece of Gilman's design for Back Bay. Modeling it on Baron Haussmann's Parisian boulevards, Gilman gave Commonwealth a breadth of 240 feet, 10-foot setbacks from sidewalks for small gardens, and a green, well-tended Mall up the middle. This showpiece boulevard was soon graced with the most ostentatious achievements of Boston's leading domestic architects. A walk up the length of "Comm Ave" is a popular tour for architecture students even today, and the Boston Society of Architects has sponsored a good guidebook for aficionados.

A peculiar collection of statues punctuates the Mall. Every few years public pressure mounts to add a statue of a woman to grace the odd lot, but for now it's a male preserve. The 1865 statue of **Alexander Hamilton** by autodidact Boston sculptor William Rimmer is perhaps one of his clumsiest pieces, but then he sculpted it in only 11 days and brought it in under budget. (Hamilton, first Secretary of the U.S. Treasury, no doubt would have approved.) The farthest reach of the mall at Charlesgate features a bronze of **Leif Eriksson** put up by a partisan who insisted that Leif the Lucky must have trod the Hub's sod in his explorations. The most successful and truly loved monument honors sailor and historian **Samuel Eliot Morison,** sculpted in an informal pose and perched atop a rock. The mall is under the zealous guardianship of the Neighborhood Association of the Back Bay, which shoos people and dogs off the grass and keeps death watch on the handful of American elms that remain of the more than 400 original such trees.

Few of the grand buildings on either side of Comm Ave are open to the public, an exception (by appointment) being the Boston Center for Adult Education. This mansion is a latecomer—1912—in the Italianate style. A 1913 wing was added to house the Back Bay's most glamorous ballroom, modeled after Petit Trianon in Versailles, for the society debut of textile industrialist Walter C. Baylies' daughter. *5 Commonwealth Ave.; 617-267-4430.*

First Baptist Church on the corner of Commonwealth and Clarendon is only one of a seemingly infinite number of Back Bay churches (19th-century Bostonians split many theological hairs, and each group of dissenters insisted on its own church), and Henry Hobson Richardson seems to have used the opportunity to warm up for his later masterpiece on Copley Square. Built of randomly laid Roxbury puddingstone, and in the Romanesque-style, the church's most innovative aspect is its nearly freestanding monumental bell tower. The decorative frieze at the

BACK BAY

An aerial view of residential blocks in Back Bay, with the Charles River and Longfellow Bridge in the background. (Robert Holmes)

Erected in 1998, the monument to the firemen killed in the Hotel Vendome fire stands at the corner of Commonwealth and Dartmouth. (James Marshall)

top was modeled in Paris by Bartholdi (sculptor of the Statue of Liberty) and carved in place by Italian artisans after the stones were set. The trumpeting angels at the corners of the tower gave the building its slightly sacrilegious nickname, "Church of the Holy Bean Blowers." *(map page 145, C-2)*

On the corner of Dartmouth Street stands the **Hotel Vendome,** one of the most technologically modern as well as sumptuous buildings of the time when built in 1871. (First public building with electric lights, it also boasted private baths and individualized steam heat.) In the 1970s, nine firefighters died in a blaze that broke out during renovations into luxury condominiums. For a generation the neighborhood stalled a proposed memorial on the Mall outside, only to relent finally in 1995. The monument was erected in 1998 at the corner of Dartmouth and Commonwealth.

■ MARLBOROUGH STREET

Marlborough Street maintains its privacy through a peculiar one-way traffic pattern that has cars converging on Clarendon Street from both directions. In 1953, writers

Robert Lowell and Elizabeth Hardwick purchased the house at **239 Marlborough Street** that figured in both of their writings. One of Hardwick's few positive passages about Boston in her autobiography *Sleepless Nights* recalls Back Bay in winter: "I am looking out on a snowstorm. It fell like a great armistice, bringing all simple struggles to an end. In the extraordinary snow, people are walking about in wonderful costumes—old coats with fur collars, woolen caps, scarves, boots, leather hiking shoes that shine like copper." Poet Lowell's memories are more mocking, noting that "even the man / scavenging filth in the back alley trash cans, / has two children, a beach wagon, a helpmate, / and is 'a young Republican.'"

One semi-public building of note is the **French Library,** where the salon is said to be modeled on Empress Josephine's private parlor at Malmaison. More than a library, the cultural center sponsors films, lectures, language classes, and events such as Bastille Day, when Marlborough hosts a festive street party. *53 Marlborough, map page 145, D-1; 617-912-0400.*

Also a host and sponsor for films, lectures, and cultural events, the German-culture **Goethe Institute** occupies a 1901 Italian Renaissance Revival building at *70 Beacon; 617-262-6050.*

Vines cover a row of Victorian homes on Commonwealth Avenue. (James Marshall)

■ **BEACON STREET** *map page 145, A to E-1*

Beacon Street is a major thoroughfare. Many of its finest mansions have been gobbled up by Emerson College, including 150 Beacon, the former site of museum founder Isabella Stewart Gardner's music room, where she had her infamous portrait painted by John Singer Sargent *(see page 47)*. Now Emerson's Abbott Library, the building is open to public view. *150 Beacon; 617-824-8670. (Administration Bldg.)*

The best look behind a Back Bay façade (in this case, an Italian Renaissance façade) is the **Gibson House Museum** at 137 Beacon. Widow Catherine Hammond Gibson and her son moved here in 1860 as pioneers decamping from Beacon Hill to build on the New Land. (She was also one of the very few women to own a Back Bay home.) One of the most modern houses of its day, the Gibson House boasted indoor plumbing in the basement, gas lighting, and coal-fired central heat.

Catherine's poet/ horticulturalist/travel writer grandson, Charles Hammond Gibson, established the home as a museum in the terms of his will, executed in 1954. He began roping off rooms in 1936, making his guests sit on the stairs to sip bathtub gin. This Gilded

Oliver Wendell Holmes
(Library of Congress)

Age time capsule still contains ornate interiors crammed with collectibles and memorabilia, just as they were left by the house's last occupant. (See "A Catalog of Boston Architecure," pages 314-15.) *137 Beacon; 617-267-6338.*

Beacon Street was the social center of the Hub in the late 19th century, especially after Dr. Oliver Wendell Holmes moved to **296 Beacon** in the 1870s, making him a neighbor of the redoubtable social reformer Julia Ward Howe (of whom it was said that when she asked you to tea, it "was like a royal invitation").

Julia Ward Howe (Library of Congress)

When *Atlantic Monthly* editor William Dean Howells bought and renovated **302 Beacon** in 1884, he wrote to his friend William James, "Sometimes I feel it is an extraordinary thing that I have been able to buy a house on Beacon Street. Perhaps the novel will pay for the house." Indeed, *The Rise of Silas Lapham* more than paid for the house. It brought hordes of tourists looking for the site of Silas's fictional Beacon Street home ("the finest house money can buy, I reckon")— much as tourists today look for Sam Malone's Cheers (actually the Bull & Finch, just a few blocks away on Beacon Street by the Public Garden.

■ COMMERCIAL BACK BAY

"Commerce" assumes all its meanings on Newbury and Boylston Streets — the discourse of ideas, the exchange of goods and services, the flirtatious language of arched eyebrow and tossed-back hair. For all their Victorian order and often gracious architecture, Newbury and Boylston generally refer to what's happening now, not yesterday in Boston.

That said, the commercial segment of Back Bay is steadily anchored by two venerable institutions. **Arlington Street Church** (corner of Arlington and Boylston, *map pae 145, D-2*) was Back Bay's first public building and the "mother church" of American Unitarianism. The congregation was once led by abolitionist preacher William Ellery Channing, whose statue stands in the Public Garden facing the church; more recently, the church served as an informal headquarters for the Vietnam War draft resistance movement. The brownstone building, which stands on 999 wooden pilings driven into the blue clay beneath, was designed by Arthur Gilman, the architect of Back Bay's overall plan and primary architect of Old City Hall *(see page 92)*. Inside are 16 Tiffany stained glass windows installed between 1898 and 1933. The church welcomes visitors daily, usually between 10:00 A.M. and 4:00 P.M.

Because the **Ritz-Carlton Hotel** (corner of Arlington and Newbury and undergoing renovation) signifies everything elegant and proper, young Bostonians assume it has been around since time immemorial. It's actually an artifact of the financial boom of the 1920s, though less overtly glamorous or imposing than most architectural paeans to wealth of that era. Instead, the Ritz impresses in the details: from the low-relief fans over the second-story windows to the white gloves of the elevator operators. Service is so legendary that the Atlanta-based Ritz-Carlton chain sends its upper-level staff to Boston to train in how one does things correctly the first time. Equally legendary is the Ritz dress code, recently relaxed in the bar to allow gentlemen to enter without benefit of a sports coat.

■ NEWBURY STREET   *map page 145, A to D-1*

The clientele of Newbury Street grows ever younger as the blocks ascend, with most shops near the Public Garden clearly addressing Ritz taste (Brooks Brothers,

Along toney Newbury Street, chic boutiques cater to the fashion-minded and pricey cafes serve the see-and-be-seen crowd. (James Marshall)

*Among the luminaries depicted on the Newbury Street Mural are John Adams and "King"
Camp Gillette, inventor of the safety razor. (James Marshall)*

Burberrys, Cartier) and those near Mass Ave (Newbury Comics, HMV Records)
proffering pop culture of Gen X. In between lies Boston's version of Fifth
Avenue: smart boutiques of Abboud and Versace, chic cafés that spill out onto the
sidewalks in good weather, exclusive art galleries, flashy grills where the clientele
outshines the entrées.

But there remain some decorous stalwarts from Back Bay's early days.
Emmanuel Church at the corner of Newbury and Berkeley claims to be the only
church in North America where the entire cycle of all 178 Bach cantatas has been
performed: part of the liturgy every Sunday at 10 is a Bach cantata with chorus
and orchestra under the baton of Craig Smith. Worth noting along the same strip
are the **Church of the Covenant** at 67 Newbury, a Gothic Revival beauty with
Tiffany windows and a Tiffany glass lantern inside; H. H. Richardson's rhythmi-
cally Romanesque **Trinity Church Rectory** at Clarendon; and the **Hotel Victoria**
at the corner of Dartmouth, which bristles with a catalog of Victorian bay window
forms. Perhaps the best enjambment of tradition and invention is the **Newbury**

Street Mural, a 1991 architectural fantasy painted as a backdrop to the parking lot at Newbury and Dartmouth. Depicting the Café DuBarry, it contains 72 portraits of the famous and obscure, from John Adams to "King" Camp Gillette, inventor of the safety razor. Keeping the mural company are the **Copley Society,** America's oldest art association, and the **Society of Arts and Crafts** (158 and 175 Newbury Street, respectively). The fortresslike structure at the corner of Exeter and Newbury was built for spiritualist activities.

■ **BOYLSTON STREET** *map page 145, A to E-2/3*
Boylston Street along the Public Garden sports several Eurostyle boutiques in a modern hotel-office-retail complex, but most of the street lacks Newbury's luster, in part because its office buildings present a less pedestrian-friendly face to the sidewalk than the Newbury townhouses.

Today, Gillette Company maintains a "World Shaving Headquarters" in downtown Boston, where workers try out new products in the shave test lab.

This outdoor cafe on Boylston Street might be the perfect resting spot for weary shoppers.
(James Marshall)

An exception is the graceful Art Deco building at the corner of Arlington and Boylston that houses **Shreve, Crump & Low, Inc.,** jeweler to Boston's best families and a courtly survivor of a more gracious era.

One might say that Boylston is where Back Bay's big buildings went. The solid French Academic block at the corner of Berkeley, for example, was built for the Museum of Natural History, the forerunner of the Museum of Science. Now it's occupied by Boston's best conservative clothier, **Louis.**

A similar building, the original home of the Massachusetts Institute of Technology, used to stand next door. It was torn down during the Depression to make way for **The New England,** 501 Boylston Street, constructed for the New England Mutual Life Insurance Company, the country's first chartered mutual life insurance company. The lobby, open during normal business hours, features eight large historical murals and a model of Old Ironsides. Several large dioramas depict, among other things, the filling in of Back Bay and use of the ancient fish weir found during excavations for the building's innovative floating slab. The company's newer home across the street (500 Boylston) has been likened to a 1930s Philco radio masquerading as a building. One knock on this Philip Johnson design is that it muddies views of Trinity Church, probably Boston's singlemost admired structure.

Apart from Copley Square, Boylston above Berkeley Street lacks much of the visual drama of the rest of Back Bay. There are, however, some humdinger exceptions. **New Old South Church** at the corner with Dartmouth is a handsomely ornamented Italian Gothic structure built in 1874-75 by the congregation that had met previously at Old South Meeting House (thus "New" Old South). Its tall campanile and Venetian lantern stand out on the skyline from every direction. *Boylston at Dartmouth.*

The Romanesque-inspired brick and stone twin building at the corner of Hereford Street was designed in 1886 by Arthur Vinal as combination police and fire station (941-955 Boylston). The fire station still occupies the corner bay and what used to be the stables that joined the two buildings. The police station, however, was renovated in 1975 under the direction of Graham Gund as a home for the **Institute of Contemporary Art**. Because the ICA has no permanent collection, exhibitions change frequently.

Across from the ICA stands the **Hynes Convention Center** (looking like nothing so much as a German rail station since its 1988 renovation) and the rest of the Prudential Center Complex.

The **Prudential Tower** was Back Bay's first real skyscraper in 1965, and while it was isolated from the rest of the area, no one really wept for the ugly railroad freight yards it displaced. The Pru's surrounding shopping complex barely muddled along for many years; an early-1990s makeover, however, enclosed the windswept walkways, established rational pedestrian traffic patterns, and joined the shopping plaza via walkway to the glitzier Copley Place across Huntington Avenue *(see page 165).*

The **Skywalk View and Exhibit** occupies the 50th of the Prudential Tower's 52 floors. It's the only 360-degree aerial observatory in the city, and a 1995 installation actually helps make sense of what you see. All the way up is the Top of the Hub restaurant, where after three decades the food is finally more than an afterthought to the view. *800 Boylston St.; 617-536-1775.*

■ COPLEY SQUARE AND ENVIRONS *map page 145, C-3*

Copley Square looks for all the world like the best-planned section of the well-planned Back Bay—proving that looks are deceiving. Originally nothing more than two triangular plots of land left over as an unresolved intersection between the gridiron and diagonal streets of Back Bay, the true square emerged from a definition imposed by the magnificent buildings erected on its perimeter—Trinity Church, the Boston Public Library, and the dignified Copley Plaza Hotel. The central plaza was still diagonally divided until 1969, and the current pleasant square of trees, grass, and water did not come about until 1990. Despite neighborhood opposition, the plaza hosts a bostix booth for same-day discount tickets to theater, dance, and music. A commemorative plaque to the Boston Marathon was inlaid on the pavement just in time for the 100th running in 1996.

■ TRINITY CHURCH *map page 145, C-3*

Trinity Church, which defines the Clarendon Street side of Copley, is easily the greatest church building in Boston and usually shows up in the American Institute of Architects poll of the 10 best buildings in the country. Arguably, the 1877 edifice is architect H. H. Richardson's greatest achievement. Built on a site described at the time as "a desert of dirt, dust, mud, and wind," Trinity's granite and sandstone Romanesque style bespeaks a faith for the ages. But the very solidity of the church was a problem, for like all Back Bay structures, it stands on soft fill. Richardson's solution was to sink 2,000 wooden piles through the mud to solid ground below, then place granite pyramids on them. On that rock he built his church, including the 12.5-million-pound bell tower.

Trinity Church benefitted from the convergence of great artistic talent. Rector Phillips Brooks reportedly told painter John LaFarge, whom Richardson had engaged to create the stained glass windows, to "put something up there that will be an inspiration to me as I stand in the pulpit to preach." Brooks was known as an orator with few peers; one contemporary timed him at an average of 213 words per minute once he got wound up. LaFarge obliged his request in a manner that would make it difficult for any preacher to fail to be inspired, let alone the charismatic Brooks. The high windows rain down heavenly colors on the walls of dull terra cotta and gold, glistening off the black walnut woodwork. The hanging barrel vaults create resonant acoustics for preacher, choir, and organ alike.

Trinity Church is reflected in the glass of the John Hancock Tower. (James Marshall)

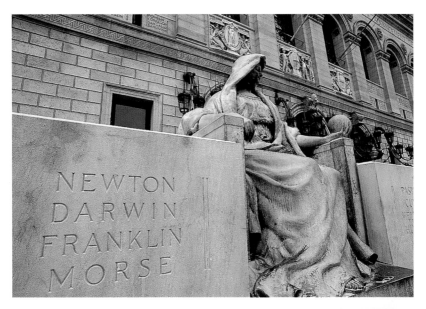

A statue outside the Boston Public Library (top) is bookended by slabs engraved with the names of great scientists. The interior courtyard of the library (bottom) reveals the influence of the Italian artisans and construction workers who helped build it. (both photos by Robert Holmes)

Brooks died in 1893, shortly before a portico and front towers were added to the building by Richardson's successor, Hugh Shepley. Shepley placed statues of nine Biblical figures on the portico—and in 1925 a statue of Phillips Brooks became the 10th "saint." Brooks was already looking out from the church, however, in the form of an Augustus Saint-Gaudens statue placed in a ground-level niche on the Boylston Street side in 1910. An active Episcopal parish, Trinity is open for viewing; there's an organ concert Fridays at 12:15 from mid-September to June.

■ **BOSTON PUBLIC LIBRARY** *map page 145, C-3*

Facing Trinity Church like the proposition for a freshman theme on the significance of their apposition, the Boston Public Library symbolizes the city's enlightened attitude toward knowledge. Even original settler William Blaxton had a library. Above the doors of the original building, built 1887-95 from the design of Charles Follen McKim, are engraved the words, "Free to All." And so it remains—the first major free municipal library in the United States and a veritable palace of the people.

McKim modeled his library on a Renaissance palazzo and the construction drew on the highly skilled force of mostly Italian construction workers and artisans who had come to Boston to build homes for the wealthy. Daniel Chester French (best known for the Lincoln Memorial in Washington) created the handsome bronze doors that represent Music and Poetry, Knowledge and Wisdom, and Truth and Romance. Murals winding up the staircase and along the second-floor corridor are by Puvis de Chavannes, whose great fame largely died with the man. Better remembered are Edward Abbey, whose Pre-Raphaelite masterpieces representing the Quest for the Holy Grail grace the book request room, and John Singer Sargent, whose murals of Judaism and Christianity cover a third-floor gallery. Restoration of all the murals was completed in 1995; again they match the grandeur of the library's rich wood and marble interior. Free tours of the library's art and architecture are conducted several times each week (tours begin at Dartmouth Street entrance; call for schecule). *666 Boylston Street; 617-536-5400.*

Philip Johnson's 1971 **Boylston Street addition** (which houses the circulating collection) echoes the dignity and monumentality of the McKim building. Its interior evokes the essence of a great library: a wealth of books suffused with light. Between the two buildings is McKim's quiet repose of a little Italian courtyard, a breather from the modernist excitement of Johnson's vault of knowledge and McKim's repository of wisdom.

BACK BAY

THE BOSTONIAN POINT OF VIEW

None but a Bostonian would ever resent being taken for a New Yorker; and so carefully do they of the sister city guard their identity by dress, action, and speech, that none but the most careless observer would ever affront them with the charge.

The Bostonian is strongly impressed with the idea that his city is the particular nucleus of all that there is great on this side of the Atlantic. He looks upon other American towns as small planetary bodies revolving about the centre of Boston Common, and deriving most of their light, heat, and strength from Cambridge University, Faneuil Hall, and Boston Harbor. He affects a wonderful degree of kinship with the English; and keeps up the connection by sharp shirt collars, short-waisted coats, and yellow gaiters. He is apt to put himself upon English stilts to look down upon the rest of the American world, which he regards complacently through an English eye-glass. He does not so much pity the rest of the American world, as he patronizes and encourages. His literary tastes being formed in the focus of western learning, are naturally correct and profound. He squats himself upon the Boston formulas of judgment, from which nothing can shake him, and puts out his feelers of opinion, as you may have seen a lazy, bottle-tailed bug try his whereabouts, without once stirring, by means of his antennae.

He likes to try you in discussion, in the course of which it will be next to impossible to tell him anything that he did not previously know; and you will prove a rare exception, if he does not tell you many things that you never knew before—unless, indeed, you have been in Boston. His stock of praises is uncommonly small, and principally reserved for home consumption; things are done *well*, only in Boston; though they are sometimes *creditably* done in other parts of the world.

—Ik Marvel, *Journals*, 1850

■ JOHN HANCOCK TOWER & COPLEY NEIGHBORS

map page 145, B&C-3&4

Copley Place, across Huntington Avenue from the Boston Public Library, occupies a roughly 10-acre space spanning the Massachusetts Turnpike. Built over four years beginning in 1980, it includes the Westin and Marriott convention hotels, several restaurants, dozens of shops and a glittering central atrium and offices. It's one of Boston's most financially successful recent developments. Spring 1996 saw a wild buzz of curiosity among the city's movers and shakers to see who would be semi-immortalized in the Palm Restaurant at the Westin Hotel, where loving caricatures of 200 celebrities now grace its walls.

Insurance companies have given Boston some of its most memorable buildings, but none as successfully as the John Hancock company. Its truncated 1947 tower at **175 Berkeley Street** (the Old Hancock Tower) cuts an unmistakable figure on the skyline with its weather beacon:

Steady blue, clear view.

Flashing blue, clouds are due.

Steady red, rain ahead.

Flashing red, snow instead.

(Flashing red in the summer means that the Red Sox game has been called.) The mirrored 790-foot rhomboid of the **John Hancock Tower** at 200 Clarendon Street, designed by Henry Cobb of I.M. Pei & Partners, amounts to a breathtakingly beautiful solution to a nearly impossible design problem: How to place a 60-story office building next to Trinity Church without overwhelming all of Copley Square. Cobb's solution was to face the razor edge into the square and turn all the skin into a mirror, making the building almost disappear. (It prompted John Updike to write, "all art, all beauty is reflection.") At one angle from Copley Square, you can see the simultaneous reflections of both Trinity Church and the original Hancock building.

The windows are the stuff of Boston legend, for even as the tower was under construction, they began to fall out—65 of them, each weighing 500 pounds. Because all parties were sworn to secrecy, myths persist to explain the problem: that the building swayed too much, that the peculiar shape created wind-shear "hot spots," that the building was twisting into the ground and popping out its windows in the process. Indeed, the tower did sway too much—giving upper floor occupants motion sickness. (The problem was fixed with a kind of gyroscopic shock absorber on the 52nd floor.) And there are hot spots of wind pressure, but they're

BACK BAY

harmless. And the building did begin to sink at first — but that was fixed before any windows went in. The problem lay in the two-layer construction of the windows, and was solved by replacing all 10,344 panes (at a cost of nearly $7 million) with single-pane tempered glass before the building was ever occupied.

The 1975 Hancock Tower will probably always reign as Boston's tallest building, especially since a zoning variance to exceed that height would make the labors of Hercules look like child's play. The observatory on the 60th floor supplies a sweeping view of Boston and includes a show narrated by historian Walter Muir Whitehill. Like tall structures everywhere, the Hancock attracts its share of odd stunts — but none stranger than the Guinness record established on September 3, 1988, by wholesale produce merchant Paul J. Tavilla of Arlington, Massachusetts, who caught in his mouth a black grape tossed by his son-in-law from a window-washing rig atop the building. What does a 110-mile-per-hour grape feel like?

"It hurts," said Tavilla.

■ MASSACHUSETTS AVENUE *map opposite, along right side*

Massachusetts Avenue, better known as "Mass Ave," represents the de facto western boundary of Back Bay today, although it was created in 1872 as one of the few thoroughfares to link Back Bay and the South End. The awkward dogleg corner at Huntington Avenue accommodates three Boston institutions.

Horticultural Hall was designed in 1901 for the Massachusetts Horticultural Society, which dates from 1829. The Society is probably best known in Boston for the Spring Flower Show, now held at one of the convention centers, and outside Boston as the founder of the grand old gardening magazine, Horticulture. Although the Christian Science Church has owned the building since 1991, the Horticultural Society still has offices on the second floor—along with the largest horticultural library in the world. The library is open for visitor use during normal weekday business hours.

The Christian Science complex began as a modest little church built in 1893-94 that sect founder Mary Baker Eddy called "our prayer in stone." That church is now the chapel behind the more grandiose basilica added in 1903-06, site of an Aeolian Skinner organ that is the largest in the Western Hemisphere. The complex acquired its orderly monumentality, however, during a makeover in 1968-1973 by the legendary design firms of I.M. Pei & Partners and Cossuta & Ponte. (Some

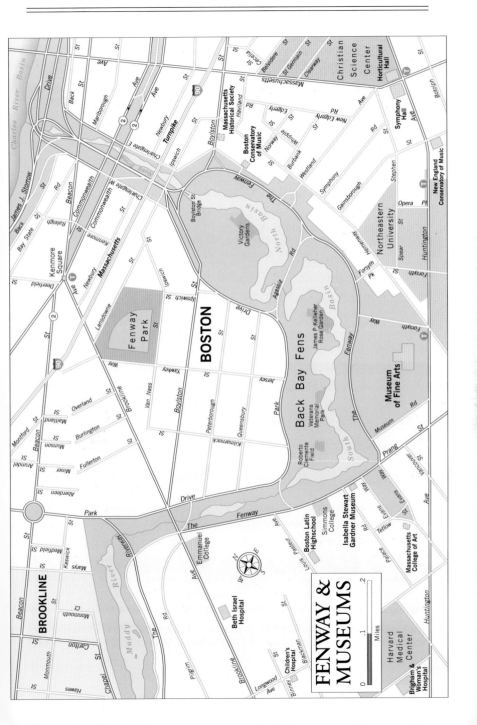

might argue that it gave the Pei firm a chance to appease the detractors of Government Center, which they had designed a few years earlier.) By adding the world headquarters building and sculpting a limestone plaza to create a new entrance on Massachusetts Avenue, they created a soaring and spacious complex that offers a modern argument for Bruneschelli's 16th-century precept that the principles of the Deity are made manifest in uncluttered religious geometry. Despite the almost severe monumentality of the plaza, the **700-foot-long reflecting pool** (part of the air-conditioning system) is a favorite summer spot for al fresco brown-bag lunches.

When the founder of the **Boston Symphony Orchestra**, Henry Lee Higginson, wanted a new hall for his orchestra, he brought in a young Harvard assistant professor of physics, Walter Sabine, to consult on the acoustics. Sabine knew his stuff. Although the 1900 Italian Renaissance exterior of Symphony Hall is simply serviceable, the interior concert hall is rich and sonorous, entirely devoid of acoustic dead spots. It's often called "the Stradivarius of concert halls." To see Brahmin Boston at its best, catch a Friday afternoon concert, where subscription seats are handed down from generation to generation. *Performs a full winter schedule; summer home of Boston Pops. 301 Massachusetts Ave. (map page 167, lower right); 617-266-1492.*

Inside the Christian Science building, visitors can marvel at the Mapparium (above), a stained glass world map. Outside, the building is mirrored in a 700-foot-long reflecting pool. (right; photo by Robert Holmes)

This corner of Huntington and Massachusetts Ais something of a cultural district in its own right. The **Boston University Theatre** resembles the Wilbur Theatre in the Theater District, although it was built 11 years later. It houses some BU student productions but is best known as the home of the Huntington Theatre Company. *264 Huntington Ave.; 617-266-8488.*

A block away is the **New England Conservatory of Music** (NEC) and **Jordan Hall** When the 1,013-seat hall reopened in 1995 after an $8.2 million restoration, the *Boston Globe* observed, "The warm, dark wood-lined, acoustically perfect space, nestled inside the walls of the New England Conservatory of Music, is considered an instrument in itself, loved the way a violinist reveres a Stradivarius." NEC offers more than 450 free concerts each year. *30 Gainsborough St.; 617-536-2412.*

■ KENMORE SQUARE AND FENWAY PARK   *map page 167, top center*

The filling of Back Bay continued all the way to Charlesgate, roughly where Route 1 crosses above Commonwealth Avenue. The "gate" refers to a water gate from Stony Brook, but today it might as well signal the entrance to Kenmore Square. (By night, Kenmore is illuminated on the skyline by the **Citgo sign**, a fine exam-

At Fenway Park baseball games, the numbers on the scoreboard are still turned by hand.

ple of animated advertising denied landmark status only because it perches on a building of "sub-landmark quality.") Kenmore is dominated by **Boston University,** which has swallowed almost all the property along the Charles River, including some striking townhouses along Bay State Road. BU students have effectively taken over Kenmore Square — except when the Red Sox are in town.

Brookline Avenue leads out of Kenmore to Yawkey Way to the sacred shrine of Boston baseball, that place John Updike called "a lyric bandbox of a ballpark." **Fenway Park** may be dowdy and confusing on the outside, but it boasts the most intimate field in Major League Baseball and the play occurs on real grass. Fenway, which opened in April 1912, is the oldest major league park. Preservationists have twice sought to make Fenway a National Historic Landmark but were stymied by team owners, who want to build a larger, more lucrative facility. On the Kenmore side of the park is **Lansdowne Street,** home to Boston's most popular late-night dance clubs.

It's difficult to see except from an aerial view, but Kenmore Square lies little more than a long home run from the Back Bay Fens portion of Frederick Law Olmsted's Emerald Necklace. *(See pages 181-83.)* Land developers had high hopes that the Fenway would sustain the building boom of Back Bay, but there were

Dance clubs on Lansdowne Street rock well into the wee hours.

only so many private fortunes in Boston. So the drained marshlands became home to a sea of apartment buildings dotted by islands of intellect, instruction, and inspiration. The Fenway contains more than a dozen colleges and universities as well as Boston's two finest art museums.

■ MUSEUM OF FINE ARTS, BOSTON *map page 167, lower center*

Boston's aristocracy made a gesture of faith in the potential of the Fens when they sited the Museum of Fine Arts (MFA) between Huntington Avenue and the Fenway in 1909 after it outgrew its 1876 Copley Square home. At the time the Fenway was yet another wild patch seemingly far from the city's heart, which enabled the trustees to acquire 16 prime acres for a comparative song. One of the largest art museums in the nation, the MFA's permanent collection comprises more than one million objects. The granite Classical Revival main building presents an imposing face to Huntington Avenue, despite the incongruous, sentimental statue on the front lawn: Cyrus Dallin's bronze of a generic Indian on horseback with outstretched arms, called *Appeal to the Great Spirit.* The permanent collection resides in this august home. The **West Wing**, designed by I.M. Pei and inaugurated in 1981, is a modernist analog of the main building. It houses temporary exhibitions, including the string of blockbusters rotating through the cavernous **Graham Gund Gallery.** The West Wing also contains the museum store, café, and restaurant.

The MFA's holdings reflect the wealth, taste, and broad interests of Boston's 19th-century collectors. The Classical department is famed for its comprehensive collection of red-figured and black-figured vases as well as bronze and terra-cotta statuettes. The Asiatic art collection is said to be the largest under one roof in the world, and represents China, Japan, Korea, the Indian subcontinent, and Islamic culture. Because the MFA joined Harvard University in key excavations in Egypt and the Sudan between 1905 and World War II, the museum's collection of Old Kingdom and Nubian art and artifacts is second only to the Cairo Museum. (Yes, the MFA has mummies—recently re-installed in stunning galleries.)

The museum also owns a world-class collection of about 1,000 musical instruments, most restored to playing condition. The MFA's chamber music concert series runs October through May in the Remis Auditorium.

Painter William Morris Hunt is indirectly responsible for many of the MFA's best works—none of them his. As a young man he hung out with other young artists

A gallery in the Museum of Fine Arts. (Robert Holmes)

in Paris in the 1850s. Returning to his native New England, he married into Boston society and convinced many of his new friends to buy art by his old friends. Under his tutelage, well-to-do Bostonians enthusiastically embraced new directions in French painting. As a result, the MFA has the largest Millet collection in the world, a group of Monet paintings surpassed only in Paris, and impressive holdings of other Impressionists and Post-Impressionists. Many of those works now rest in the MFA's most popular main building gallery, the "Impressionism" gallery, second floor right.

The museum's strong holdings in American fine and decorative arts illuminate an even earlier generation of wealth. John Singleton Copley, perhaps America's most talented 18th-century painter, is said to have grumbled that "were it not for portraits, art would be unknown in this place." More than 60 of his portraits—including the Revolutionary triumvirate of John Hancock, Paul Revere, and Samuel Adams—serve as barometer of late Colonial social values and capture the merchant princes for whom Boston's streets are named. More than 40 works by his near-contemporary Gilbert Stuart complete the era's iconography, especially his

Painted anonymously circa 1855, A Street in Winter: Evening *is one of the works in the vast permanent collection at the Museum of Fine Arts. (courtesy Museum of Fine Arts, Boston)*

unfinished portrait of George Washington, now engraved on the dollar bill, and his heroic painting, *Washington at Dorchester Heights,* showing the Revolutionary general driving the British from Boston.

Sometimes it can be hard to separate art from history. Along with two cases of smaller pieces of Revere silver, the MFA gives pride of place to Paul Revere's "Liberty Bowl." The 1768 commission by the Sons of Liberty brought together Revere's careers as patriot and silversmith to honor Massachusetts legislators for taking a stand against the Townshend Acts. The MFA purchased this icon of the Revolution in 1949 with funds raised by Boston schoolchildren and by general public subscription.

Not all the silver is simply for display. From September through April it's possible to enjoy a civilized afternoon Ladies Committee Tea: a homey assortment of cookies baked by MFA volunteers who also pour tea from great silver urns surrounded by fresh flowers and candles. Consider it a cultural lesson—a holdover from the salon days of the society folk who founded the MFA.

One of the MFA's quirkier strengths is the work of John Singer Sargent, an American expatriate painter who was a frequent guest at those very salons. Sargent did his best work as a muralist in the Boston Public Library, in Harvard's Widener Library, and in the central rotunda of the MFA (Boston is the only place in the United States where Sargent murals can be seen). The MFA series, painted 1916-1925, depicts charac-

John Singleton Copley's famous portrait of Paul Revere, ca. 1768–70 (Gift of Joseph W., William B., and Edward H. R. Revere, courtesy Museum of Fine Arts, Boston)

BACK BAY

ters from Greek myth to glorify the arts and pay tribute to the power of knowledge and the imagination. Sargent also worked on a more intimate scale as a master portraitist. Witness the luminous *Mrs. Fiske Warren and Her Daughter,* posed at Fenway Court, now known as the Isabella Stewart Gardner Museum. *MFA; 463 Huntington Ave.; 617-267-9300.*

■ ISABELLA STEWART GARDNER MUSEUM   *map page 167, lower left*

Isabella Stewart Gardner was a pioneer in moving to the Fenway, but this New Yorker who married into a Brahmin family delighted in defying convention. Her husband, John Lowell Gardner, first thought about building a new home in the Fens, but when he died suddenly in 1898, Isabella decided to construct her own palace with the primary purpose of housing her art collection. "Mrs. Jack" worked with architect Willard T. Sears for two years on the project, showing up daily to supervise the construction and the installation of architectural elements that she and Jack had purchased in Europe.

The three-story Venetian palazzo at 280 The Fenway was finished in 1901, and Isabella spent the next two years arranging her collections on the three floors, which surround a central garden courtyard filled with flowering plants and trees. She opened Fenway Court officially on New Year's night, 1903, serving doughnuts and champagne to a select group of friends. (Bostonians seem to remember such things.) Isabella lived on the fourth floor until her death in 1924, opening her galleries to public view on occasion. The grand style suited the woman whom art historian Bernard Berenson (an advisor and friend) described as "the one and only real potentate I have ever known." In 1925, Fenway Court became a full-fledged museum.

Berenson and other advisors helped Gardner assemble a collection of about 2,500 objects spanning 30 centuries. The museum's strengths are Italian Renaissance paintings as well as French, German, and Dutch masters. The modern collections are also impressive, including works by Degas, the first Matisse to enter an American collection, and paintings by Gardner's friends James McNeill Whistler and John Singer Sargent. Among them is a Sargent portrait of Isabella judged so scandalous when unveiled in 1888 that it was withdrawn from public view until after her death.

Notoriety again touched Fenway Court on March 18, 1990, when thieves absconded with 13 works conservatively valued at $200 million, the world's largest art theft to date. The losses included Vermeer's *The Concert,* two major Rembrandts, five works by Degas, a Manet oil, and a Shang dynasty bronze beaker.

Under the terms of Gardner's will, the museum must remain as she created it: No works may be sold or purchased. As a result, blank spots and discreet cards mark the empty places on the walls. Yet the restrictions permit Isabella Stewart Gardner's psyche to rule the rooms. Whatever else one might say, the Gardner has distinct personality. And because it is frozen in time, it remains what one critic called "the most authentic slice of the 19th century anywhere."

Isabella Stewart Gardner's passion for art extended to horticulture and music. Today many visitors attend the museum as much for its gardens and extensive concert series (125-130 per year) as to view Titian's powerful *Rape of Europa* or Emperor Nero's chair. *Gardner Museum; 280 The Fenway; 617-566-1401.*

The Raphael Room (above) and courtyard (right) at the Isabella Stewart Gardner Museum.
(courtesy Isabella Stewart Gardner Museum, Boston)

EMERALD NECKLACE
THE FENS TO FRANKLIN PARK

Let your buildings be as picturesque as your artists can make them. This is the beauty of a town. Consequently, the beauty of a park should be the other. It should be the beauty of the fields, the meadow, the prairies, of the green pastures, and the still waters. What we want to gain is tranquility and rest to the mind.
— Frederick Law Olmsted, "Public Parks and the Enlargement of Towns,"
A paper presented to the American Social Science Association, February 25, 1870

IT OFTEN SEEMS THAT HALF THE CITIES in North America claim Frederick Law Olmsted as architect of their parks. But Boston is the home he chose for his mature practice, and it is Boston that most indelibly bears his mark. New York's Central Park and hundreds of other projects were behind him when Olmsted moved his family and his practice to Brookline, retiring in place when he finished the Boston Parks in 1895.

The Boston Parks Commission approached Olmsted during the 1870s in search of two things: a showpiece park system akin to those Olmsted had designed for New York and Chicago, and a way to ameliorate some of the public health problems spawned by rapid population growth and overcrowding. America's first professional landscape architect delivered on both counts with a series of linked parks, ponds, and green spaces stretching from the erstwhile swamp at the end of Back Bay across the isthmus that links Shawmut Peninsula to the mainland.

Olmsted integrated his new green spaces with existing open areas, which is why the imprecisely termed "Emerald Necklace" also takes in the Boston Common, the Public Garden, Commonwealth Avenue Mall, and sometimes the Charles River Esplanade. But the master's personal hand touched only the outer reaches: Back Bay Fens, Muddy River Improvement, and Jamaica Pond on the Brookline border, the Arnold Arboretum in Jamaica Plain, and Franklin Park in Roxbury. Each segment is a variation on rusticity in an urban surround, each a locus for the restorative "contemplation of pleasing rural scenery"—Nature's antidote to urban stress, Olmsted believed.

In practice, the five-mile swath of the Emerald Necklace has devolved into a series of neighborhood parks: prized green space within the heart of a residential area. A few playing fields and ball courts attract a spontaneous athleticism, and runners rule the paths in the early morning. But most often the paths are dominated by folks simply out for a stroll: singles and couples ambling along, families with young children, small packs of school friends, the occasional young man or woman jogging with a Labrador retriever on a leash.

It is more than possible to cover the entire length of the Necklace as a day trip on foot or bicycle, especially to leave the bustle of the urban center behind to enjoy, as Olmsted envisioned, "tranquility and rest to the mind."

■ THE BACK BAY FENS

A pragmatic civil engineer as well as a Wordsworthian romantic, Olmsted solved a significant public health problem with Back Bay Fens. When he began in 1878, the Fens area was a fetid saltwater marsh cut off from tidal flushing and flooded with waste from the Muddy River and Stony Brook. Olmsted created water gates to regulate the tidal flow and holding marshes to control flooding; at the same time, his design evoked a pre-colonial landscape.

The arrival of modern sanitation codes and the 1910 damming of the Charles River a mile downstream have rendered moot the practical function of the Back Bay Fens and transformed the landscape by killing the salt-tolerant vegetation and displacing water with new land. Purists decry the current Fens landscape because it departs from Olmsted's vision, but the park fills a niche different from the one Olmsted conceived. Fenway dwellers use it heavily for energetic athletic pursuits rather than for the meditative perambulations that Olmsted anticipated. In addition, the Fenway today serves as a scenic approach and backdrop for Boston's largest art museums. (For specific sights in the Back Bay Fens, see map page 167.)

The Bay Back Fens begin at the end of Commonwealth Avenue Mall at **Charlesgate**, a block above Massachusetts Avenue, where a trickle of **Stony Brook** is visible beneath the overhead highway interchange. More obscured is the park's original formal entrance, H. H. Richardson's **Boylston Street Bridge**, built of Cape Ann granite. Its medieval formality, reminiscent of Richardson's Trinity Church, satisfied Olmsted's request for an unadorned, instantly ancient artifact.

It's more practical to approach the Fens on foot or bicycle from Kenmore Square (see "BACK BAY," pages 170-71) by taking Brookline Avenue to Yawkey Way, which becomes Jersey Street as it passes Fenway Park. Jersey runs directly into the South Basin of the Fens. Alternatively, head across Massachusetts Avenue on Boylston Street to its apparent conclusion.

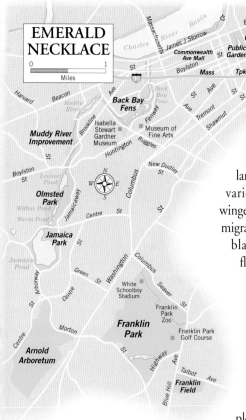

The **North Basin,** to the left, is surrounded by tall *Phragmites communis,* a freshwater grass that invaded once tidal action ceased. Biologists are exploring ways to suppress the grass, but it does provide excellent cover for mallard ducks, Canada geese, and a wide variety of songbirds, especially red-winged blackbirds. In the fall and spring migrations, the North Basin often turns black with Canada geese as entire flocks bank and turn and swoop to its surface.

Along the path are the ornamental **Victory Gardens,** created in 1942 from fill excavated from the nearby Kenmore Square MBTA station. Intended as supplemental food gardens, these small but highly prized plots have evolved into personal expressions of gardeners from nearby tenements and apartment buildings. Faced with small living spaces, some gardeners have turned their 100-square-foot spaces into outdoor rooms, complete with garden furniture and well-established plantings of spring bulbs and summer roses. Others opt for a wild profusion of cutting annuals, with some plots virtually disappearing by late July in a jungle of sunflowers —a dozen different strains of them.

The land around the **South Basin,** with its many public-spirited "improvements," attracts more strollers and sightseers than North Basin. Veterans Memorial Park is dominated by a gargantuan angel offering a sheathed sword—a memorial to Boston's casualties of World War II, the Korean War, and the Vietnam War. Olmsted would not have approved; he disliked war memorials, opining that "they

A mock suspension bridge spans the lagoon in the Public Garden, part of the Emerald Necklace.

scare small children." Nearby, the **James P. Kelleher Rose Garden,** a beautiful if incongruous addition, perfumes the basin with a heady scent in June and July. Still farther along the path is **Roberto Clemente Field,** where two baseball diamonds, two basketball courts, and a cinder track attract residents from the neighborhood to the urban traditions of sandlot baseball and pickup basketball. Olmsted's Victorian preference for cerebral contemplation over muscle-swelling recreation has been entirely overwhelmed. A bas relief of Clemente notes "Sus Tres Amores: Puerto Rico, El Beisbol y los Niños." Naming the field for Clemente, who had no particular link to Boston, hints at the ethnic transformation of the neighborhood in recent decades.

Small footbridges across the South Basin lead to the **Fenway,** the highway version of the carriage road designed by Olmsted. On that road are the Museum of Fine Arts and the Isabella Stewart Gardner Museum. (See pages 172-79.)

■ MUDDY RIVER, THE RIVERWAY, AND OLMSTED PARK

Asphalt has largely buried Olmsted's transition between Back Bay Fens and Muddy River, but the Muddy River section of the Emerald Necklace demonstrates Olmsted's wisdom of advising that the best way to manage a landscape on limited funds is to leave it alone. Aside from annexing the carriage road to create a winding four-lane motorway known as the Riverway, Boston and neighboring Brookline have done little to this park. The happy result is that most of the landscape remains as Olmsted envisioned it: a bit more than a mile of woodsy paths along a pleasant, meandering stream.

Walking beneath the leafy canopy along Muddy River (really a large brook), it's hard to believe that this landscape is manmade. It certainly looks natural unless you're a botanist and observe that all the trees on the far side of the water are native species, while most of those on your side come from Europe and Asia. The Muddy River serves as a border between Boston and the town of Brookline. Back in the 1880s, Olmsted chose what he thought were pretty trees (many of which were exotic species); as a Darwinian disciple who believed the "fittest" had demonstrated themselves by dominating natural ecological niches, Brookline's park commissioner insisted on native species. The argument (the two men didn't speak to each other for years) was moot; both plantings flourished.

Like the Fens, Muddy River is frequented mostly by those who live near it, and they use the park extensively. You might even encounter former governor and presidential candidate Michael Dukakis out for his daily constitutional. Olmsted's plan for separate pathways for pedestrians and carriages pays off here. Today, young families with strollers and tykes on plastic tricycles take the quiet paths, while whizzing, helmeted athletes on bicycles or in-line skates speed along the old carriage route.

The upper reaches of Muddy River broaden into ponds, and the park chain widens around the water to include the rolling green meadows of what is now called Olmsted Park (essentially the Emerald Necklace from Perkins Street to the far end of Jamaica Pond).

■ JAMAICA POND AND NEARBY BROOKLINE SITES

Jamaica Pond is one of the least humanly altered landscapes in the Emerald Necklace. Olmsted knew a good thing when he saw it and merely tidied up the area with graded banks and new plantings. The largest of three kettle ponds in the area, Jamaica Pond is surrounded by glacial knobs and drumlins. This irregular topography saved the neighborhood from early development. The 120-acre pond, fed by 50-foot-deep springs, holds some of the city's purest water. Until 1848, the pond was a major water source for Boston, after which it was used extensively to make ice. An 1859 Winslow Homer wood engraving shows skaters on Jamaica Pond; barely visible behind them is one of the pond's two vast ice houses.

The pond's natural one-mile circumference seems designed by Nature for aerobic walkers, joggers, and runners in training. But the paths are clear for vigorous workouts only in the very early morning before neighborhood families head to the **natural beaches** on Perkins Street and along the Jamaicaway. These shorelines are covered with rocks where box turtles haul themselves out to take the sun and with grassy patches popular for picnics despite the profusion of mendicant Canada geese and wild and domestic ducks.

Of Olmsted's planned improvements, only his boathouse at the end of Pond Street on the east side was built. Dating from 1912, the current structure—with nearby picnic tables, and lawns—is the focus of recreation at the Pond. During July and August, the Metropolitan District Commission rents rowboats and small sailboats that bank and glide on the patch of placid blue water.

Within a 10-minute walk from Jamaica Pond, at 99 Warren Street in Brookline, the **Frederick Law Olmsted National Historic Site**—or "Fairsted"—serves both as an archive of the Olmsted firm's work over 75 years and as a living example of

EMERALD
NECKLACE

the master landscape designer's aesthetic. The 1810 farmhouse (onto which Olmsted added a wing) housed the first full-time professional landscape design firm in the country; today scholars come here to peruse the massive collection of drawings and photographs. In keeping with the style of the master landscape designer, the grounds feature carefully crafted lines of sight that borrow vistas from surrounding properties, rusticated features such as a tiny grotto in a sunken garden, and natural features such as a stone outcrop and a meadow-like back lawn presided over by a stately (and healthy) American elm.

On a somewhat more sumptuous Brookline estate about a half mile from Jamaica Pond at 15 Newton Street is the **Museum of Transportation,** an assemblage of automobiles ranging from some of the earliest Model-Ts through the exuberant tailfinned behemoths of the late 1950s.

■ THE ARNOLD ARBORETUM

Of all the links in the Emerald Necklace, the Arnold Arboretum remains closest to Olmsted's original design, perhaps because it has been under constant, loving care

EMERALD NECKLACE

Scenes from the Arnold Arboretum (right; photo by Robert Holmes) and at Brookline Park (above).

since its inception. Better than any other surviving Olmsted landscape, the arboretum demonstrates the success of the designer's penchant for curving vistas on gentle slopes and his use of vanishing point perspectives. On any given summer Sunday, the arboretum's lawns are dotted with the blankets of picnickers and the easels of amateur painters following Boston's long tradition of making art *en pleine aire*. From the Fens, it's well worth the short trip: it's but a half-mile on the Arborway from the southern tip of the Fens to the northern tip of the arboretum.

Arnold Arboretum is an unusual joint project of Harvard University, which established and continues to manage the collection of trees and woody shrubs, and the city of Boston, which owns the land and maintains the roads. Plantings of the permanent tree collection concluded in 1894 and, a century later, it's possible to behold what Olmsted and Charles Singer Sargent, the founding director, wrought. Olmsted predicted it would take that long for the design to become manifest, and today the 15,000 or so specimens on 265 acres create a series of both narrow and broad vistas of most of the species that flourish in temperate zones around the planet. The Arnold, in fact, has the most comprehensive collection of Asian trees and shrubs outside Asia, thanks largely to turn-of-the-century collecting expeditions. Arborists here are deeply involved in propagating endangered species from around the world.

Because most specimens are tagged with both scientific and common names (as well as date of planting), gardeners and homeowners use the arboretum as a reference collection to examine species of trees and shrubs under consideration for planting. Even more come for extravagant displays that no domestic landscape could ever duplicate.

During peak bloom periods the arboretum truly looks like a Victorian park, as the roads throng with walkers who range from youthful dogwalkers in blue jeans and tank tops to nattily attired Brahmins of the Horticultural Society making a formal promenade. **Lilac Sunday,** the third Sunday in May, attracts up to 20,000 visitors to the most comprehensive *Syringa* collection in the world. (Actually, various lilacs bloom from early May through late June, and a few rebloom in September.) Memorial Day weekend marks the beginning of peak bloom for mountain laurels, azaleas, and other rhododendrons. By mid-June the gardens of roses and their relatives are similarly spectacular and form a pictorial library of non-hybrid rose types.

One of the nicest spots in the entire park is atop the mound known as **Bussey Hill,** named for the family who donated their farm for the park. It was once a solemn stand of American elms, all since lost to Dutch elm disease. The resulting open hillside is a favorite for picnics, for it offers soaring views of green canopies in the foreground and of the Prudential and Hancock towers of Back Bay on the horizon.

■ FRANKLIN PARK

Olmsted considered Franklin Park, which lies east of the arboretum on Arborway (Route 203), one of his three finest achievements, ranking it with Manhattan's Central Park and Brooklyn's Prospect Park. Its clever design isolated active from passive recreation so that untrammeled landscapes could be preserved. (Olmsted preferred unstructured recreation, but he was attuned to the then-new-fangled interest in golf, tennis, and other organized activities.) Years of neglect have damaged the original design, and the open meadows, once mown by grazing sheep per Olmsted's instruction, have been converted largely to the **Franklin Park Golf Course,** a public facility spurned by country club golfers but enthusiastically embraced by those with less disposable income. Small playing fields have been superseded by **White Schoolboy Stadium,** a seemingly ironic title since most of the surrounding residents are African American.

The small zoo Olmsted planned has expanded dramatically and dynamic current leadership is starting to bring **Franklin Park Zoo** the popularity it deserves. The seven-acre **Bird's World** contains hundreds of species in naturalistic habitats, many within a free-flight cage. At the center is the delightful 1912 **Oriental Bird House,** one of the few remnants of the early zoo. In recent years the zoo has transformed itself into a leader in ecological education. The **African Tropical Forest,** one of the world's largest indoor exhibits of western lowland gorillas, lets animals move freely through zones of African desert, tropical forest, veldt, and bush forest. Visitors mingle with wallabies and emus along the **Australian Outback Trail,** while the tent-like **Butterfly Landing** provides amateur lepidopterists close encounters with butterflies and moths. Lions, cheetahs, snow leopards, and giraffes each have crowd-pleasing exhibits that reproduce their natural habitats.

Although portions of Franklin Park have been appropriated for uses Olmsted never intended, vast sections have been allowed to revert to overgrown heaths and woodlands. Every few years the city announces that it will begin to restore the 520-acre park, raising the hope that Olmsted's vision of the 19th century may be reborn in the 21st.

EMERALD
NECKLACE

ON THE WATERFRONT

*Whoever has been down to the end of Long Wharf
and walked through Quincy Market has seen Boston.*

— Henry David Thoreau, "Cape Cod," 1855

MOST COMMERCIAL FLIGHTS INTO LOGAN AIRPORT follow the same landing path: the plane swings over the South Shore and out past Boston Light, then tilts and whirls to swoop straight down the 10-mile length of Boston Harbor, trimming altitude until the wingtips almost graze the tops of whitecaps. Asphalt materializes as the landing gear clears the seawall at Logan's east runway and the plane rolls down to the terminals. It's a thrill that never fades. A single three-minute pass scans the entire harbor that shaped—and was shaped by—the city at the point of its funnel.

The neighborhoods of East Boston, Charlestown, downtown, Fort Point, South Boston, and Dorchester all touch the sea. Yet by the middle of the 20th century, Boston had long forgotten that it had been born on the shore and had risen to

Clamdiggers at work in Boston Harbor, not far from the runways at Logan Airport.

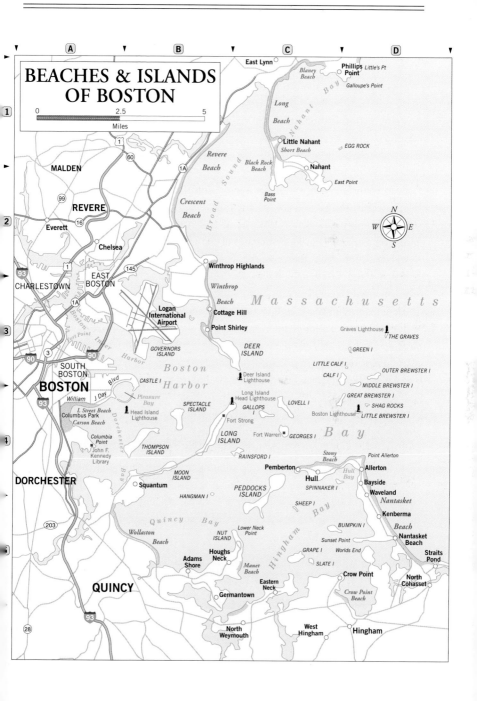

BEACHES & ISLANDS OF BOSTON

0   2.5   5
Miles

greatness on the high seas. A once mighty harbor lay despoiled—its fish choking on waste, its piers and docks in shambles. In his presidential campaign speeches in 1988, candidate George Bush accurately portrayed Boston Harbor as the nation's most polluted, blaming the governor of Massachusetts, Michael Dukakis, for dragging his heels to clean it up. Yet since the federally mandated $3.4 billion cleanup, harbor waters have shown surprising resilience. Seals and porpoises have returned; schools of bluefish and striped bass roil the waters. Once grim beaches now fill with sunbathers and swimmers.

Even before the cleanup of the waters, Bostonians began to reclaim the shoreline, especially the portion that closely follows the old outlines of Shawmut Peninsula. The complete metamorphosis of this orphaned strip of coast will take another generation, but long stretches of the waterfront have been recaptured for recreation, commerce, and industry. The fishing and shipping piers have moved farther out into the channel, leaving the inner harbor to other uses. Former chandleries have re-emerged as shops, great stone warehouses as housing. New docks for cruise ships and private yachts are underway, and aquaculture is gaining a toehold.

The last barrier to unification of land and sea is the Central Artery, the 1950s elevated highway scheduled for dismantling by 2010 when its underground replacement is ready. In place of steel support beams and an overhead concrete roadway will be a swath of parkland under foot, linking the downtown and the docks.

Plans also call for a 43-mile walking path from Milton to Revere between two of the best-preserved urban salt marshes in America. Large segments of the path already exist from the former Navy Yard in Charlestown to Fan Pier's Federal Courthouse, and from Castle Island in South Boston to Columbia Point in Dorchester, where Boston meets the suburbs of the South Shore. Even with the substantial lacunae, the existing portions of this path along the rim of Boston Harbor's bowl provide breathtaking vistas of both natural and human origin. The seawalls and docks and wild marshes speak of Boston's history of living on and from the ocean.

■ CHARLESTOWN NAVY YARD *map page 196, A/B-1/2*

The innermost portion of Boston Harbor is the mouth of the Charles River, flanked by Boston's North End on the southeast and by the peninsula of Charlestown on the northwest. Long since absorbed by the more vigorous Boston,

Charlestown nonetheless figures significantly in the maritime life of the area, most prominently today at the Charlestown Navy Yard, sited where British troops landed for the Battle of Bunker Hill. Now part of Boston National Historic Park, this was one of six navy yards established in 1800 by President John Adams. Newport, Rhode Island, had been Adams's first choice for a New England navy yard, but Charlestown offered the deeper harbor and longer tides necessary to work on large ships. It also provided a more defensible position: even today the view from the drydocks sights down the straits toward South Boston and Boston Light. They're not visible from the Navy Yard, but ancient batteries still flank the length of the channel.

For 174 years, as wood and canvas gave way to steel and electronics, the facility played a key support role to America's Atlantic fleet. When the yard was decommissioned in 1974, 30 acres were preserved to interpret the art and history of naval shipbuilding under the National Park Service. The remaining combination of open land and long granite structures was sold and developed as luxury housing, offices, and industrial space.

Innovation and ingenuity conspired at the Navy Yard to revolutionize naval support. The entire yard, principally designed by Alexander Parris (architect of Quincy Market), is one of the earliest examples of "purpose-built" industrial architecture. The long, narrow **Rope Walk building** is perhaps the most extreme example. Most of the U.S. Navy's cordage was produced here for more than 100 years —until Navy Yard workers invented die-lock chain in Building 105 in 1926. The Rope Walk's walls are two-and-a-half feet thick and the structure is made so that isolated sections can be closed off to smother the many fires that used to break out in the ropemaking process.

■ USS CONSTITUTION *map page 196, A-2*

Drydock #1 was another of Charlestown's innovations: the second drydock on America's Atlantic coast when it was built in 1802. Essentially a giant bathtub, the drydock is opened to the ocean and a ship is floated in. Then the drydock is sealed and drained while the ship is braced in place. When the hull is repaired, the drydock is refilled and the ship floats again. The first—and most recent—occupant of Drydock #1 was the venerable USS *Constitution*.

Perhaps better known as "Old Ironsides," the ship is the centerpiece of buildings and vessels in the park. This first of America's superfrigates slid down the ways

The USS Constitution *at the Charlestown Navy Yard.*
(James Marshall)

from Edmund Hartt's North End shipyard in October 1797. She soon saw action in the Mediterranean, protecting American vessels against the Barbary pirates, but earned her fame and nickname during the War of 1812. During her first upset victory—over the *Guerriere,* a formerly French ship recommissioned in the British Navy— lore has it that a sailor who saw cannonballs bounce off the *Constitution*'s oak planks cried out, "Huzza! Her sides are made of iron."

It was a natural mistake, since her resilient planking was painted black. The nickname stuck. Over 84 years of active service, the "overbuilt and oversailed" floating fortress bristling with guns won 42 battles, lost none, captured 20 vessels, and was never boarded by an enemy.

But, as one wag observed, the *Constitution* protected America better than America protected the ship. Several times she was nearly scuttled, reduced at one point to serving as a demasted floating barracks, and very nearly became a target for cannon practice. Oliver Wendell Holmes, while still a Harvard student, first rallied public support to save the ship with his 1830 poem, "Old Ironsides." Congressman John "Honey Fitz" Fitzgerald prevailed again in 1897 to convince Congress to pony up for repairs. And in the 1920s, a children's campaign of pennies and nickels once more saved the ship.

The Navy has long since grasped the symbolic and historic significance of the USS *Constitution,* the oldest commissioned ship afloat. The ship received a major overhaul for the 1976 national bicentennial and another in anticipation of its own bicentennial in 1997. Artisans from around the world worked to refit the *Constitution* from her keel up, using live oak cut from South Carolina and the Georgia sea islands. On July 21, 1997, the *Constitution* sailed under her own canvas for the first time in 116 years. "To sail her was what the hearts and minds of the American people wanted," said her commander Michael Beck. Each year she reverses position at the pier to ensure equal weathering on both sides.

Two museums stand close to the ship. The **USS *Constitution* Museum** *(near Drydock #1)* rounds out the ship's history with displays of log books, journals, charts, weapons, and other artifacts. Adjacent to the Navy Yard is a small building devoted to the Battle of Bunker Hill. **Bunker Hill Pavilion** *(map page 196, B-1)* presents a multimedia re-creation of the battle from a site as close as possible to where British troops gathered to assault Breed's Hill.

A modelmaker at work at the Charlestown Navy Yard. (Robert Holmes)

THE WATERFRONT

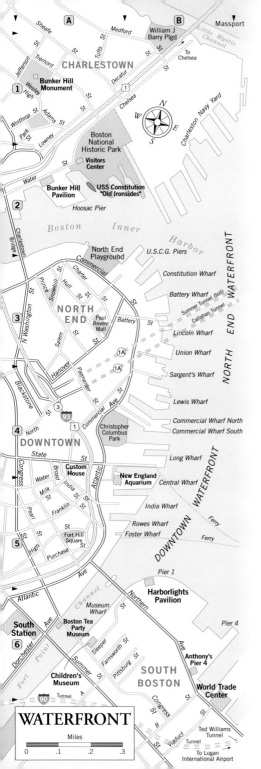

■ BOSTON HARBOR WALK

On the Boston side of the footings of the Charlestown Bridge stands a granite sea-wall promenade, the beginning of a walkway that outlines the modern Shawmut side of the Charles River's mouth. Once waves lapped between the piers at the foot of Copp's Hill, but when the Charles River was tamed with a dam, the silted wharves were claimed as dry land. The broad passageway of **Commercial Street** defines the old waterfront perimeter; everything on its water side has been wrested back from the sea. This seawall is the prototype of the long-contemplated walk around the entire Boston Harbor perimeter—a place where community and waterfront intersect, where dogwalkers pass shipwatchers and everyone admires the broadside view of the USS *Constitution*.

■ NORTH END WATERFRONT

North End Playground

map A-3

Facing the Charlestown Navy Yard along this promenade is North End Playground, where the inhabitants of the neighborhood's claustrophobic 17th-century streets spill out into the open air. Given the North Enders' chiefly Italian heritage, it is no wonder that the bocce courts are in steady use. But so are the tennis courts, the green baseball fields, and, in their respective seasons, the swimming pool and the freshly restored ice skating rink. But the sea's melancholia is never far: in mid-park stands a simple granite statue of a sinking vessel, dedicated to the radio operators who went down with their ships in World War II.

The promenade ends abruptly at the Coast Guard base that commands the tip of Shawmut Peninsula.

Wharves
map opposite, B-5

The promenade picks up again with the first cluster of wharves—Battery, Lincoln, Union, Sargent, Lewis, Commercial—that complete the lineup of the North End's waterfront. These survivors from the 80 or so Boston wharves of the early 18th century are in the midst of change.

Battery Wharf, long the aromatic home of Bay State Lobster's wholesale and retail operations, is gaining residential condominiums.

Boston Yacht Haven Marina on Commercial Wharf is being rebuilt to handle oceangoing yachts up to 130 feet.

Commercial Wharf still evokes some of the old Boston waterfront in the surviving businesses of John G. Alden and Son Co. (builder of grand yachts) and the Robert Eldrige White Instrument Co., publisher of *Eldrige's Tide and Pilot Tables,* a yellow-bound essential for clamdiggers, beachcombers, and mariners.

Lewis Wharf condominium conversions have not softened the massive commercial aura of the indestructible granite warehouses.

Christopher Columbus Park
map opposite A-4

North End and Downtown waterfronts meet at this broad swath of green field broken by a wisteria vine arbor and a path along the water's edge. The channel once ran right through the park to the east door of Faneuil Hall but this land was recaptured from the sea as old wharves silted in. Now the park exists, one suspects, as a connector between street patterns, for here the waterfront thoroughfare shifts from Commercial Street to Atlantic Avenue, a city planning relic of the 1860s designed to connect the railheads with the wharves.

◄○►

■ DOWNTOWN WATERFRONT
map opposite, A/B-4/5

Long Wharf
map opposite, B-4

In 1948, poet and essayist David McCord wrote that "the outstretched fingers of the great Boston wharves still carry the old romance in their length and look."

If any wharf upholds that tradition today, it's Long Wharf, built in 1710 as a triumphal path from ship to Custom House, then on to the Old State House and the banks of State Street (called King Street in those days). Long Wharf was where Boston traders came home to see their bankers. With its continuing bustle of tour boats, water taxis, and ferries (including those to Georges Island), Long Wharf remains the portal between land and sea.

Sea otters being fed by their trainer at the New England Aquarium. (James Marshall)

Custom House

map page 196, A-4

Land has crept up Long Wharf's shanks since the 1750s, when young John Copley hid behind his mother's skirts at her tobacco shop. For example, when the Custom House (now two streets inland) was built in the 1840s, it sat at the water's edge. The tower on the Custom House was Boston's first skyscraper. Although city zoning specified a 125-foot height limit, the federally owned building was exempt. When the 16-story tower rose in 1913, it created a good deal of grumbling about Washington arrogance. Now the clock tower is a beloved city landmark—and home to a pair of peregrine falcons who hunt waterfront rodents and pigeons in the glass canyons of the Financial District. Free tours of the tower are offered daily at 10 A.M. and 4 P.M. *3 McKinley Sq.; 617-310-6300.*

New England Aquarium

maps: page 11, central right, and page 196, B-5

In its day, Central Wharf was as much a wonder as Long Wharf, but it was so derelict by 1962 that the city sold it to some visionaries for $1. Their dream? A resurrection of Boston Harbor through a centerpiece attraction that would recapture the wharves and help focus attention on the marine life of the city. Some six million private dollars and seven years later, their vision was realized in the New England Aquarium, the first such design by the now-famed aquarium designers, Cambridge Seven Associates. Within its modernistic confines stands the spiraling Giant Ocean Tank with fluttering tropical fish, zipping sharks, powerful sea turtles, and sleek moray eels gliding in the currents. Smaller tanks and exhibits display aquatic environments from the Amazon Rain Forest to the Antarctic. Designed for 600,000 visitors per year, the aquarium hosts more than 1.3 million, and is in the midst of a $70 million expansion. *Central Wharf; 617-973-5200.*

The stretch of wharves and walkways, overlooks and cafes, boat piers, and windbreaks that connect the aquarium's broad plaza to the water taxi docks at Rowes Wharf offer a vision of what Boston's waterfront can be.

India Wharf *map page 196, B-5*

Next to the aquarium is India Wharf, where the twin Harbor Towers thrust 40 stories into the air, relieved only by external zipper-like metal balconies. It is easy to pass through the stainless steel sculpture at the base of the towers (stepping over sunbathers capitalizing on its reflective properties) and walk directly onto Rowes Wharf with no apparent transition.

Rowes Wharf
  map page 196, B-5

A triumph of good city planning, intelligent architecture, and human desire can be found here. The **Boston Harbor Hotel** dominates the wharf while water taxis from the airport and commuter boats from South Shore all land here, spilling their passengers onto the inviting multi-level plazas. Several harbor cruises and large sightseeing boats dock at Rowes Wharf as well, drawing people from all over the city to the water. And on a hot August night, there's hardly a cooler spot in the city than the Boston Harbor's outdoor plaza bar.

■ FORT POINT CHANNEL:
WHARF MUSEUMS AND SEA TRADE DISTRICT

The Harbor Walk continues past Rowes Wharf, but is abruptly interrupted after crossing Fort Point Channel. This old industrial inlet marks the passage into **South Boston,** a district annexed in 1804 over the protests of the town of Dorchester (which has since joined the Boston fold). The area in and around the channel includes **South Station**—a subway and Amtrak terminal now wonderfully restored to its Neoclassical Revival splendor—at the Summer Street bridge, as well as **Museum Wharf** between the Congress Street and Northern Avenue bridges.

Boston Tea Party Museum
  map page 196, A-6

Halfway across the Congress Street bridge is the Boston Tea Party Museum, including the replica of the brig *Beaver,* one of the ships that lost its cargo to rebellious colonists that fateful December night in 1773. The channel was open water in those days. (The actual site is at 470 Atlantic Avenue, where a plaque describes the colonists'

THE WATERFRONT

action against a "trivial but tyrannical tax.") The buildings of the South Boston side of the channel represent the now-defunct "wool district." In fading paint on some of them it is possible to make out "Boston Wharf Company"— the still-surviving mercantile giant which developed Fort Point Channel.

Children's Museum
map page 196, A-6
The Children's Museum easily identified by the giant milk bottle in front. The renovated warehouse provides simple, open spaces for colorful, interactive exhibits. Children's Museum exhibit designers pioneered many of the now-familiar exhibits at similar museums around the world—

giant soap bubbles, marble ramps, and an area where surplus office and industrial products are sold for use in children's art projects. *Museum Wharf; call 617-426-8855 for hours.*

Boston SoHo district
Other warehouses along the channel have become a Boston SoHo district, housing live-work space for artists. In a show of strength, artists banded together to purchase and rehab the old buildings at **249 A Street** and **300 Summer Street** (the latter now includes a gallery). Open space—so surprisingly accessible to the Massachusetts Turnpike and the airport—has been eyed for everything from a new convention center to a baseball park to a football stadium.

Visitors to the Boston Tea Party Museum have their photos taken while posing behind Colonial figure cutouts (above). The Children's Museum is easily identified by the milk bottle out front. (opposite, photo by Robert Holmes)

THE WATERFRONT

As the 21st century gets underway, the harborfront on the South Boston side of Fort Point Channel stands poised for the largest in-town development in decades. Anchoring the downtown side, the **U.S. Courthouse** makes a dramatic architectural statement—its wraparound architecture and soaring glass wall open to the sea while presenting an impassive wall to inland Boston. It's worth visiting the interior (and going through the metal detectors) for the wonderful harbor views from the upstairs cafeteria (weekdays only). The small park between the courthouse and the water is also a fine spot for a picnic or for watching harbor fireworks.

The adjoining parcels remain as parking lots until development gets underway, although shuttle bus service from South Station already makes the area reasonably accessible. Various proposals present a high-density, mixed-use South Boston waterfront of offices, condominiums, shops, and pocket parks, but infighting among the players could delay construction for many years. The linchpin of the development will be a modernistic new convention center for Boston along with a massive convention hotel. What this will spell for the legendary **Anthony's Pier 4** restaurant, with its sweeping harbor views and retro menu, remains to be seen.

Meanwhile many small trade shows and conventions use the **World Trade Center,** which links via an overhead walkway with the pleasant Seaport Hotel and Convention Center. The docks beside the **World Trade Center** are busy in warm weather with ferries across Massachusetts Bay to Provincetown and with excursion and party boats (see page 311). Boats of a more practical nature call at the adjoining **Fish Pier,** which still lands half the shoftshell crabs and about a third of the lobsters caught in Massachusetts. Every weekday morning the live fish auction draws the city's restaurateurs to select their haddock, cod, flounder, and monkfish.

Still heading south along the water, the vast weathered wooden stretch of **Jimmy's Harborside** fish restaurant seals Northern Avenue from the harbor. As old-fashioned as Anthony's but less class conscious, Jimmy's represents a type of Boston institution endangered by development capital now that the harbor is clean and inviting. The restaurant is flanked by wholesale fish dealers, and directly across the street stands a school of smaller fish houses. During July and August, the billowing sail-like tent of the FleetBoston Pavilion, Boston's largest in-town outdoor concert venue, flaps between Jimmy's and the cruise ship terminals.

THE WATERFRONT

Farther out on the peninsula the U.S. Naval Reservation and U.S. Army base have been leased for commercial use. The latter, which lies on the deep Reserved Channel (an Army Corps of Engineers creation from World War I), houses the **Black Falcon Cruise Terminal,** port of call for oceangoing cruise ships. Because Boston lies 200 miles closer to Europe than any other large United States port, it was a major cruise port until World War I. But decaying facilities and the popularity of air travel cut into the cruise business. Slowly but surely, the lines are returning after a lackluster three-quarters of a century.

The far side of the channel, now approaching the community of South Boston, is brawny **Castle Island Terminal.** This container port facility handles a substantial portion of the $8 billion in goods that move through Boston piers each year.

Fishmongers display a nice catch of flounder.

(top) Hanging out on a South Boston street corner. (bottom) A day in the sun at Castle Island.

■ SOUTH BOSTON AND CITY POINT

Although the shipping piers lie within South Boston limits, the residential districts of this principally Irish enclave stand south and west. Some Yankees abandoned Beacon Hill for City Point (the easterly portion of South Boston) in the early years of its development, but by the 1860s new residents were almost exclusively Irish immigrants. Middle-class immigrants favored the sea views and fresh breezes of City Point, while working-class immigrants settled for the cramped quarters on filled land, an area they called alternately Little Galway or the Lower End.

First-generation Irish American William J. Day embodied the kind of hope that brought so many Irish to America in general and to Boston in particular. Working his way through Boston College, then through Boston University Law School, he established a law practice in Boston and flourished, eventually rising to a judgeship and a position on the board of a bank. Beginning in the Lower End, within 30 years he was an established figure in City Point. When he died, South Boston's beachside boulevard was renamed in his honor.

A long tale to tell how a road was named? Perhaps, but South Boston is a neighborhood with a very long memory. Every name on a square or a street or a school has an associated story, more often than not emphasizing the triumph of an underdog through hard work and tenacity.

■ CASTLE ISLAND   *map page 191, B-3*

The northeastern terminus of William J. Day Boulevard is the Castle Island parking lot, where the waterfront promenade picks up again after the long hiatus at Fort Point Channel. It begins at the **Steel Pier,** one of the most popular fishing spots along the harbor. Depending on tide and season, fishermen catch anything from flounder to mackerel to striped bass. An obelisk at Steel Pier honors Donald McKay, the native Nova Scotian whose East Boston shipyards directly across the channel (now a Logan Airport runway) turned out some of the greatest clipper ships ever known.

The pier stands on Castle Island, which has been fortified continuously since 1634. The basis of the much-rebuilt fort was erected in 1779 under orders from General George Washington. It was christened **Fort Independence** in 1799—and never saw action again, although its formidable batteries were credited with keeping the British Navy from attacking Boston during the War of 1812.

Fort Independence was manned through the Civil War, when it served as a prisoner of war camp. Among the odd tales told of the fort is the legend that friends of a man killed in a duel in 1817 walled up the killer in one of the dungeons. Apparently the story was current a decade later, when an 18-year-old private heard it. The ex-soldier, Edgar Allan Poe, later changed the principals and the locale but kept the gruesome conclusion in "The Cask of Amontillado."

Frederick Law Olmsted created much of the design for Castle Island and the surrounding beachscapes as the logical conclusion to the Emerald Necklace—a scheme thwarted by the high cost of purchasing a right of way between Franklin Park and Marine Park, as the area was designated.

■ **BEACHES**   *map page 191, B-3*

As part of the park plan, the strait between the mainland and Castle Island was filled in 1891. The former island, now a head, anchors one end of aptly named **Pleasure Bay**, a recreational area with one of the city's finest and cleanest swimming beaches. The mile-long causeway across the bay, recently restored, has been a popular spot for residents of South Boston to take constitutional walks since it was constructed in 1886. (In 1888, the Causeway attracted 44,000 people one hot July day.) South Boston is one of America's top markets for high-priced, imported baby carriages, and most

Head House used to dominate Marine Park at City Point. Designed by Olmsted in the 1880s, the 32-acre park gradually fell into disrepair; fire destroyed the mansion in 1942. (Boston Public Library)

The L Street Brownies in all their glory.

of them are on display at the causeway. But all walks of life strut the strand. Until reputed South Boston underworld boss James J. "Whitey" Bulger disappeared on January 5, 1995, this black-sheep brother of the then-president of the state Senate regularly gathered his colleagues for a brisk walk along the open and windy Causeway just beyond the reach of FBI binoculars and microphones.

Of the seven Boston mainland beaches, the four that lie along William J. Day Boulevard are the best swimming beaches in the city. This sandy strand became an unsavory shore during the height of harbor pollution and the once-proud bathhouses were allowed to decay. Thanks to the harbor cleanup, the beaches are open for swimming on most summer days (a blue flag signals clean water, a red flag means "stay out").

With entrances off K, L, and M Streets, the **James Michael Curley Recreational Facility** (locals call it the "L Street Bathhouse") has been refurbished in a style befitting the flamboyant politician. Every January 1, the hardy "L Street Brownies" brave the frigid season to take their first ocean dips of the year. Next door the grand wooden bathhouse at **Carson Beach** has also been renovated.

The view from the beaches commands Boston's outer harbor, looking eastward to the harbor islands and the peninsula of Hull, southward to Quincy and the

THE WATERFRONT

TAHKIN' IN BAHSTAWN

Americans used to think that if they could imitate Jack Kennedy's speech, they were speaking fluent Bostonian. Nope. The Kennedy accent is spoken only by born Kennedys. The rest of Boston speaks a tongue almost incomprehensible to someone from places where the King's English is spoken—places like the states of *Jawjaw* and *Ahkansore*. Herewith, a guide to understanding the natives:

PRONUNCIATION

The key to Boston English is the lost *AH*, the letter that comes between *Q* and *S*, and the breadth of the letter *A*, the beginning of the alphabet. As in French, Bostonians consider a concluding *R* to be silent. In true Yankee economy, we save our orphaned *R*s to attach to words that might otherwise end with an undifferentiated vowel sound, usually an "uh" sound in the rest of the country. In practice, *Ah final AHs simply disappeah, but wheah they go we have no idear.* Perhaps Boston has spawned so many poets because Bostonian English provides nearly as much opportunity for rhyme as some Romance tongues.

These linguistic oddities create unfortunate cognates between Bostonian and American English. In most places, *khakis* denote casual tan trousers. In Boston, they're inserted in the ignition to *staht the cah.*

VOCABULARY

Many peculiar Boston terms apply to traffic. Hence, a *gahkablahka* is a traffic jam caused by drivers staring at an accident on the other side of the road. It's attributed to WEEI traffic reporter Kevin O'Keefe, who also coined *stall-n-crawl, cram-n-jam,* and *snail trail*—all terms used to describe the Central Artery from 5 A.M. until midnight. There's nothing odd about the pronunciation of *breakdown lane,* which is a Boston oxymoron referring to a highway shoulder and the last place to break down, especially when it becomes the high-speed lane during rush hour.

Place names bedevil visitors. Just remember that *Public Garden* and *Boston Common* are both singular, never plural. *Tremont,* as in the street, is pronounced "TREH-mont" and the square with the beautiful architecture is always "COP-lee," never "COPE-lee"— regardless of how John Singleton probably said it. The Cradle of Liberty is pronounced "FAN-yuhl HALL." *The othah side* is an East Boston locution for the rest of the city, while *across the rivah* is a derisive term applied to Cambridge, especially to *Hahvahd.*

And, oh yes, *scrod* is fish with an identity complex. (There's a hoary vaudeville joke involving this dish and the Boston accent.) Some Bostonians insist that if spelled with an *H* (schrod), it's young haddock, and without the *H* it's young cod. It's whichever is cheaper that day at Fish Pier.

Neponset River gas storage tanks, one of which bears a colorful abstract painting designed by artist Corita Kent. The best view of all is from the top of Telegraph Hill, better known to history as **Dorchester Heights.** The monument behind South Boston High School on top of the hill is the most farflung portion of Boston National Historic Park. This spot where geography and history intersect provides instant understanding of General Washington's strategy for breaking the siege of Boston. By fortifying Dorchester Heights, Washington had the entire British naval force literally under his guns. They could neither run nor hide, so they accepted his offer for a peaceful retreat, and returned Boston to its inhabitants on March 17, 1776.

■ COLUMBIA POINT AND KENNEDY LIBRARY
map page 191, A-4

The rocky, windswept peninsula that begins at the end of Carson Beach is Columbia Point—home to the University of Massachusetts Boston campus, the Commonwealth Museum, and the John F. Kennedy Library and Museum.

The Commonwealth Museum, located in the Massachusetts Archives building near the tip of the point, has permanent and rotating exhibits focusing on the people, places, and politics of Massachusetts.

Far out at the end of the peninsula, the 9.5-acre park surrounding the **Kennedy Library** is landscaped with pine trees, shrubs, and roses in a manner that hints of President Kennedy's Cape Cod compound. The building—a soaring triumph of white concrete and glass designed by I. M. Pei and Partners—stands on the precipice of Columbia Point, high above the water and looking out to the lonely sea through a 50-foot-high glass wall. A profoundly spiritual and symbolic structure, the Kennedy Library seems simultaneously as permanent as the rock on which it stands and as evanescent as a whitecap on the waters of the outer harbor.

The **museum at the JFK library,** rededicated in 1993, takes full advantage of the fact that John F. Kennedy was the first politician to fully comprehend and

THE WATERFRONT

The interior of the Kennedy Library was designed by architects I. M. Pei and Partners.

master the power of media to inspire, to rule, and to control. The man is gone, but archives of his moving image make the key events of his presidency seem fresh and immediate. For example, short films on the Cuban Missile Crisis and the beginnings of the U.S. space program are gripping. The assassination, on the other hand, is handled as it happened—in shocking brevity that poignantly recaptures a nation's loss. *Columbia Point, One JFK Rd.; museum: 617-929-4500.*

■ THE HARBOR ISLANDS

More than 30 islands link Boston's inner and outer harbors in an archipelago embracing 1,200 land acres over 50 square miles. All but the outermost rocks share a common origin with such famous mainland features as Breed's Hill, Dorchester Heights, and Beacon Hill: they are glacial drumlins, heaps of glacial debris shaped like the back of a teaspoon. The glacial melt inundated the bases of the hills, leaving their rocky, rubbly tops to dot the harbor. Ranging in size from less than an acre to 214 acres, the harbor islands have a long history of their own. Like the Shawmut peninsula, some were summer fishing camps for Native Americans and at least one was regularly planted in corn. (The earliest direct evidence of human habitation in New England—a man's skeleton carbon-dated to 4,100 years ago— was unearthed by a gardener on Peddocks Island in the late 1960s.)

Colonists farmed some of the islands into the early 1800s, a few became retreats for the yachting rich, and fishermen continued to use others into the 20th century. Over the centuries the nearest islands were annexed by a land-hungry population—and the others became places to dump unsightly or unsavory facilities such as prisons, reform schools, poorhouses, hospitals, quarantine centers, prisoner of war camps, police shooting ranges, missile bases, garbage dumps, and sewage treatment facilities.

Since the 1950s, however, most of the islands were simply abandoned, although a few summer cottages persist on Peddocks Island. In 1970, the state began to acquire the remaining privately held islands (municipalities own many of them) to create **Boston Harbor Islands State Park.** On October 1, 1996, Congress designated the islands as a National Recreation Area, to be administered by the National Park Service in cooperation with local governments.

Ferries take passengers from downtown docks out into the waters of Boston harbor. (James Marshall)

THE WATERFRONT

No other major city in the United States has so many islands so close—especially islands that remain undeveloped—but only a handful are accessible by public transportation and even those have only rudimentary facilities for visitors. Summertime ferries land at Georges Island in the middle of the system, where shuttles usually service Bumpkin, Gallops, Grape, Lovells and Peddocks. Long and Moon islands are accessible by causeway from the city of Quincy. Thompson, the only privately owned island, is the base for Outward Bound's program; some public access is available by its boat.

Georges Island

map page 191, C-4

Seven miles from downtown Boston, Georges Island is strategically located in the throat of the harbor between the main shipping channel and the secondary Nantasket Road channel. Georges has a small grassy area with picnic tables, a modest gravel beach and a large dock that is one of the best lookouts for harbor traffic. But the 28-acre island is dominated by Fort Warner, which was begun in 1833 and finished nearly two decades later. Its 10-foot-thick walls of Quincy granite still stand, though parts of the fort have decayed. The highlights of this partially restored National Historic Landmark include labyrinths of dungeon prisons (it was a POW camp during the Civil War), officers' quarters and stalwart parapets still standing watch on both Boston and the open sea.

Grape and Bumpkin Islands

map page 191, C&D-5

Far closer to the South Shore than to Boston, these islands are popular with runners and hikers. Grape is perhaps the more inviting, with a rocky northern end and tidal salt marshes and gravel beaches on its south side. Although Grape is only 500 yards from the mainland at Weymouth, its raspberry, blackberry, and beach rose thickets teem with songbirds and rabbits. A 70-foot-high drumlin on the western edge of the island is a king-of-the-mountain lookout for a panorama of coastline and harbor. Crumbling ruins on the smaller Bumpkin suggest a melancholy abandonment. The story actually is rather sad; they mark an abandoned hospital that burned in 1945. The trails above the ruins, however, provide a particularly picturesque sunset view back to the mainland.

Gallops Island

map page 191, C-4

Little (16 acres) Gallops Island has an association with pirates going back to the 18th century. Treasure hunters still seek the diamonds that Boston Harbor historian Edward Rowe Snow claims were buried by Long Ben Avery. A channel marker just north of Gallops used to be the island of Nix's Mate, where pirates' bodies were allegedly hung in chains as a warning to rogue ships entering the harbor. The island's natural features (including a heron rookery) are more interesting than its ruins (another hospital and the foundation of a World War II Maritime Radio school).

THE WATERFRONT

Covered with wild roses in the summer, the grassy bluffs of Gallops offer spectacular views of the entire Boston harbor, especially Boston Light in one direction and the city skyline in the other. In addition to hiking trails, Gallops has well-kept picnic areas and state-of-the-art composting toilets.

Lovells Island

map page 191, C-4

Some of the World War I–era fortifications of Lovells Island still stand, offering an interesting contrast with the 19th-century fort on Georges Island. This substantial piece of land (62 acres) has the best amenities in the islands park—the only supervised swimming beach (the water is very cold), boat and fishing piers, extensive picnic grounds, walking trails, campsites (permit required), and public restrooms.

Peddocks Island

map page 191, C-4&5

Peddocks Island—four separate drumlins on a single 188-acre land mass—is the most diverse of the harbor islands. Sprawling in various states of decay on the eastern end of the island are the remains of 26 buildings that made up Fort Andrews, built in 1900. Andrews was a coastal artillery garrison in World War I and a pow camp for Italian prisoners during World War II. Yet war seems very far away as the maple, pine, and birch trees overtake the east end, burying the fort. It seems Peddocks is always in bloom: with apple blossoms from decrepit orchards on the uplands, followed by the purple-tinged beach plums on the sand spit dunes in May and June, then wild roses continuously into October. In fact,

Peddocks is a popular spot in the fall for gathering rosehips and beach plums to make jelly. The abundance of fruit and the excellent cover provided by the dense shrubbery on Peddocks makes the island an ideal habitat for many birds. The Massachusetts Audubon Society lists one of only two rookeries of black-crowned night herons in a clump of Peddocks Island apple trees.

Deer Island

map 191, B&C-3

In an important sense, Deer Island is key to the other harbor islands. Now attached by land to the town of Winthrop, Deer Island is devoted largely to a wastewater treatment plant for 43 cities and towns, the latest such facility since the first sewage pumping facility was built in 1889. Completed in 1999, it is the largest sewage treatment plant in New England. Deer Island also has a large wildlife population of ring-necked pheasants, red-winged blackbirds, raccoons, and snowy owls.

Spectacle Island

map 191, B-4

No island in the harbor group has been so transformed as Spectacle Island. Used alternately for agriculture in the 1660s, as a quarantine island in the 1700s, a summer resort with illegal gambling in the 1800s, and a horse rendering plant in the late 1800s and early 1900s, Spectacle suddenly began to grow dramatically in the 1950s, when Boston began using it as a city dump. When the dump was abandoned in 1959, trash towered 70 feet high. The familiar Boston story of filling to create new land is

Aircraft that take off from Logan Airport often pass directly over Little Brewster and Boston Light.

being played out again on Spectacle with clay from the excavation for the Ted Williams Tunnel. In the next few years, Spectacle will have a new look: a visitors center, a marina, and a green park.

The Brewsters

map page 191, C&D-3&4

The outermost islands of Boston Harbor are the Brewsters, principally used as summer staging grounds for offshore fishermen until this century. These rocky ledges are not part of the drumlin field comprising the other islands, but their remoteness and bleak topography provide safe rookeries for herons, cormorants, and gulls. Little Brewster holds Boston Light, the first lighthouse built in the United States (1716) and the last offshore light to be staffed. On a clear day, Boston Light is visible 27 miles away. A small Coast Guard museum stands at the base of the National Historic Landmark lighthouse, including a restored 1719 cannon that was the first fog signal used.

■ EAST BOSTON

"Eastie," as its residents call it, has been part of Boston since 1637, though in no place does East Boston land touch Boston proper. In 1830 developers began filling the marshes between five islands to create the large Noddles Island that became East Boston. They promoted it as a resort community for well-to-do Bostonians,

At play on Revere Beach.

and a few large mansions were built on tree-lined boulevards. But East Boston soon became an immigration processing center, second on America's East Coast only to Ellis Island, and many of the Irish, Italians, and Eastern European Jews remained to work in the industrial areas that grew up along the waterfront. Among those immigrants was the Nova Scotian naval architect Donald McKay, who opened a shipyard on the waterfront and turned out some of the fastest and largest sailing ships ever built. As the population swelled, house lots were sliced smaller and smaller and triple-decker tenements became the dominant building style. In the 1960s, new waves of immigrants, mostly Hispanic and Asian, began to replace earlier groups.

Construction of Boston Airport in 1923 changed East Boston forever. Now **Logan International Airport** covers more than a third of the area of East Boston. In 1995, the city opened **East Boston Piers Park,** a handsome 6.5-acre waterfront plot with extensive playgrounds and gazebos on a pier looking back at Boston's downtown skyline. Piers Park is an ideal vantage for harbor fireworks displays. Moreover, the Boston Natural Areas Fund and the Trust for Public Land received a substantial grant to begin work on a "greenway" path from Piers Park to Constitution Beach (a recreational beach dwarfed by an airport runway) to Belle Isle Marsh. The last surviving pre-Colonial salt marsh, Belle Isle lives on as the final link of a 21st-century city to its 17th-century origins.

THE WATERFRONT

SECRET GARDEN OF EASTIE

*H*ow broad and low the sky seemed over East Boston, with almost no trees on the streets to soften it, with the houses built flush to the sidewalks. Everything was white or grey or bleak pastels, so that even the occasional brick school or very occasional brick apartment building seemed harsh in color by contrast. All the lushness was hidden from the streets. Between every house there was a walkway, often barred by a high gate padlocked or bolted. No stranger could guess the secret world of the backyards, where in May the peach trees blossomed all over Eastie, where grapevines were trained to arbors and roses coiled over fences, where tomatoes offered their lush fruits, where right outside the back door a terrace of patterned bricks or patio blocks had often been laid so that it offered an outdoor table, some chairs, an external room under the flapping of the perennial multitiered laundry. Backyard barbecues and blue and white madonnas stood side by side. This was the world of her childhood.

—Marge Piercy, *Fly Away Home,* 1984

Revere Beach in the mid-1930s. (Underwood Photo Archives, San Francisco)

A DAY AT THE BEACH(ES)

Revere Beach: On warm summer weekends, Revere Beach attracts up to 100,000 people to its broad crescent of sand and sea, where bathers can catch the surf and watch jetliners coming and going at Logan Airport. The first publicly owned beach in America, Revere celebrated its centennial in 1996 by refurbishing the historic bathhouses, bandstand, and other facilities. *Take the Blue Line to Eliot Circle for the south end, the Revere Beach stop for the center, or the Wonderland (named for the big-band era ballroom) stop at the end.*

Wollaston Beach: Wollaston is in Quincy, south of Boston: three miles of coarse sand across a highway from a string of classic clam shacks. *Take the Red Line to the Wollaston Beach stop or the Ashmont bus #217.*

L Street Beach: This best of the beaches on the "Irish Riviera" in South Boston is a neighborhood favorite. The classic bathhouses were Mayor Curley's reward to his most loyal constituents. This is where the "L Street Brownies" take their annual January 1 dip. *Take the Red Line to South Station, then change to City Point bus #7.*

Lovells Island Beach: The only good swimming beach on the Harbor Islands has stretches of fine sand, clean water, and a lovely lighthouse view. *Take the Harbor Islands ferry from Long Wharf, then the water taxi from Georges Island.*

C A M B R I D G E

The sun goes down over Cambridge with as much apparent interest as if he were a Harvard graduate: possibly he is; and he spreads a glory over the Back Bay . . . .
— William Dean Howells, Letter to Henry James

SOMETIMES IT'S HARD TO TELL where Harvard University and the Massachusetts Institute of Technology (MIT) end and the city of Cambridge begins. Municipality and academia are entwined in a friendly, even symbiotic embrace. The universities elevate Cambridge's vision beyond merely parochial concerns, while the city keeps the tenured sages grounded in the verities of working class life. An annual flood of fresh-faced and frequently brilliant new students imbues Cambridge with a youthful sense that all things are possible. And a certain number of these modern Candides remain to become Panglosses, believing that they have, indeed, found the best of all possible worlds.

Although only one of us was educated at Harvard, we have chosen to make our home in the weedier city outside the sheltering academic groves. We speak of Cambridge with a lover's affection, and perhaps a lover's blindness to her flaws.

■ HARVARD SQUARE

Even most Bostonians think Harvard Square is Cambridge, and in a sense they are right. This is where the city was born and the best place to begin an exploration.

Cambridge is linked to Boston by eight bridges, but most people arrive in Harvard Square on the Red Line subway. The main exit leads up to a small traffic island next to **Out of Town News**, the city's chief dealer in national and international magazines and newspapers. Chances are good that half the people standing between Out of Town and the Cambridge information kiosk will be turning in slow circles, scanning the surrounding streets. "Let's meet at Out of Town" is a standard rendezvous arrangement between Cantabrigians and their visiting friends.

This is Ground Zero, as the *Omphalos* sculpture makes clear in obscure reference to Cambridge thinking of itself as Delphi, the navel of Earth's human realm and the gateway to divine knowledge. True enough, the world swirls around this

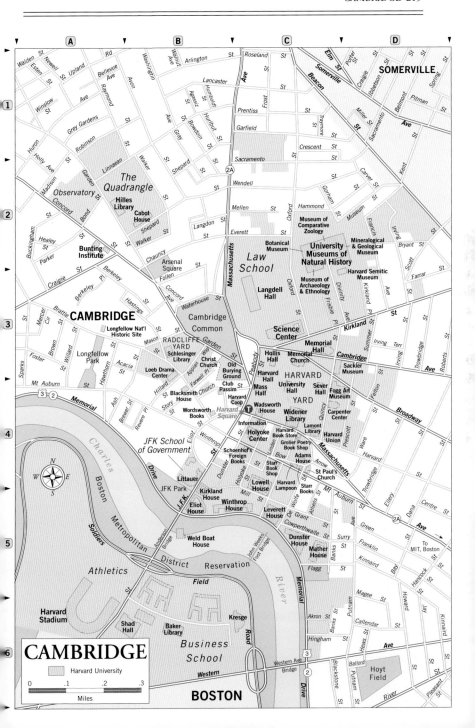

CAMBRIDGE

Harvard University

0   .1   .2   .3
Miles

isle of the printed word—or at least the traffic does. From Out of Town one can survey the three historic overlays of Cambridge: the colonial town, the university, and the lively commercial square. To east and northeast lie the high brick walls one of the world's most prestigious universities; to the south and west stand the shops, bookstores, and cafes of the mercantile square. Due north past the statue of Charles Sumner lies the oldest extant portion of the city, Cambridge Common.

■ THE LEGACY OF COLONIAL CAMBRIDGE

The street layout of Harvard Square has been augmented but little altered since the 17th century, when the square was the market area between the palisaded town and the common pasture. This is where Cambridge was founded in 1630 by a handful of Puritan settlers who called their home "Newtowne." The Massachusetts Bay Colony established a college here in 1636 "to advance Learning and perpetuate it to Posterity; dreading to leave an illiterate Ministry to the Churches, when our present Ministers shall lie in the Dust," according to a 17th-century account. In 1638 young cleric John Harvard died in Charlestown, leaving half his fortune and all his books to the college. In recognition, the Great and General Court called the school Harvard College and rechristened Newtowne as Cambridge to honor the alma mater of many of the colony's leaders.

Cambridge Common
map page 219, B-3

Precious little remains of pre-Revolutionary Cambridge except the Cambridge Common and some of its surrounds. Set aside in 1631, the Common originally encompassed 86 acres but was trimmed to its present 16 acres in 1724 as Cambridge mercantile life flourished and farming was pushed farther out into the suburbs. Crisscrossed with asphalt paths lined with venerable trees, the Common today serves more as an exercise area than as either pasture or drill ground. On the same grounds where Little Leaguers play baseball, more than 10,000 soldiers huddled during the winter of 1775–76, trying to keep warm. More than two centuries later, the Common in winter is a place of austere beauty, where bare branches arch over a snowfield tracked with the narrow trails of cross country skis.

Washington Elm: The Common is dotted by plaques and monuments, including one plaque beneath a scion of the Washington Elm indicating the spot where, according to Cambridge lore, Washington took command of the Continental Army on July 3, 1775. (Historians argue that Washington actually assumed command the day before and merely reviewed the troops on July 3.) The original elm toppled in 1923 when workmen were trying to trim a branch. A

CAMBRIDGE

traffic island cast adrift from the Common proper contains cast hoofprints indicating the route of William Dawes on his midnight ride of April 18-19, 1775. In 1997, the first American memorial to the victims of the Irish Famine was unveiled on the Common. The statue shows a woman cradling a dead child as she sends her remaining two children off to the New World.

Old Burying Ground

map page 219, B/C-3/4

The first set-aside from the Common was the area known alternately as **God's Acre** or

The Old Burying Ground. The simple stones, set apart from the Square's clamor by a black iron fence, mark the remains of many Harvard presidents, the first colonial printer Stephen Daye, and several veterans of the Revolution, including African Americans Cato Stedman and Neptune Frost.

Christ Church

map page 219, B-3

Contemplative tranquility also rules at the adjacent **Christ Church**, designed for Cambridge Tories in 1761 by Peter Harrison, who was also the architect of Boston's King's Chapel. Most of the Anglican

A view of Harvard Yard in 1726. (Massachusetts Historical Society)

congregation fled Cambridge in 1774, and the church served as a barracks for colonial troops, who melted its organ pipes for bullets. It was restored and reopened for services on New Year's Eve 1775, when George and Martha Washington worshipped here. With the exception of electric lighting, the church has changed little since. Perhaps because it lacks a tall spire and sits back from the street, gray-shingled Christ Church creates a diminutive impression. Yet the interior is airy, bright, and spare, reflecting a simple asceticism that recalls Puritan meeting houses.

Brattle Street and Tory Row
map page 219, A/B-3

Even in the 17th and 18th centuries the amenities of life in a college town drew some of the colony's wealthiest merchants to build in Cambridge. Many of their architectural testaments still stand along the portion of Brattle Street called Tory Row, which begins a block behind Christ Church and extends about a mile out of Harvard Square. Surrounded by long, green lawns and Georgian gardens, these stately mansions sit far back from broad, tree-lined Brattle Street as models of proportion and order. Seven of the grand houses seized by the Massachusetts government after the Revolution and auctioned off to patriots still stand and two are open to the public: the **Hooper-Lee-Nichols House** (159 Brattle Street), home of the Cambridge Historical Society and the oldest (1688) house in Cambridge, and the Longfellow National Historic Site (see below).

Longfellow National Historic Site
map page 219, A-3

The Tory family that built the latter house had made its fortune in the West Indies plantations and fled home to England at the beginning of the Revolution. George Washington definitely did sleep here, as he made it his quarters during the siege of Boston. Henry Wadsworth Longfellow became a lodger in 1837, and when he married Frances Appleton (of the Boston Brahmin line of Appletons), his father-in-law purchased the house as a wedding gift. The Longfellow family maintained the house until 1974, when they turned it over to the National Park Service. A moving and intelligent house tour interprets the joys and tragedies of the Good Gray Poet's family life. Even apart from the house's association with celebrity, the tour provides an intimate peek at comfortable upper middle-class life of the latter 19th century. The spacious, large-windowed rooms (a mark of the first owners' wealth) are padded with Empire-style furniture, Victorian wallpaper, the family's souvenirs of their European trips, and a flood of graphic and fine art. (The poet's son was a painter.) Among the furnishings is a chair given to Longfellow by Cambridge schoolchildren; it was made from the "spreading chestnut tree" that had stood in front of the village blacksmith's house. That building, found at 56 Brattle Street, now houses the Cambridge Center for Adult Education and the bakery and cafe of the Hi-Rise Pie Company.

Longfellow National Historic Site: *105 Brattle St.; 617-876-4491.*

CAMBRIDGE

A Tale of Many Plots: Mount Auburn Cemetery

In 1831, when the Massachusetts Horticultural Society founded Mount Auburn Cemetery in the rural outlands of the city, they transformed the American way of death. In place of the austere practicality of colonial graveyards, the founders envisioned a woodland burial ground on the west end of Cambridge to commemorate the dead and comfort the bereaved with the beauty of the natural world. This adaptation of Paris's Père Lachaise cemetery was so well-received that within a generation it inspired both the garden cemetery and public parks movements. By the late 19th century it had become such a tourist attraction that the management finally established rules for visitors: closing the gates at night, banning horseback riding and bicycles, forbidding pets and picnicking, and prohibiting visitors from digging up souvenir plants.

Not that Mount Auburn wished to keep visitors away. On the contrary, from the outset the 174-acre cemetery was designed to be used by the people above ground, providing that they show the proper respect for those below. Still an active cemetery, Mount Auburn remains a must-see site for visiting horticulturalists and birdwatchers. More than 300 species of trees and 130 species of shrubs and ground covers provide sanctuary for urban wildlife, including eighty-plus species of spring migratory birds.

In fact, birding is a rite of spring at Mount Auburn, when the nights begin to warm, the dogwoods, apples, and cherries begin to bloom, and the warblers, vireos, orioles, and scarlet tanagers arrive. During the peak migration around May 10 as many as 1,000 birders per day visit Mount Auburn, lured by the possibility of seeing up to 100 species in a single day. A "Bird Sightings" bulletin board is posted at the Brattle Street gatehouse. Mount Auburn's birding hotline is 617-547-7105, ext. 824.

Mount Auburn Cemetery also provides an interesting comparison of changing fashion in gravestones and mortuary art. Among the architects and artists whose memorial work stands in the cemetery are Arthur Gilman, Horatio Greenough, Augustus Saint-Gaudens, and Stanford White.

Along the 10 miles of roads and paths are buried 87,000 people, including many named elsewhere in this volume. The illustrious dead include navigator Nathaniel Bowditch, architect Charles Bulfinch, Christian Science founder Mary Baker Eddy (no, there is not a telephone in her tomb), Fannie Farmer, Buckminster Fuller, Isabella Stewart Gardner, Oliver Wendell Holmes, Winslow Homer, Julia Ward Howe, Edwin Land (of Polaroid's "Land Camera" fame), Henry Wadsworth Longfellow, Harrison Gray Otis, and B.F. Skinner.

Mount Auburn Cemetery is open daily 8-5, 7-5 during daylight saving time. A map and walking tour guide are available free at the main gate.

Radcliffe

map page 219, B-3

Where James Street forks from Brattle is an arched entrance to Radcliffe Yard. At one end of three linked buildings within the yard is the **Schlesinger Library on the History of Women in America,** including an exhaustive culinary collection. Radcliffe College began in 1879 as the "Collegiate Institution for Women," women who until 1943 attended female-only classes taught by Harvard College faculty. The two colleges are now completely interwoven under the auspices of Harvard University, though Radcliffe on its own continues to host special programs for visiting scholars and artists as well as symposia on women's issues.

Loeb Drama Center

map page 219, B-3

Also sandwiched between the two Longfellow sites is the **Loeb Drama Center,** an innovative 1959 building with a flexible stage that can be changed from proscenium to thrust to theater-in-the-round. Built for student productions, it is also home to the **American Repertory Theatre,** an innovative leader in America's current regional theater movement.

An interior and an exterior view of Longfellow House. (Both photos by Robert Holmes)

■ HARVARD YARD ET CIRCUM   *map page 219, C-3/4*

Harvard University looms large in Cambridge. It is the sixth largest employer, owns more than 360 acres of land and 400 buildings in the Cambridge-Boston area, and accounts for a population of about 18,000 students scattered among its two colleges and 10 graduate and professional schools.

The university's own literature laments that no brief walking tour can do Harvard justice. Yet Harvard Yard remains the sanctum sanctorum: the physical manifestation of the soul of the oldest institution of higher learning in the United States.

"Other American colleges have campuses, but Harvard has always had and always will have her Yard of grass and trees and youth and old familiar ghosts," wrote poet and essayist David McCord, alumnus and recipient, in 1956, of Harvard's first honorary Doctor of Humane Letters degree.

Harvard itself believes so strongly in the Yard that it houses all Harvard College freshmen here, perhaps to inculcate the weight of history and the gravity of the education on which they are embarking. This segregation by age often leads visitors to conclude that all Harvard students are as perilously young as the scrubbed youth sitting beneath the towering trees as they pore over Plutarch, Hobbes, or Byron while their classmates scale Frisbees over the hallowed lawn.

■ TOURING THE YARD   *map page 219, C-3/4*

The area in and around the Yard is a must for architecture buffs: over the years Harvard has commissioned works by many famous architects, prompting British architect James Stirling to describe his contribution to the collection, the Sackler Museum, as "the newest animal in Harvard's architectural zoo."

The college's cloistering brick wall is punctuated by nine major and several minor gates, allowing any pedestrian to go through Harvard without passing an entrance exam. The gate on Massachusetts Avenue opposite Dunster Street opens into "old" Harvard Yard, which dates from the 1630s.

Wadsworth House
map page 219, C-4

Abruptly on the right stands the yellow clapboard Wadsworth House, built in 1727 for the ninth president of Harvard and inhabited by eight of his successors. George Washington lived here briefly in July 1775 before moving out to Tory Row.

Massachusetts Hall
map page 219, C-4

The cluster of Colonial-era brick structures diagonally ahead to the left begins with Massachusetts Hall, the oldest surviving Harvard building, which was constructed at public expense in 1720 and housed 640 colonial soldiers during the siege of Boston.

CAMBRIDGE

Harvard Hall

map page 219, C-3

Just beyond lies Harvard Hall, the third building to bear that name since 1642. In 1764, a fire burned the second one and also destroyed John Harvard's book collection, except for one volume a student had taken out the night of the fire. The next day the young man returned the book to the college president who, the story goes, thanked him profusely for saving the book—then expelled him for removing it without permission.

Hollis Hall

map page 219, C-3

Just past Harvard Hall is Hollis Hall, the 1763 dormitory where Ralph Waldo Emerson and Henry David Thoreau lived when students here. The steps and bricks in front are dented and pockmarked because, before a furnace was installed, students would roast cannonballs in a fire to radiate warmth all night in their rooms. When spring arrived, the "heaters" went out the windows.

John Harvard Statue

map page 219, C-4

On the opposite side of the "old" Yard is one of the most-photographed sites at Harvard: the "statue of three lies," or, more properly, the John Harvard Statue. The inscription reads "John Harvard, Founder, 1638." For the record, Harvard was a benefactor of the school, which had already been founded in 1636, before he arrived in the New World. Nor is the statue a likeness of

---

HARVARD POSERS

*B*arker spun his chair to face the window behind his desk. Across the green a woman was pointing a camera at a man posing in front of the statue of the putative John Harvard; this configuration occurred many times a day, as if Harvard was Abe Lincoln or Mahatma Gandhi. Barker had never understood why anyone would want to have their picture taken with a statue—what was it they hoped to capture in such a pairing? It eluded him even as he assumed it must reflect some universal, albeit primitive, need for association with the sacred. And to anyone who watched it from afar, Harvard was the Vatican, its president the pope. When Barker joined the Harvard faculty, Von Stampler had assured him that he would thenceforth be considered, both by those within it and those not so fortunate, to be a member of the Upper Class. Barker wondered first whether this was true, and secondly whether it was, per se, a good thing to be a member of the Upper Class. To what did that entitle you except a slew of responsibilities and a set of expectations on the part of your fellows? The man and woman now exchanged places; he pointed the camera at her. They would go home and show the pictures to their children, who would, Barker guessed, say "so what?," a response Barker considered not only plausible but altogether rational. Children didn't give a shit about that kind of worship.

—Anne Bernays, *Professor Romeo*, 1989

the minister; because Harvard's visage was a mystery, sculptor Daniel Chester French is thought to have modeled the head on a popular member of the class of 1882.

University Hall

map page 219, C-4

Harvard's statue sits in front of University Hall, designed by Charles Bulfinch and completed in 1816. Handsomely classical on both front and back, it neatly divides Harvard Yard into "old" and "new" sections. On the grassy expanse of the "new" Yard, commencement exercises are held each June, rain or shine (usually "shine"—as Howells observed, the sun is probably a Harvard man).

Sever Hall

map page 219, C-4

Facing University Hall, Sever Hall, by Henry Hobson Richardson, is a Romanesque intrusion in a field of New England Colonial Revival edifices.

Widener Library

map page 219, C-4

A long sweep of steps mounts to the Olympian Widener Library, the Yard's other backdrop for Kodak moments. Widener is the third largest library in the brary in the world, with more than 4.5 million books on more than five miles of shelves. The building is named for Harry Elkins Widener of the class of 1907. When

Harvard students and sightseers flood the streets on a fall weekend in Cambridge (above). A classic Commencement Day photo opportunity: a class marshall and his family pose with John Harvard. (opposite)

he perished in 1912 on the *Titanic,* his mother honored young Harry's wishes to donate his books to Harvard—and threw in the funds to build a memorial library to house them. Although a Harvard University library card is required to enter the remarkable stacks, where volumes dating back to the 17th century are still shelved, visitors are permitted to view the John Singer Sargent murals and the historical dioramas of Cambridge and Harvard in the lobby. Widener Library serves as the hub of Harvard's library system, which consists of 90 libraries in all.

Houghton and Pusey Libraries

Two other major libraries stand on Widener's southeast side: Houghton, which often mounts exhibitions from its collection of rare books, manuscripts, and portraits; and Pusey, which holds, among other treasures, Harvard's collection of theatrical costumes and memorabilia.

THE NUTTY PROFESSOR

*O*ne spring morning his first remark was: "Mrs. James is house-cleaning to-day. You know that awful upheaval—and she says I can't come home to luncheon. Won't you all come over to the club and have luncheon with me?" The question seemed to us a valuable creative idea, and in due time we were gathered round the table of a delightful host. In the midst of the cheerful conversation he turned to me and said in a confidential tone: "Did you ever take enough of anything stimulating so that you felt yourself just going off, letting go of the present and grasping for a moment a real conception of the unity of the universe?" Having been brought up in a conservative New England village, I had never even seen anyone grasping for cosmic unity in just that way; so I replied with a hesitating negative. Then our host went on to describe certain emotions he had experienced while experimenting with strange drugs.

Occasionally he would report these experiences in class and quote the words he had spoken as they were carefully taken down by his devoted wife. Two that I remember are: "The only differences in the world are differences of degree between degrees of difference and no difference at all"; and: "School, high school, normal school, law school, divinity school, school, school. Oh my God!" Perhaps the last of these psychological experiments he tried the following year with mescal. A medical friend sent him a bud telling him that it would give the most glorious visions of color and gild every common object with splendor. The net result was nothing but twenty-four hours of dangerous illness—and no visions.

—Mary E. Raymond, *Memories of William James,* ca. 1895

■ OUTSIDE THE GATES OF HARVARD YARD

Science Center
map page 219, C-3

North of "old" Harvard Yard through **Holworthy Gate** sprawls the Science Center, a modernist masterpiece designed by the Catalan architect José Luis Sert, who once headed Harvard's Graduate School of Design and whose own innovative home is encircled by a brick wall on nearby Francis Avenue. The technologically adroit **Tanner Fountain** in front of the Science Center shuts off whenever the wind gets strong enough to spray passersby; in the winter it emits steam.

Memorial Hall
map page 219, C-3

Memorial Hall is the massive brick structure diagonally to the right of the Science Center. Designed by a pair of 1850s Harvard grads, Memorial Hall is the Boston area's largest surviving example of the Victorian style known as Ruskin Gothic. The plan is a Gothic cathedral with the transept serving as the entrance. The religious reference is apt, for the immense bulk of Memorial Hall is a monument to genuine grief for the Harvard men who died in the Civil War (that is, the 136 Union men, but not the 64 Confederate soldiers, who died). The 21 stained glass windows include several from the Tiffany and LaFarge studios. In recent years, the central nave has been restored to its original function as a dining hall.

The apse of Memorial Hall holds the 1,200-seat **Sanders Theatre,** a major concert, lecture, and poetry reading venue. Folksinger (and Harvard dropout) Pete Seeger claims its acoustics are perfect for singers—"like singing in a bathtub"—though younger singer Cheryl Wheeler likens its intimate scale to "singing in a rolltop desk." Cambridge-based Rounder Records often uses Sanders to record singer-songwriters on its roster.

■ UNIVERSITY ART MUSEUMS

Harvard's university art museums lie along Quincy Street. *Also see pages 232-333.*

Sackler and Fogg Museums

The Arthur M. Sackler Museum, at the corner of Quincy and Broadway, and the Fogg Art Museum on Quincy lie opposite Harvard Yard. The entrance to the Sackler, which opened in 1985, looks incomplete because it is. Architect James Stirling planned a bridge over Broadway to connect the two museums, but neighbors raised such a fuss that Cambridge refused to grant the necessary zoning variance and Harvard left the pilings on the front of the Sackler as a reminder of its neighbors' intransigence.

Carpenter Center for the Visual Arts
map page 219, C-4

The 1963 Carpenter Center, next to the Fogg, is the only building in North America designed by Swiss-French architect and Harvard visiting professor Charles-Edouard Jeanneret, known as Le Corbusier. Viewed from across Quincy Street, the Carpenter

(continues page 235)

CAMBRIDGE

HARVARD'S MUSEUMS

Cambridge's museums of art, culture, and natural history rank among the best of their kind in the world, far outshining the holdings in many good-sized urban museums. Harvard has a long record of making history and making taste, and these museum collections are the sources from which both were fashioned.

Each of Harvard's three art museums claims its own turf but share the same phone number: *617-495-9400*

Fogg Art Museum

map page 219, C/D-4

The principal gem in Harvard's artistic crown is the Fogg Art Museum, a 1927 structure built around a central courtyard adapted from a 16th-century church in Montepulciano, Italy. This liturgical architecture ultimately suits the collections, which cover the sweep of the last millennium of Western art. Superb Gothic religious art graces the walls of the lower courtyard, and Renaissance paintings line the spiraling marble staircase. Second level galleries reveal deep holdings in French art from Ingres to the Impressionists, old master prints and drawings, the mystical paintings of the Pre-Raphaelite Brotherhood, fine American and English silver, and other exquisite decorative objets. Because it is a small museum with a rotating collection, the Fogg is never fatiguing and always surprising. *32 Quincy Street.*

Busch-Reisinger Museum

map page 219, C/D-4

Werner Otto Hall was grafted onto the rear of the Fogg in 1991 to house the Germanic art of the Busch-Reisinger Museum. Walter Gropius and Lyonel Feininger chose the Busch-Reisinger as the depository of their personal papers and drawings, thereby ensuring that the museum would thoroughly document the work and philosophy of the Bauhaus. The collection is very deep in German Expressionism, with major works by such 20th-century masters as Max Beckmann, Lyonel Feininger, Wassily Kandinsky, Paul Klee, Oskar Kokoschka, Franz Marc (the beautiful *Red Horses)*, Lazlo Moholy-Nagy, and Emil Nolde. *In Otto Werner Hall, 32 Quincy Street.*

Sackler (Arthur M.) Museum

map page 219, C-3

Housing Harvard's Ancient, Asian, Islamic, and later Indian art, this building's interior is also a work of art, with a long narrow staircase that rises into light. The Greek black- and red-figured vases at the top of the stairs establish the tone: imagine John Keats contemplating his urn in this minimalist setting. The Sackler has one of the finest collections of archaic Chinese bronzes and jades in the West. Other strengths include Korean ceramics and Buddhist sculptures. *485 Broadway; 617-495-9400.*

CAMBRIDGE

Harvard Museums of Cultural and Natural History

map page 219, C-2/3

A single building with two entrances houses the Harvard Museums of Cultural and Natural History. Don't expect bells and whistles in the natural history collections. The straightforward presentation of labeled objects exudes an infectious Victorian charm in its naivete, yet these are some of the most formidably complete accumulations of their kind. *24 Oxford St.; 617-495-3045.*

The **Botanical Museum's** unique collection of glass flowers is easily the most popular exhibit in the building: Cantabrigians invariably bring visiting great aunts to see these marvels. Hand-blown and shaped by Leopold and Rudolph Blaschka between 1887 and 1936, the 3,000 models of 850 plant species are extraordinary examples of the glassblower's art. Each species is illustrated with a scientifically accurate lifesize model and magnified parts.

The **Museum of Comparative Zoology** has one of the most extensive collections in the world of type specimens, including Louis Agassiz's 19th-century personal arachnid collections. True, the stuffed animals in the cases look a little threadbare, but the fossils and skeletons

The Botanical Museum's collection of hand-blown glass flowers is popular among students, Cambridge residents, and visitors alike. (Robert Holmes)

make up for the mustiness. Among this dizzying labyrinth of cases are a skeleton of the giant sea serpent *Kronosaurus*, as well as the first scientifically described *Triceratops*.

The plain cases in the **Mineralogical and Geological Museum** detail specimens discovered as far back as 1783, including samples of most major New England ore and gem finds. The simplicity of the presentation obscures the significance and breadth of the museum's holdings. Highlights include meteorites (one of the world's premier collections) and rough and cut gemstones.

Peabody Museum of Archaeology and Ethnology

The Peabody was founded in 1866 as the first museum in the Americas devoted exclusively to anthropology. In the late 19th century, scientists at the Peabody began groundbreaking systematic archaeological and ethnological research in North and Central America. As a result, great strengths in the Peabody's holdings include Mayan objects from Copán and Chichen Itza; gold figures from Panama; findings from predynastic Egypt (Harvard joined the Museum of Fine Arts in some of the seminal digs in Egypt and the Sudan); materials from the Lewis and Clark Expedition; and holdings from the Mimbres and Pecos Pueblos of the American Southwest.

The exhibits mounted since 1990 demonstrate the sea change of attitudes in anthropological museums from trophy exhibition to serious lifestyle interpretation. The multi-million dollar interactive "Change and Continuity," for example, narrates interactions in North American between Europeans and the indigenous peoples—with a concentration on major adaptations that occurred in the 19th century. *11 Divinity Ave.; 617-495-3045.*

Harvard Semitic Museum

map page 219, C-3

This museum has also served as a center for archaeological exploration, pioneering excavations in the Holy Land at Samaria in 1908-12. Since reopening in 1982, it has presented small exhibitions from its deep holdings from Assyrian, Babylonian, Hebrew, and Phoenician cultures, among others. Currently the museum is directing an excavation at the ancient seaport of Ashkelon in Israel. *6 Divinity Ave.; 617-495-4631.*

Collection of Historical Scientific Instruments

map page 219, C-3

Gadgeteers love the small but fascinating instruments displayed in the basement of the Science Center. These run the gamut from a beautifully crafted astrolabe (ca. 1450) to modern radar apparatus. *Basement of Science Center.*

CAMBRIDGE

(continued from page 231)

Center is a fascinating interplay of planes and curves, opened and closed elements, massive heaviness and hovering lightness. The Prescott Street side of the building has achieved a long-delayed architectural resolution. The sweeping grace Le Corbusier envisioned was finally realized when the rear of the building was linked in 1991 to **Otto Werner Hall,** which houses the Germanic art collection of the **Busch-Reisinger Museum.** *(See page 232.)*

Holyoke Center

map page 219, C-4

The south side of the Yard faces Holyoke Center, another outsized Sert-designed hulk that raises the bile of the preservation-minded Harvard Square Defense Fund. Yet few visitors to Cambridge even notice Holyoke Center: they're drawn to the plaza cafe in front on Massachusetts Avenue, or they simply pass through the open gallery en route to Mount Auburn Street.

■ YARD TO RIVER

Harvard buildings continue along the 17th-century banks of the Charles River to the present, more contained river. This area also became a flourishing commercial center in Colonial times because it was the gateway from Boston to areas north and west via ferry service at the foot of Dunster Street (where the colony's first tavern was licensed) and, after 1662, by the Great Bridge at the foot of what is now JFK Street. The district now contains a mix of restaurants, small shops, and Harvard buildings. The main street, Boylston, was renamed JFK to honor Harvard's illustrious alumnus. Down Plympton Street stands **Adams House,** one of the dormitories of Harvard's "Gold Coast" (its dome is still painted gold). Diagonally across Bow Street from Adams House is the flatiron-shaped **Lampoon Castle,** home of the legendary *Harvard Lampoon* humor magazine. Fittingly enough, the building's architectural elements make a silly face in the direction of Harvard Square. Harvard upperclass dormitories occupy much of the prime real estate on Memorial Drive along the river from **Eliot** and **Kirkland Houses** on JFK Street to **Dunster** and **Mather Houses** at the corner of Flagg Street. A block away, **20 Flagg Street** bears a small historical marker. It notes that Harvard student W. E. B. Du Bois rented a room here in the late 1880s and early 1890s (his landlady was descended from Jamaican slaves) because African Americans were not welcome in the dormitories. "I was in Harvard but not of it," DuBois later wrote.

■ MERCANTILE HARVARD SQUARE

Commercial Harvard Square has taken on a life and culture of its own as an urban ecosystem of diverse ideologies and lifestyles. Here the contradictions of the city collide in a sort of freefloating, Fellini-esque scene that blends patrician and proletarian, professor and panhandler. Cult movies start here. Street singers outnumber boomboxes, strangers challenge each other to chess duels, and pedestrians freely commandeer the roads.

That the existing buildings—mostly brick, mostly low—date chiefly from the late 19th and early 20th centuries does not keep a local preservation society from fighting further alterations. As a result, the eclectic mix of small merchants and restaurants includes few chain operations. That's not to say there isn't change. Each generation returning to Harvard for a 20th reunion inevitably (and loudly) laments the loss of this shop or that restaurant. During that week in early June, the phrase most often overheard in the Square is "used to be."

Plus ça change ... Harvard Square remains, as ever, a mart for the young and the affluent as well as for the intellectual and intellectual manqué.

Students and locals enjoy a warm evening at a Cambridge wine bar.

CAMBRIDGE

Bookstores

Appropriately for the first city in the British colonies with a printing press, Harvard Square boasts one of the world's densest concentrations of bookstores. At least 15 dealers in new and used books can be found in and near the Square.

Wordsworth Books, the largest of the group, keeps long hours seven days a week, stocks more than 100,000 titles, and discounts everything except textbooks. *30 Brattle St.; 617-354-5201.*

Harvard Book Store *(1256 Massachusetts Ave.; 617-661-1616)* and the beautifully renovated bookstore and café of the **Harvard Cooperative Society** *(1400 Massachusetts Ave.; 617-499-2000)* are more selective but easier to browse.

Grolier Poetry Book Shop's proprietor Louisa Solano wedges 15,000 slim titles into a store the size of a small cafe, managing to carry thousands of poetry books literally unavailable anywhere else. *6 Plympton St.; 617-547-4648.*

Schoenhof's Foreign Books fills orders from around the globe for scholarly and literary books in dozens of languages. *76A Mt. Auburn St.; 617-547-8855.*

James & Devon Gray Booksellers specializes in books printed before the year 1700. *12 Arrow St.; 617- 868-0752.*

Starr Book Shop in the rear of the Lampoon building is one of the long-time dealers in used books. The Square has as much life of the street as life of the mind. Cambridge is one of the best cities in the world for street performers, according to Stephen Baird, political puppeteer, musician, and founder/director of the International Street Artists Guild—a task he calls "organizing anarchists." *29 Plympton St.; 617-547-6864.*

Street Performers

Singing in the Square is a venerable tradition and apocryphal tales circulate of Bob Dylan, Joan Baez, Tracy Chapman, and Bonnie Raitt playing for change. In 1990, the city council passed a resolution honoring street performers and an ordinance limiting their volume to 80 decibels to settle what musicians were calling "the volume wars." Now it's possible to stroll the Square on a balmy summer evening and hear a scruffy Dylan wannabe, a Haitian tenor performing Edith Piaf, or an Ecuadoran troupe with panpipes and armadillo-shell mandolins. One fixture is Leonard Solomon, virtuoso of his own musical contraptions, the Bellowphone and Callioforte.

Club Passim

A relic from the Great Folk Scare of the late 1950s and '60s, when it was called Club 47, Club Passim gave Joan Baez her debut mike in 1959. Others who went on to fame from Club 47/Passim include Jimmy Buffett, Jackson Browne, Leon Redbone, and Tom Waits. Tiny Club Passim remains the national paragon of acoustic music venues, more recently helping to nurture the careers of singer-songwriters Suzanne Vega, Nanci Griffith, and Shawn Colvin. *47 Palmer St.; 617-492-7679.*

Cantabrigians dress flamboyantly for Carnaval.

■ THE OTHER SQUARES OF CAMBRIDGE

With the possible exception of MIT, Cambridge outside the immediate vicinity of Harvard is terra incognita to most casual visitors. Like Boston, Cambridge is a conglomeration of villages arranged around large traffic intersections. In the 19th century, Old Cambridge tried to disown its offspring and form a separate city, but Puritan bluebloods were outvoted by the not-so-English municipal majority.

Cambridge expanded quickly in the industrial revolution as bridges spanning the Charles River linked the city to the port and railyards of Boston. Even today, the other squares remain strung like pearls along Cambridge Street, Broadway, and Massachusetts Avenue, each of which runs from a Boston bridge to Harvard Square. ("Mass Ave," as it's known, continues north toward Arlington through Porter Square.) Industrial Cambridgeport (which never really became a port) sprang up after the West Boston Bridge opened in 1793. East Cambridge grew rapidly when an 1805 bridge linked the Lechmere industrial canal to Boston's West End. As massive bakeries and assembly plants were built in the 19th century, workers' housing went up nearby, attracting immigrant workers. Although Cambridge's principal product today is knowledge (the first e-mail message was issued from Cambridge), the city spawned Lever Brothers, the nation's first ladder factory and carriage works, the first galvanized iron pipeworks, and the first factories to produce reversible collars, waterproof hats, piano keys, and mechanical egg-beaters. A few manufacturers persist: Cambridge produces candy (Junior Mints, Skybars, and NECCO wafers), house paint, titanium bicycles, and human skin and knee cartilage. Lotus and Polaroid make their world headquarters here.

■ MIT AND KENDALL SQUARE

map pages 10-11, center

Kendall Square, the most industrial section of Cambridge, boasts both the remnants of a once-great foundry industry and the seeds of a newly sprouted biotechnology cluster. MIT sprawls across the area, low and gray like a robust lichen colony, spawning many of the nearby corporate software, internet, and biotech companies. Several former mill buildings along the rail tracks near Broadway have metamorphosed into a bustling little shopping, dining and entertainment center with a brewery and a very Cantabrigian multiplex cinema screening independent and repertory films.

Because MIT's back is turned to Kendall Square, "Tech" is more approachable from Massachusetts Avenue, where the scale of its buildings hints at the university's status as one of the world leaders in engineering and scientific research. These

A vintage postcard with a view of the MIT campus. (courtesy Patricia Harris)

buildings are numbered rather than named, making navigation easy if you know the code, but dull. The main administration building on Mass Ave, rendered in a vaguely Greek temple style, is called simply **Building 10**. Sailing buffs may wish to visit the **Hart Nautical Museum** here, which contains a wide range of ship models, including one of Donald McKay's *Flying Cloud* clipper.

MIT's commitment to architecture (its own program is very distinguished) has resulted in some interesting, if often hidden, structures. The **Wiesner Building,** which contains the **List Visual Arts Center**, is a collaboration among architect I. M. Pei and several artists, among them Kenneth Noland, whose relief mural dominates the atrium. Two of the most visually exciting buildings on the campus are W16 and W15, the elegant shallow dome of **Kresge Auditorium** (1954-55) and the brick cylinder of **Kresge Chapel** (1955), respectively. Both are extraordinary marriages of art and engineering by Eero Saarinen. The small MIT **Museum** at 265 Massachusetts Avenue runs the gamut from geeky (the history of slide rules) to astonishingly beautiful (holographic art). The **Harvard Bridge** on Massachusetts Avenue, joining MIT to Boston, is marked in a unit of measurement known as the smoot, based on the 1958 survey using Lambda Chi Alpha pledge Oliver R. Smoot as a human yardstick. The bridge is 364.4 smoots and one ear long. Twice a year, pledges renew the painted information.

■ EAST CAMBRIDGE AND BULFINCH SQUARE

East Cambridge owes much of its physical character to Andrew Craigie, a real estate speculator who convinced the Commonwealth of Massachusetts to place the county courthouse here, thereby boosting the value of the tracts Craigie owned nearby. The old county buildings on Thorndike Street between Second and Third Streets—including Charles Bulfinch's 1814 **Middlesex County Courthouse**— were rescued from demolition in the 1980s and renovated by Graham Gund's architectural firm as public and private offices. This handsome group of Federal-period buildings around a central plaza epitomizes classical harmony. The **Cambridge Multicultural Arts Center** (41 Second Street) occupies a portion of the courthouse with a small gallery on the Second Street level and an intimate theater space on the next level up.

While much of East Cambridge is tenement housing—Craigie and his successors built many tenements to shelter immigrants who settled here to work the factories—the old Lechmere industrial canal has been recaptured as a scenic lagoon with condominiums on one side and a highly successful shopping mall, Cambridge-side Galleria, on the other. Boat and bus shuttles connect the mall to public transportation. Although the adjacent roads are difficult for pedestrians to cross, the mall is very close to Boston's Museum of Science and Charlestown's City Square.

■ CENTRAL SQUARE

More residential than Kendall Square and grimier than Harvard Square, gritty Central Square on Massachusetts Avenue abounds with incongruities. At one end of the Square, indie rock clubs attract the skaters, hipsters, and garage-band true believers of the 20-to-30-year-old set, while the other end holds the Cambridge Senior Center, City Hall, and the main Post Office. Central Square is home of the food bank, the grocery co-op, social service agencies, and thrift shops.

The upside of this low-rent ambience is that Central Square has evolved into a mecca for inexpensive ethnic dining—Indian, Caribbean, Ethiopian, Middle Eastern—and live performances of music, dance, and poetry. The same venues that feature alternative rock also spotlight emerging local jazz and pop musicians, while blues pours through the doorways of other lounges. Two bars and two coffeehouses regularly feature poetry readings and slams. The **Dance Complex,** an artist-controlled teaching and performing facility, occupies an H. H. Richardson building at 536 Massachusetts Avenue.

■ INMAN AND PORTER SQUARES

Inman and Porter squares skirt the edge of Cambridge's blue-collar neighbor, Somerville. Inman Square, where Cambridge, Prospect, Hampshire, and Beacon streets meet, was a primarily Italian neighborhood a century ago, but its modern streets are dominated by Portuguese social clubs, restaurants, and shops. Language links their clientele, as most of the recent immigrants come from Brazil and the Azores islands off Africa. Inman is also a jazz spot, and a great place to eat. Late-night diners have long fancied the **S&S Deli,** but foodies invaded the neighborhood when small chef-owned restaurants began to pop up.

Porter Square and North Cambridge have yet to generate the critical mass of shoppers and diners to qualify as a destination in their own right, although they did become more tightly linked with the rest of Cambridge in the early 1980s when the Red Line subway was extended to Porter. The area remains a largely Irish enclave, known to the world as the home where Tip O'Neill alighted during his long career in Congress to draw strength, like Antaeus, from touching the earth.

THE CHARLES RIVER BASIN *map pages 10-11*

Boston and Cambridge are separated by the Charles River, which runs between them and empties into Boston Harbor. But they share the park-lined Charles River Basin, a nine-mile stretch of slow water between the Watertown Dam and the Charles River Dam. The basin dates from 1910, when, following on the heels of the successful creation of Back Bay's fashionable neighborhood, the lower dam was constructed to block the tidal flow from Boston Harbor and thereby stabilize the riverbanks. Inspired by great European river cities, Boston began to build parks along the newly tamed river—a process that continues today.

Three boat clubs, four colleges, and two preparatory schools maintain boathouses along the Charles, which has become a center for intensive training for competitive rowers, including many Olympians. Even before all the ice clears from the river in March, a few dedicated rowers (often in wetsuits) will begin their early morning workouts, hauling and heaving between bridges as they punch their stopwatches. The **Head of the Charles Regatta** in October is the largest two-day rowing event in the world.

Boston owes the lovely white sails of the basin, however, to Joseph Lee, Jr., who recruited Boston youth to help build a fleet of sailboats on the rooftops of apartment buildings in the 1930s. Their efforts were subsequently launched in the Charles as the basis of a grassroots sailing program. In 1941, **Community Boating** opened at the base of the Longfellow Bridge and is now the oldest and one of the largest public sailing programs in the country.

Eighteen miles of walkway

The pathways on each side of the river form an 18-mile loop for walking, jogging, and biking between the Charles River Dam and the Watertown Dam. During the last two weeks of May, the Watertown Dam glints with silvery herring making their

Sculling along the Charles River. (James Marshall)

spawning run, many of them driven by their biological imperative to ignore the fish ladder and jump the five-foot dam.

Esplanade

By far the most popular stretch of riverfront is the embankment along the Beacon Hill "Flats" and the series of islands and lagoons perpendicular to the Back Bay streets from Arlington to Fairfield. This section is popularly known as the Esplanade, a term that captures both the area's quiet splendor and its principal use as an arm-in-arm promenade ground. In 1929, Boston Pops conductor Arthur Fiedler chose the Esplanade as the site for his pioneering outdoor concerts to bring orchestral music to the people. Fiedler conducted free concerts on the Esplanade through 1979, before retiring and ceding the orchestra to John Williams, who has since handed the baton to the exuberant, youthful Keith Lockhart.

Hatch Memorial Shell

The Shell was constructed in 1939 and stands just across the 1953 **Arthur Fiedler Footbridge** from the junction of Arlington Street and Beacon Street. The bridge's dedicatory plaque honors the man who "has here brought the music of the masters to countless thousands in these concerts." Indeed, on the Fourth of July, countless hundreds of thousands fill the riverbanks and hundreds of boats cluster in the Basin for the concert and its rousing conclusion as fireworks begin. *(See page 307.)*

Science Park *map page 11, center left*

Museum of Science: moved from Back Bay to assume buildings atop the Charles River Dam in 1951, it has since expanded dramatically to create Science Park, a complex so vast that many Bostonians are unaware that the dam lies beneath it. This popular museum features interactive exhibits on physical science principles conceived for school-age children.

Hayden Planetarium: offers a daily afternoon show of that night's star patterns

Mugar Omnimax Theater: shows sensational wide-format films on a 180-degree screen.

To reach the museum, planetarium, or theater, call 617-723-2500.

New Riverside Park

The tidal containment function of the dam was superseded in 1981 by a new dam farther down the river, creating a section of abandoned commercial waterfront sometimes called "the lost half-mile." A decade of reconstruction designed to link the Charles River parks with Boston Harbor across this "lost" riverfront began in 1995. When it is finished, bikeways and walkways will complete the century-old dream of a river basin equal to the great riverine parks of Europe.

(following pages) The Boston Pops performs at the Hatch Memorial Shell every Fourth of July

BOSTON LITERARY PORTRAIT GALLERY

Ralph Waldo Emerson

May 25, 1803 - April 27, 1882 After attending Harvard Divinity School, Boston native Emerson served as a Unitarian minister for three years before leaving the church in 1832 and developing his own philosophy of Transcendentalism. He wrote the early Transcendentalist work, *Nature* (1836), at his family's Concord home, The Old Manse, then published it anonymously in Boston. He then lived at Emerson House in Concord while writing essays describing his idealistic views of self-sufficiency and spiritual potential.

Nathaniel Hawthorne

July 4, 1804 - May 19, 1864 Born in Salem, Hawthorne is best known for the novel *The Scarlet Letter* (1850). For three years Hawthorne and his wife rented Emerson's Old Manse, where he wrote the stories in *Mosses from an Old Manse*. The House of Seven Gables belonged to a cousin of Hawthorne's in Salem, and was the setting for that 1851 novel. After a seven-year stint as U.S. Consul in Liverpool, England, Hawthorne returned to Concord to live at The Wayside.

Henry David Thoreau

July 12, 1817 - May 6, 1862 After graduating from Harvard, Thoreau began his friendship with Emerson in Concord, his hometown. He lived his Transcendentalist philosophy during a two-year "experiment" of self-reliance and observation—sleeping in a one-room cabin he built at Concord's Walden Pond and writing essays which would be seminal in the American nature writing tradition. His advocacy of civil liberties and abolition and his night in jail for refusing to pay a poll tax are chronicled in *Civil Disobedience*.

Henry Wadsworth Longfellow

February 27, 1807 - March 24, 1882 The most popular American poet of his day, Longfellow was also a modern language professor at Harvard and a critically acclaimed translator. Longfellow wrote the wildly successful "Song of Hiawatha," as well as *Tales of a Wayside Inn,* the first poem of which is "Paul Revere's Ride." He wrote many of his works between 1837 and 1882 while living at the mansion now known as the Longfellow-Craigie House, 105 Brattle Street in Cambridge.

Louisa May Alcott

November 29, 1832 - March 6, 1888 Alcott spent most of her life in Boston and Concord, often in the company of Thoreau and Emerson. To meet her family's pressing financial needs, Alcott wrote several potboilers, but it would be the letters she wrote while volunteering as a nurse in the Civil War (published as *Hospital Sketches)* which made her known. Her most famous work, *Little Women,* is based on her girlhood at The Wayside (which Hawthorne bought in 1852). She wrote most of her novels while living at Orchard House in Concord.

Henry James

April 15, 1843 - February 28, 1916 A great admirer of both Hawthorne and George Eliot, Henry James became a great literary figure on both sides of the Atlantic. He is today best known for his compelling stories of Americans in European society—as in *Portrait of a Lady* (1881), the study of an American woman abroad. *The Bostonians,* meanwhile, with its tale of suffragettes, conservatives, and reformers, is a vivid picture of the city's late 19th-century idealism. James finished his novella *Daisy Miller* while living on Beacon Hill.

D A Y T R I P S

HOW MANY NEW ENGLANDERS DOES IT TAKE to change a light bulb? Two: one to change the bulb, the other to talk about how nice the old one was. Like Boston, these three day-trip destinations look back with fondness and pride on the history they have seen. In one fashion or another, they have been major spokes in the wheel of New England (Boston, of course, being the Hub). Each trip can be accomplished in a day, for each of the three lies within an hour's drive of Boston.

■ LEXINGTON AND CONCORD

These one-time farming communities northwest of Boston played pivotal roles in America's early history and letters. Fighting here set the American Revolution in motion. Two generations later, Concord gave the nation its first truly American literature, sparking a literary and intellectual renaissance which continues today. The simplest way to reach them is to drive on Route 2 west from Cambridge, following the signs to Lexington Center, where you will proceed west on Route 2A to Concord.

Walden Pond State Reservation. (Robert Holmes)

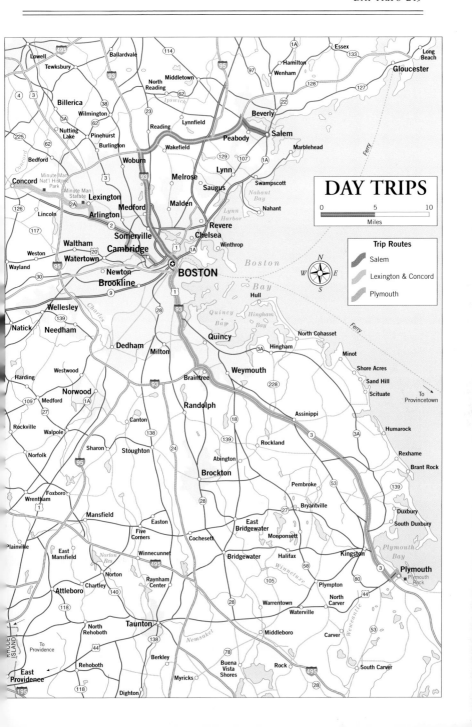

DAY TRIPS

0   5   10
Miles

Trip Routes

Salem

Lexington & Concord

Plymouth

■ REVOLUTIONARY HISTORY

Lexington's Battle Green

It remains unclear who fired first on whom, but the first shots of the American colonies' war for independence rang out at dawn at the Battle Green in Lexington. The colonists who fell on the now-peaceful grassy common were the Revolution's first casualties.

Buckman Tavern

Opposite the green is the yellow clapboard Buckman Tavern (ca. 1690), where 77 militiamen gathered before the battle on the Green; *781-862-5598*

Hancock-Clarke House

John Hancock and Samuel Adams were staying here on the night of April 18 when Paul Revere and William Dawes rode out to warn them of the approaching columns of Redcoats. Now a museum, the house stands on its original site at 36 Hancock Street, although it was moved several times after it was built in 1698. *Information: 781-861-0928.*

Minute Man National Historic Park North Bridge Visitor Center

Like the British soldiers, you should continue west on Massachusetts Avenue (Route 2A) to the **Visitor Center**, where you can pick up a map of the park and surrounding areas. Call 617-484-6156 for more. The park preserves the scene of the fighting between Colonial militiamen and British regular troops on April 19, 1775.

Within the park you'll see Concord's North Bridge, immortalized by local boy Ralph Waldo Emerson in his poem, "Concord Hymn":

> *By the rude bridge that arched the flood,*
> *Their flag to April's breeze unfurled,*
> *Here once the embattled farmers stood,*
> *And fired the shot heard 'round the world.*

Minute Man Statue

At the entrance to the trail to the bridge is the Minute Man Statue by Daniel Chester French, who is best known for the seated Lincoln in Washington's Lincoln Memorial. The militiamen at Lexington had been in a state of disarray, but those who faced the British at North Bridge did so with fixed purpose and stern military discipline. The first ordered firing upon British troops here resulted in the first British fatalities of the day.

Battle Road

The path of the British retreat is called the Battle Road. It leads to Meriam's Corner in Concord, through Lincoln, to Fiske Hill in Lexington, then onward to Boston. For six hellish hours the Redcoats beat their retreat, all the while enduring Colonial musketfire until, exhausted, they finally reached Boston Harbor.

Minute Man Bikeway

Much of Battle Road is now the Minute Man Bikeway, marked with signs showing Paul Revere in tricorn hat riding a bicycle. The entire 10.5-mile route begins in Bedford, just over the Concord border, and ends at the Alewife subway station in Cambridge.

DAY TRIPS

■ LITERARY HISTORY

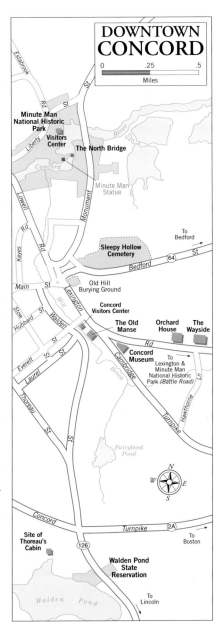

The Old Manse

Concord minister William Emerson watched the battle from the windows of his 1770 house, which overlooks North Bridge. In 1836, his grandson Ralph Waldo Emerson wrote Nature, his first book, here. The building acquired its moniker, The Old Manse, from Nathaniel Hawthorne, who lived here for three years after his marriage, during which time he published a collection of stories called Mosses from an Old Manse. While her husband was busy scribbling, Sophia Hawthorne scratched graffiti into the window panes of Emerson's former study, noting completion dates of the paintings she did there, as well as epigrams like "Man's accidents are God's purposes."

The Wayside

In 1852, Hawthorne purchased The Way-side, the only house he ever owned. Now administered by the National Park Service, the Wayside was once home of a Revolutionary patriot, but gained its lasting fame as an important literary site. Between 1845 and 1848, a young Louisa May Alcott lived here when the home was called The Hillside. At the tender age of 16, she penned here what would be the first of many published writings. 455 Lexington Road.

The Old Manse in Concord was once the home of Ralph Waldo Emerson, and, later, of Nathaniel Hawthorne. (Robert Holmes)

The Orchard House

Alcott wrote her most famous work, *Little Women* (based partly on her experiences at The Wayside) while living with her family at The Orchard House, today a private museum. Alcott's father, A. Bronson Alcott, was a Utopian dreamer with little head for business, leaving Louisa as the family's chief breadwinner for many years. *399 Lexington Rd.; 978-369-4118.*

The Emerson House

The house remains very much as it was in Ralph Waldo's day, right down to the furniture and books. Its modesty serves as a reminder that great fame and influence in letters does not always bring great wealth. Emerson was a generous and sociable man, often inviting his fellow Concord literati to sup. Henry David Thoreau came almost every Sunday to dinner during his "exile" at Walden Pond. At 28 Cambridge Turnpike; *978-369-2236.*

Concord Museum

The town operates the Concord Museum, where period rooms and galleries give an introduction to Concord history. Among the displays are Emerson's study, a plethora of Thoreau memorabilia, and assorted relics of the Revolution. *200 Lexington Rd.; call 978-369-9609 for hours.*

Sleepy Hollow Cemetery

Outside town on Route 62 is Sleepy Hollow Cemetery, which contains the graves of several of the Transcendentalist writers clustered together on Authors' Ridge. The last to die was Emerson, in 1882, but more than a century later, visitors leave offerings of poems, letters, and odd objects on the authors' graves.

Walden Pond State Reservation

Thoreau's cabin at Walden Pond has long since turned to dust, probably just the way he'd have wanted it. But the Walden Pond State Reservation on Route 126 makes it possible for Thoreau fans to walk those same woods and contemplate the pond's waters. Trails to the cabin site are well marked; *call 978-369-3254.*

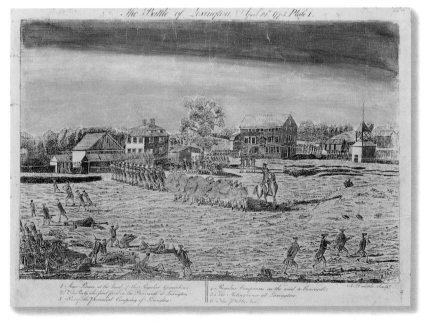

The Battle of Lexington *by artist Amos Doolittle depicts the famous moment—the first shots of the American Revolution. (Connecticut Historical Society)*

■ PLYMOUTH   *map page 256*

Before there were Puritans in Boston, there were Pilgrims in Plymouth, which consequently calls itself "America's Home Town." Even today, one Plymouth resident in ten claims to be descended from *Mayflower* Pilgrims.

To reach Plymouth, drive south from Boston on the Southeast Expressway and follow signs to Route 3.

Plimoth Plantation

Probably the best way to get a real feel for life in the New England wilderness in the 17th century is to visit the living history museum Plimoth Plantation (Exit 4, Route 3). This recreation of the Pilgrims' settlement circa 1627 emphasizes historical accuracy. Highly skilled actors (who could probably take day jobs as social historians, in a pinch) portray specific, historically documented colonists. They're happy to answer questions—as long as they're phrased in 17th-century terms. Method acting is rarely taken to such limits, which makes the experience simultaneously perplexing, entertaining, and educational. Information: *508-746-1622.*

Plymouth Information Center

Most of the Pilgrim sites are found in the town itself. The Plymouth Information Center on Water Street has maps, guides, and brochures aplenty. The self-guided walking tour of Pilgrim sites is marked on the sidewalks with stenciled Pilgrim hats. *508-747-7525.*

Mayflower II

Moored in Plymouth Harbor, this is a recreation of the Pilgrims' tight-quartered ship; its cramped size inevitably surprises first-time visitors. Nearby is Plymouth Rock: look for the Greek portico designed by McKim, Mead and White. The rock itself, which tradition claims is where the Pilgrims first stepped ashore in Plymouth, is more a symbol than a sight. After centuries of sand have washed up on the shore, the rock now lies down a hole—perhaps a justification for the anomalous portico.

Howland House

The various little museums of Plymouth do an impressive job of conjuring the Pilgrim past. Start at 33 Sandwich Street with Howland House, the 1667 home of the son of a *Mayflower* Pilgrim. When his parents' farm burned, they moved in—hence the claim that this is "the last house left in Plymouth whose walls have heard the voices of the *Mayflower* Pilgrims." Take note of the many items typical of the 17th century. Call the Howland House at *508-746-9590.*

Harlow Old Fort House

Built in 1677 with timbers from the original Plymouth fort. Costumed guides tell about 17th-century life. *119 Sandwich; check hours by calling 508-746-0012.*

A replica of the Mayflower *rests in Plymouth Harbor. (Robert Holmes)*

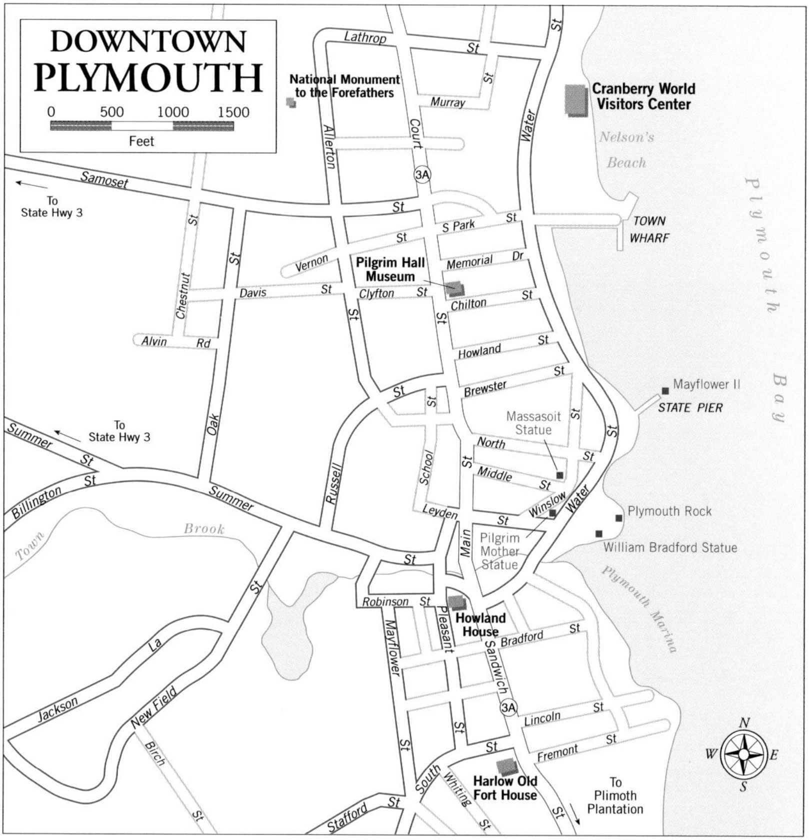

DOWNTOWN PLYMOUTH

0   500   1000   1500
Feet

Pilgrim Hall Museum

Bills itself as "America's Museum of Pilgrim Possessions." No gee-whiz exhibits here, just modest personal belongings—a tankard, a razor, some broken pottery—to remind you that the Pilgrims were ordinary human beings clinging to a stony life at the edge of the wilderness. *75 Court St.; 508-746-1620.*

Statue of Massasoit

Coles Hill is topped by a **statue of Massasoit,** the Wampanoag leader who befriended the Pilgrims. The hill was the scene of

secret night burials of those who died during the first winter of the settlement: only 51 of the original 102 settlers survived. The Pilgrims planted corn over the graves so that the Native Americans would not know how many had perished. A sarcophagus now contains many of their remains.

William Bradford statue

Honors the longtime governor of the Plymouth colony. The design by Cyrus Dallin was commissioned as part of Plymouth's tercentenary celebration in 1921.

DAY TRIPS

Pilgrim Mother statue

In 1921 this Pilgrim Mother statue was erected at the corner of Water and North streets, a gift from the Daughters of the American Revolution.

National Monument to the Forefathers

The 1889 monument is the largest solid granite monument in the United States. At 216 times life size, it was a prototype for the Statue of Liberty.

Cranberry World Visitors Center

Plymouth's modern history revolves largely around cranberry farming and processing. Not far from the waterfront is Cranberry World Visitors Center, run by the Ocean Spray cooperative of growers. The exhibits explain everything you ever wanted to know about cranberries—and probably a little more. On the way out are various refreshments, all cranberry. *225 Water St.; 508-747-2350.*

■ SALEM   *map page 258*

Salem used to call itself the Witch Town, acknowledging the enduring morbid appeal of the witch-hunting hysteria of 1692, perhaps best dramatized in Arthur Miller's play, *The Crucible.* But Salem would prefer to be remembered for its reputation of a century later, when it was known as the "New World Venice:" a capital of the mercantile seas. Salem's role in opening and maintaining the China Trade spread its name to every port.

The easiest way to get to Salem is on the Rockport/Ipswich commuter rail line, which departs from North Station. It's about a 30-minute ride to Salem Depot. The easiest drive to Salem (also about 30 minutes) is to take I-93 north to exit 37A (I-95 north) to Route 128 north. From 128, take exit 25A to Route 114 east, following the signs to downtown Salem.

Salem Maritime National Historic Site

At 2 New Liberty off Essex Street, the Chamber of Commerce and **Salem Maritime National Historic Site** share a spacious and modern Visitor Service Center where you should pick up the excellent walking map and the National Park brochure; call 978-740-1650. If you must indulge in modern witch hysteria, you'll also find brochures of the wax museum and various other things-that-go-bump-in-the-

night attractions. Salem is also a world center of New Age mysticism and witch-centered mystic feminism, industries that also offer brochures for herbal supply shops, crystal vendors, palmreaders, and so forth.

Peabody Essex Museum

Maritime history is what makes Salem worth visiting. Essex Street is the center of commercial activity and the home of the Peabody Essex Museum, an institution

DOWNTOWN SALEM

born of the merger of two earlier museums The Peabody, founded in 1799, was the repository of trophies and curiosities acquired by Salem's merchant sailors from across the globe. The oldest continuously operated museum in the country, it presents an eclectic mix of Asian art, export porcelain, and maritime history and trade. *At 132 and 161 Essex St.; call 978-745-9500 for either location.*

Three House Museums

The former Essex Institute was the historical society of the county, and emphasizes the now equally exotic life of those who stayed home. The Peabody Essex offers tours of three house museums from three centuries: the 1684 John Ward House, the 1727 Crowninshield-Bentley House, and the 1804 Gardener-Pingree House, a brick mansion by Salem's foremost architect, Samuel McIntire. Among them they trace the evolution of a global outlook and the rising tide of Salem fortunes as expressed in architecture: a dark medieval cottage, a rationalist Georgian home for the king of the black pepper trade, and a splendid, self-satisfied statement of Federal-era merchant wealth.

DAY TRIPS

Salem Common

Just a few blocks away, the nine-acre park of Salem Common rivals any common in New England with its central bandstand, surrounding trees, and 19th-century cast-iron fence. The Common is ringed by some of the most beautiful houses in Salem: those at 74, 82, and 92 Washington Square East are all associated with Samuel McIntire. A **bronze statue of Roger Conant,** Salem's founder, surveys the scene from the corner of Brown Street.

Salem Witch Museum

Beyond the Conant statue, the Salem Witch Museum at Washington Square occupies the former Second Church of Salem. This attraction features an emotionally charged voice-over narrative intoning the tragic events of 1692 as illustrative dioramas are suddenly lit in the otherwise pitch-dark building. Surprisingly, the Halloween hokiness rather effectively conveys the details of the witch hysteria, an episode during which more than 150 townspeople were imprisoned, and 20 were executed. *Call 978-744-1692 for hours.*

Salem Witch Trial Memorial

A more reflective response to this darkest moment of Salem's past is the Salem Witch Trial Memorial, near the old cemetery—a.k.a. the Old Burying Point—in the center of town.

The Grand Turk *was built in Maine but managed by a group of Salem businessmen. (Peabody Essex Museum, Salem. Gift, Joseph A. Sibley. Photo by Markham Sexton.)*

The Wonders of the Inviſible World.

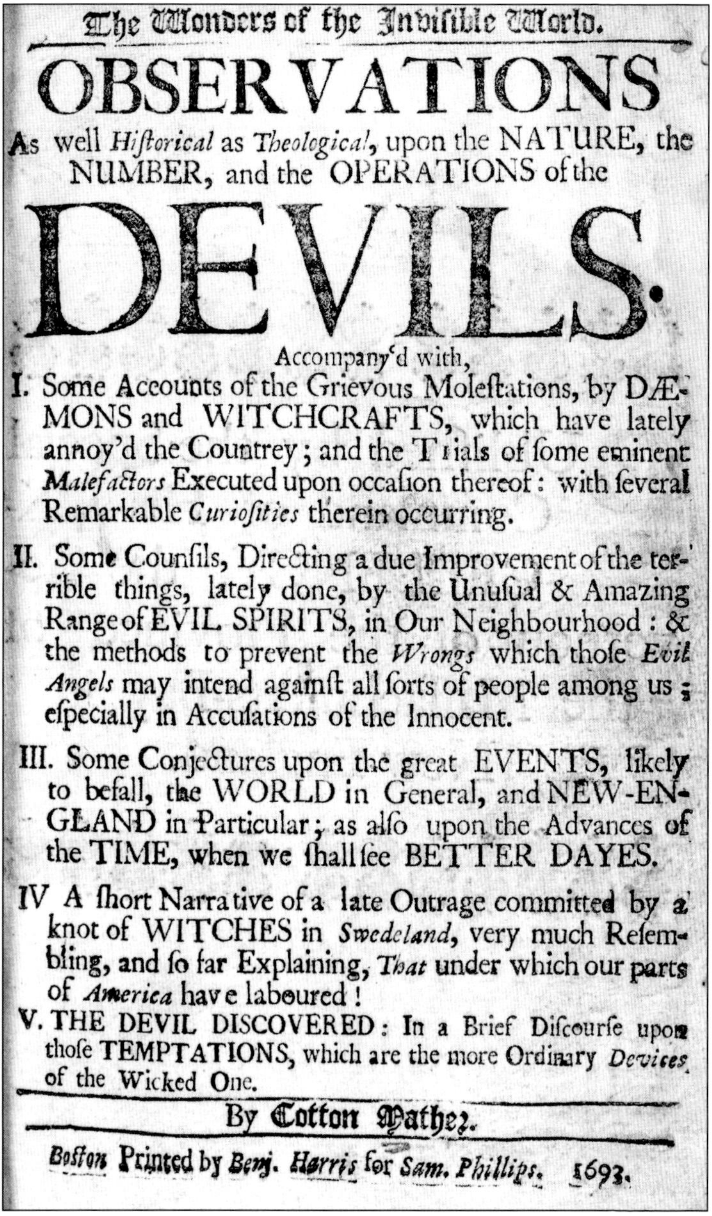

OBSERVATIONS

As well *Hiſtorical* as *Theological*, upon the NATURE, the NUMBER, and the OPERATIONS of the

DEVILS.

Accompany'd with,

I. Some Accounts of the Grievous Moleſtations, by DÆMONS and WITCHCRAFTS, which have lately annoy'd the Countrey; and the Trials of ſome eminent *Malefactors* Executed upon occaſion thereof: with ſeveral Remarkable *Curioſities* therein occurring.

II. Some Counſils, Directing a due Improvement of the terrible things, lately done, by the Unuſual & Amazing Range of EVIL SPIRITS, in Our Neighbourhood: & the methods to prevent the *Wrongs* which thoſe *Evil Angels* may intend againſt all ſorts of people among us; eſpecially in Accuſations of the Innocent.

III. Some Conjectures upon the great EVENTS, likely to befall, the WORLD in General, and NEW-ENGLAND in Particular; as alſo upon the Advances of the TIME, when we ſhall ſee BETTER DAYES.

IV A ſhort Narrative of a late Outrage committed by a knot of WITCHES in *Swedeland*, very much Reſembling, and ſo far Explaining, *That* under which our parts of *America* have laboured!

V. THE DEVIL DISCOVERED: In a Brief Diſcourſe upon thoſe TEMPTATIONS, which are the more Ordinary *Devices* of the Wicked One.

By Cotton Mather.

Boſton Printed by *Benj. Harris* for *Sam. Phillips*. 1693.

Salem Maritime National Historic Site

Only two blocks from the Common, Salem Harbor, Derby Wharf is dominated by the spirit (and name) of Elias Hasket Derby, America's first millionaire and a pioneer in lucrative overseas trade.

The centerpiece of the Salem Maritime National Historic Site, Derby Wharf is representative of those which dominated Salem's waterfront during the China Trade era. The ports of Salem and Boston were arch rivals until trading vessels simply became too large for Salem's shallow, narrow harbor.

National Park Service rangers lead tours from the orientation center at *174 Derby St.; 978-740-1660.*

The Friendship

This replica of an East Indiaman mercantile tall ship built in Salem in 1797, is docked for boarding at Derby Wharf much of the year. The largest wooden sailing vessel constructed in New England since the 19th century, *The Friendship* is typical of trading ships that helped amass Salem's fortunes.

Salem Custom House

Across Derby Street from the wharf is the Salem Custom House of 1820, where author Nathaniel Hawthorne worked as a customs official, thanks to an appointment by his college roommate Franklin Pierce, after the latter became President of the United States.

House of Seven Gables

Farther down Derby Street at water's edge you can tour this 1668 mansion that Nathaniel Hawthorne appropriated as the setting for the novel of the same name. Part of the tour takes in the small house where Hawthorne himself grew up with is widowed mother, dreadfully cognizant of the role one of his ancestors played as a judge in the Salem witch trials of 1697.

The house stands at *54 Turner St.; call 978-744-0991 for more information.*

Chestnut Street Mansions

Beginning three blocks west of Old Town Hall is Chestnut Street, a one-way street worth walking rather than driving. Often cited as America's most beautiful street, it is lined with elegant Federal mansions designed or inspired by Samuel McIntire. Most of these homes were built in the early 19th century by prosperous merchants and sea captains. The **Stephen Phillips Memorial Trust House** is open for tours at *34 Chestnut St.; 978-744-0440.*

Boston cleric Cotton Mather, author of The Wonders of the Invisible World *(left), initially supported but later helped to end the witchcraft hysteria of 1692. (Massachusetts Historical Society)*

H O T E L S & I N N S

Reservation Services

A B&B Agency of Boston
47 Commercial Wharf;
617-720-3540 or 800-248-9262

Bed & Breakfasts of Cambridge
& Greater Boston
617-720-1492 or 800-888-0178

Citywide Reservations Services
839 Beacon St.;
617-267-7424 or 800-468-3593

Discount Hotel Rates
800-511-5739
www.hoteldiscount.com

Boston Hotels

BOSTON HOTELS are among the most expensive in the United States. Always ask about promotions, weekend specials, and affiliation discounts. For a listing of YMCAs and hostels, please see page 282.

Room Rates:

Per night during tourist season, double occupancy, before tax:
$ = under $100; $$ = $100–200; $$$ = $200–300;
$$$$ = $300–400; $$$$$ = over $400

Hotel and Motel Chains

Best Western	800-528-1234	Marriott Hotels	800-228-9290
Days Inn	800-325-2525	Radisson Hotels	800-333-3333
Doubletree	800-222-8733	Sheraton Hotels	800-325-3535
Hilton Hotels	800-HILTONS	Sonesta Hotels	800-SONESTA
Holiday Inn	800-HOLIDAY	Suisse Chalet	800-524-2538
Howard Johnson	800-654-2000	Westin Hotels	800-228-3000
Hyatt Hotels	800-233-1234		

BACK BAY HILTON

A solid business hotel (not a plush Hilton) located near the Hynes Convention Center.

BEST WESTERN BOSTON, INN AT LONGWOOD MEDICAL

This 152-room modern hotel is adja-cent to Children's Hospital in the Longwood Medical Area. The many efficiencies accommodate families of patients at Children's.

$$$$
Neighborhood: Back Bay
Address: 40 Dalton St.
Phone: 617-236-1100
Reservations: 617-236-1100
Fax: 617-867-6104
Website: www.hilton.com
Number of Rooms: 385
Gym/Spa Facilities: Yes
Parking: $24 per night
Pets: Yes, conditional
Business Services: Yes
Restaurant: Boodles
Bar: Boodles

$$-$$$
Neighborhood: Fenway
Address: 342 Longwood Ave.
Phone: 617-731-4700
Reservations: 800-528-1234
Fax: 617-731-6273
Website: www.bestwestern.com
Number of Rooms: 160
Gym/Spa Facilities: Yes
Parking: $16 per night
Pets: No
Business Services: Yes
Restaurants: Longwood Grill & Bar
Bar: Longwood Grill & Bar

BOSTON HARBOR HOTEL

Probably the most gorgeous location in Boston, this hotel and its surrounding landscape feel like part of the life of the city. Ask for a harbor view.

BOSTON PARK PLAZA HOTEL

Rooms at this centrally located tower run the gamut from small and plain to large and luxurious. McCormick & Schmick's is right downstairs and the commercial theaters are just around the corner.

$$$$-$$$$$
Neighborhood: Waterfront
Address: Rowes Wharf, Atlantic Ave.
Phone: 617-439-7000
Reservations: 800-752-7077
Fax: 617-330-9450
Website: www.bhh.com
Number of Rooms: 230
Gym/Spa Facilities: Full spa
Parking: $28 per night
Pets: Pet friendly
Business Services: Yes
Restaurants: Intrigue and Rowes Wharf Restaurant
Bar: Rowes Wharf Bar

$$-$$$
Neighborhood: Back Bay/Theater District
Address: 64 Arlington St.
Phone: 617-426-2000
Reservations: 800-225-2008
Fax: 617-426-5545
Website: www.bostonparkplaza.com
Number of Rooms: 950
Gym/Spa Facilities: Yes
Parking: $21 per night
Pets: No
Business Services: Yes
Restaurant: McCormick & Schmick's
Bar: Captain's Bar

CAMBRIDGE CENTER MARRIOTT

A little out of the way unless you're doing business at MIT, but the Red Line can take you to downtown Boston or Harvard Square in minutes.

CAMBRIDGE HOUSE BED & BREAKFAST INN

This grand home (circa 1900) is elegantly decorated in Waverly fabrics and wall coverings and filled with antiques and representative period furnishings.

$$$

Neighborhood: Kendall Square
Address: Broadway at Third St.
Phone: 617-494-6600
Reservations: 800-228-9290
Fax:617-494-0036
Website: No
Number of Rooms: 431
Gym/Spa Facilities: Yes
Parking: $18 per night
Pets: No
Business Services: Yes
Restaurant: Parmizzano
Bar: Characters Bar & GrillA

$$-$$$

Neighborhood: Porter Square
Address: 2218 Massachusetts Ave..
Phone: 617-491-6300
Reservations: 800-232-9989
Fax: 617-868-2848
Website: www.acambridgehouse.com
Number of Rooms: 15
Gym/Spa Facilities: No
Parking: Free
Pets: No
Business Services: Yes
Restaurant: No
Bar: No

CHARLES HOTEL IN HARVARD SQUARE

Great location in the heart of Harvard Square. Ten minutes by car or bus to downtown Boston. Two great restaurants ameliorate the spareness of the very modern rooms. Regatta Bar is the top jazz club in the city.

$$$-$$$$

Neighborhood: Harvard Square
Address: One Bennett St.
Phone: 617-864-1200
Reservations: 800-882-1818
Fax: 617-864-5715
Website: charleshotel.com
Number of Rooms: 293
Gym/Spa Facilities: Yes
Parking: $23 per night
Pets: Yes
Business Services: Yes
Restaurant: Henrietta's Table, Rialto Restaurant
Bar: Regatta Bar, Tini Bar

CHARLES STREET INN

Romantic urban hideaway with nine spacious Victorian-style rooms, each with a carved marble fireplace and period furniture, and modern touches such as small Sub-Zero refrigerators and high-speed net access. Probably the best-kept antique on the street where the antiques industry began.

$$-$$$

Neighborhood: Beacon Hill
Address: 94 Charles St.
Phone: 617-314-8900
Reservations: 877-772-8900
Fax: 617-371-0009
Website: www.charlestreetinn.com
Number of Rooms: 9
Gym/Spa Facilities: No
Parking: No
Pets: No
Business Services: Yes
Restaurant: No
Bar: No

COLONNADE HOTEL

A recently renovated large business hotel with capacious and plush public rooms and large, comfortable guest rooms. Sports Boston's only rooftop swimming pool. A favorite with upscale bus groups.

COPLEY INN

This traditional brownstone B&B offers 20 guest rooms with kitchenette and private bath near Copley Place. The entire guesthouse is smoke-free.

$$$-$$$$$
Neighborhood: Back Bay/South End
Address: 120 Huntington Ave.
Phone: 617-424-7000
Reservations: 800-962-3030
Fax: 617-424-1717
Website: www.colonnadehotel.com
Number of Rooms: 285
Gym/Spa Facilities: Yes
Parking: $26 per night
Pets: Yes
Business Services: Yes
Restaurant: Brasserie Jo
Bar: Brasserie Jo

$$
Neighborhood: Back Bay
Address: 19 Garrison St.
Phone: 617-236-0300
Reservations: 800-232-0306
Fax: 617-536-0816
Website: www.copleyinn.com
Number of Rooms: 20
Gym/Spa Facilities: No
Parking: No
Pets: No
Business Services: No
Restaurant: No
Bar: No

COPLEY SQUARE HOTEL

A reasonably priced alternative in Copley Square with the most unusual combination of dining on premises: the Original Sports Saloon for barbecue and Cafe Budapest for Hungarian cuisine.

THE ELIOT SUITE HOTEL

The 95 suites at this four-star and five-diamond European-style hotel attract many European travelers as well as musicians playing at Symphony Hall.

$$$-$$$$
Neighborhood: Back Bay
Address: 47 Huntington Ave.
Phone: 617-536-9000
Reservations: 800-225-7062
Fax: 617-267-3547
Website: www.copleysquarehotel.com
Number of Rooms: 143
Gym/Spa Facilities: No
Parking: $26 per night
Pets: No
Business Services: Yes
Restaurant: Original Sports Saloon, Cafe Budapest
Bar: Speeder & Earl's

$$$-$$$$
Neighborhood: Back Bay
Address: 370 Commonwealth Ave.
Phone: 617-267-1607
Reservations: 800-44-ELIOT
Fax: 617-536-9114
Website: www.eliothotel.com
Number of Rooms: 95
Gym/Spa Facilities: Associated
Parking: $28 per night
Pets: Yes
Business Services: Yes
Restaurant: Restaurant Clio
Bar: Restaurant Clio

FAIRMONT COPLEY PLAZA HOTEL

Known as the "Grande Dame" of Boston since its gala opening in 1912, this newly restored, beautiful Edwardian-style hotel anchors one end of Copley Square. It features both an award-winning restaurant and one of the coolest jazz bars in the city.

XV BEACON HOTEL

Housed in a 1903 Beaux-Arts building, this luxury boutique hotel has just 40 rooms, but it boasts stylish design as well as the latest in 21st century amenities, including T-1 lines and loaner mobile phones.

$$$-$$$$$
Neighborhood: Back Bay
Address: 138 St. James Ave.
Phone: 617-267-5300
Reservations: 800-441-1414
Fax: 617-267-7668
Website: www.fairmont.com
Number of Rooms: 379
Gym/Spa Facilities: Yes
Parking: $16–29 per night
Pets: Conditional
Business Services: Yes
Restaurant: The Oak Room
Bar: The Oak Bar

$$$$-$$$$$
Neighborhood: Beacon Hill
Address: 15 Beacon St.
Phone: 617-670-1500
Reservations: 877-992-3220
Fax: 617-670-2525
Website: www.xvbeacon.com
Number of Rooms: 60
Gym/Spa Facilities: Yes
Parking: $28 per night
Pets: No
Business Services: Yes
Restaurant: The Federalist
Bar: The Federalist

FOUR SEASONS HOTEL

Chic, cosmopolitan, but not stiff. The only Mobil five-star/AAA Five-diamond hotel in New England. Great restaurants complement good rooms, some with excellent Public Garden views.

463 BEACON STREET GUEST HOUSE

This Edwardian-era brownstone is the least well-kept secret of Boston B&Bs, but remains a great deal. Most rooms have kitchenette and private bath.

$$$$$
Neighborhood: Back Bay
Address: 200 Boylston St.
Phone: 617-338-4400
Reservations: 800-332-3442
Fax: 617 423-0154
Website: www.fourseasons.com/boston
Number of Rooms: 274
Gym/Spa Facilities: Yes
Parking: $27 per night
Pets: Yes (within guidelines)
Business Services: Yes
Restaurant: Aujord'hui, The Bristol
Bar: The Bristol Lounge

$-$$
Neighborhood: Back Bay
Address: 463 Beacon St.
Phone: 617-536-1302
Reservations: 617-536-1302
Fax: 617-247-8876
Website: www.463beacom.com
Number of Rooms: 20
Gym/Spa Facilities: No
Parking: $9
Pets: No
Business Services: Yes
Restaurant: No
Bar: No

A FRIENDLY INN AT HARVARD SQUARE

A well-kept and pleasant B&B behind the city high school and library and less than five minutes on foot to Harvard Yard. Public transportation to downtown Boston. All rooms have private baths, TV and A/C.

THE GRYPHON HOUSE

The capacious rooms in this 1895 brownstone townhouse—a short walk from Fenway Park—verge on the size of studio apartments; all have gas fireplaces, wet bars, and high-speed internet access.

$-$$
Neighborhood: Harvard Square
Address: 1673 Cambridge St
Phone: 617-547-7851
Reservations: 617-547-7851
Fax: 617-547-7851
Website: afinow.com/afi
Number of Rooms: 20
Gym/Spa Facilities: No
Parking: Free
Pets: No
Business Services: Yes
Restaurant: No
Bar: No

$$-$$$
Neighborhood: Fenway
Address: 9 Bay State Rd.
Phone: 617-375-9003
Reservations: 877-375-9003
Fax: 617-425-0716
Website: www.innboston.com
Number of Rooms: 8
Gym/Spa Facilities: No
Parking: Free
Pets: No
Business Services: Yes
Restaurant: No
Bar: No

HARBORSIDE INN

Located in a former spice warehouse built in 1858, this 54-room hotel with exposed brick-and-granite walls and Victorian-style furnishings opened in 1998 as a modest boutique hotel in the Financial District.

HARVARD SQUARE HOTEL

A former motor inn with great location and motor inn rooms, renovated in 1996.

$$
Neighborhood: Downtown
Address: 185 State St.
Phone: 617-723-7500
Reservations: 617-723-7500
Fax: 617-670-2010
Website: www.hagopianhotels.com
Number of Rooms: 54
Gym/Spa Facilities: No
Parking: No
Pets: No
Business Services: Yes
Restaurant: Margo Bistro
Bar: Margo Bistro

$$
Neighborhood: Harvard Square
Address: 110 Mt. Auburn St.
Phone: 617-864-5200
Reservations: 800-458-5886
Fax: 617-520-3711
Website: www.theinnatharvard.com
Number of Rooms: 113
Gym/Spa Facilities: Access to ymca
Parking: $30 per night
Pets: No
Business Services: Yes
Restaurant: The Atrium Restaurant
Bar: The Atrium Bar

HYATT REGENCY CAMBRIDGE

Dramatic central atrium with good-sized rooms, many with little balconies and great Charles river and Boston skyline views. Awkward location eased somewhat by shuttle van.

INN AT HARVARD

An unadvertised gem, alas, often booked for Harvard functions. Guests have dining privileges at Harvard Faculty Club. Soaring atrium lobby with real library and comfortable seating.

$$$-$$$$
Neighborhood: Cambridge
Address: 575 Memorial Dr.
Phone: 617-492-1234
Reservations: 800-233-1234
Fax: 617-491-6906
Website: www.cambridge.hyatt.com
Number of Rooms: 469
Gym/Spa Facilities: Yes
Parking: $17 per night
Pets: No
Business Services: Yes
Restaurants: Spinnaker and Zephry
Bar: Spinnaker and Zephry

$$$-$$$$
Neighborhood: Harvard Square
Address: 1201 Massachusetts Ave.
Phone: 617-491-2222
Reservations: 800-222-8733
Fax: 617-520-3711
Website: www.theinnatharvard.com
Number of Rooms: 113
Gym/Spa Facilities: No
Parking: $30 per night
Pets: No
Business Services: Yes
Restaurant: No
Bar: No

IRVING HOUSE

In the heart of Cambridge since 1945, right around the corner from A Friendly Inn, this B&B offers 60 rooms in two buildings. Wheelchair accessible, 24 hour desk service.

ISAAC HARDING HOUSE

In 1997, a handsome renovation of a historic 1860s mid-Cambridge Victorian produced this superb, fully accessible B&B halfway between Harvard and Central Squares. A five minute walk to the Red Line.

$$

Neighborhood: Harvard Square
Address: 24 Irving St.
Phone: 617-547-4600
Reservations: 877-547-4600
Fax: 617-576-2814
Website: www.irvinghouse.com
Number of Rooms: 44
Gym/Spa Facilities: No
Parking: Free
Pets: Yes
Business Services: Yes
Restaurant: No
Bar: No

$-$$

Neighborhood: Cambridge/ Harvard Square
Address: 288 Harvard St.
Phone: 617-876-2888
Reservations: 877-489-2888
Fax: 617-497-0953
Website: www.irvinghouse.com
Number of Rooms: 14
Gym/Spa Facilities: No
Parking: Free
Pets: No
Business Services: Yes
Restaurant: No
Bar: No

MARY PRENTISS INN

This 18-room Greek Revival–style inn was a country estate when it was built in 1843; now it's in a residential neighborhood between Harvard and Porter squares off Massachusetts Avenue. Some rooms have working fireplaces.

LE MERIDIEN BOSTON

Housed in the former Federal Reserve Bank—a beautiful piece of architecture in the Financial District —this Meridien rises above many in North America. The restaurants are outstanding.

$$-$$$
Neighborhood: Cambridge/ Porter Square
Address: 6 Prentiss St.
Phone: 617-661-2929
Reservations: No
Fax: 617-661-5989
Website: www.maryprentissinn.com
Number of Rooms: 20
Gym/Spa Facilities: No
Parking: Free
Pets: No
Business Services: Yes
Restaurant: No
Bar: No

$$$$$
Neighborhood: Downtown
Address: 250 Franklin St.
Phone: 617-451-1900
Reservations: 800-543-4300
Fax: 617-423-2844
Website: www.lemeridienboston.com
Number of Rooms: 326
Gym/Spa Facilities: Yes
Parking: $32 per night
Pets: Yes
Business Services: Yes
Restaurant: Café Fleuri, Restaurant Julien
Bar: Julien Lounge

LENOX HOTEL

Freshly renovated 1900 landmark hotel one block from Copley Square features fireplaces in the more expensive rooms.

MARRIOTT LONG WHARF HOTEL

Built on historic Long Wharf with a facade that echoes more venerable wharf structures, this Marriott is a bit brash inside, but the location (steps from Faneuil Hall Marketplace) is hard to beat.

$$$-$$$$$
Neighborhood: Back Bay
Address: 710 Boylston St.
Phone: 617-536-5300
Reservations: 800-225-7676
Fax: 617-266-7905
Website: www.lenoxhotel.com
Number of Rooms: 212
Gym/Spa Facilities: Yes
Parking: $28 per night
Pets: Yes
Business Services: Yes
Restaurant: Anago
Bar: Sam Adams Brewhouse

$$$-$$$$
Neighborhood: Waterfront
Address: 296 State St.
Phone: 617-227-0800
Reservations: 800-228-9290
Fax: 617-227-2867
Website: marriotthotels.com/boston
Number of Rooms: 402
Gym/Spa Facilities: Yes
Parking: $30 per night
Pets: No
Business Services: Yes
Restaurant: Oceana
Bar: Waves Bar & Grill

NEWBURY GUEST HOUSE

It's hard to believe that such nice rooms are available at these prices on Back Bay's toniest street, but they are. Breakfast included.

$$
Neighborhood: Back Bay
Address: 261 Newbury St.
Phone: 617-437-7666
Reservations: 800-437-7668
Fax: 617-262-4243
Website: www.hagopianhotels.com
Number of Rooms: 32
Gym/Spa Facilities: No
Parking: $15 per night
Pets: No
Business Services: Yes
Restaurant: No
Bar: No

OMNI PARKER HOUSE

The longest continuously operating hotel in America, the Parker House gave the world its rolls and Boston cream pie. The plush lobby has cases that display evidence of its past glory as the head of Boston society and the hotel has just finished a $70 million upgrade to restore all that lost luster.

$$$-$$$$
Neighborhood: Downtown
Address: 60 School St.
Phone: (617) 227-8600
Reservations: 800-the omni
Fax: 617-742-5729
Website: www.omnihotels.com
Number of Rooms: 551
Gym/Spa Facilities: Yes
Parking: $30 per night
Pets: No
Business Services: Yes
Restaurants: Parker's, Last Hurrah
Bar: Parker's, Last Hurrah

REGAL BOSTONIAN HOTEL

Offers a surprisingly plush and sheltered retreat from the bustling marketplace next door. Check out the display of archaeological treasures that were uncovered when the hotel was built.

$$$-$$$$$

Neighborhood: Downtown
Address: Faneuil Hall Marketplace
Phone: 617-523-3600
Reservations: 800-343-0922
Fax: 617-523-2454
Website: www.millennium-hotels.com
Number of Rooms: 201
Gym/Spa Facilities: Yes
Parking: $30 per night
Pets: No
Business Services: Yes
Restaurant: Seasons Restaurant
Bar: Atrium Lounge

ROYAL SONESTA

Spectacular views of Charles River and skylines of Beacon Hill and Back Bay. Nice patio dining in warm weather. Across the street from the Cambridgeside Galleria Mall and next door to the Museum of Science.

$$-$$$$

Neighborhood: Charles River
Address: 5 Cambridge Pkwy.
Phone: 617-806-4200
Reservations: 800-SONESTA
Fax: 617-806-4232
Website: www.sonesta.com/boston
Number of Rooms: 400
Gym/Spa Facilities: Yes
Parking: $18 per night
Pets: No
Business Services: Yes
Restaurant: Davio's and Gallery Café & Patio
Bar: Davio's Lounge

SEAPORT HOTEL & CONFERENCE CENTER

Next to and managed by the World Trade Center in South Boston, the Seaport opened in mid-1998 as a 426-room hotel geared for business clients. Great views and an award-winning restaurant compensate for location slightly stranded from the rest of the city.

$$-$$$$
Neighborhood: Waterfront
Address: One Seaport Lane
Phone: 617-385-4000
Reservations: 877-seaport
Fax: 617-385-4001
Website: www.seaporthotel.com
Number of Rooms: 426
Gym/Spa Facilities: Yes
Parking: $22 per night
Pets: Conditional
Business Services: Yes, 24-hour
Restaurant: Aura Restaurant
BAR: AURA LOUNGE

SHERATON BOSTON HOTEL & TOWERS

Attached to the Hynes Convention Center and the renovated Prudential shopping complex, it's a classic Sheraton business hotel with great service.

$$-$$$$
Neighborhood: Back Bay
Address: 39 Dalton St.
Phone: 617-236-2000
Reservations: 800-325-3535
Fax: 617-236-1702
Website: www.sheraton.com-boston
Number of Rooms: 1.200
Gym/Spa Facilities: Yes
Parking: $28 per night
Pets: Yes
Business Services: Yes
Restaurant: Apropos
Bar: Turning Point

SHERATON COMMANDER HOTEL

Fits old-style Harvard types like a velvet smoking jacket. This Cambridge grande dame on Cambridge Common has undergone extensive renovation, though some rooms and halls remain small.

SWISSOTEL BOSTON

This stunning hotel, with impeccable service and excellent restaurant, is located downtown, convenient to shopping, Financial District, and the last remnants of the old Combat Zone.

$$-$$$$

Neighborhood: Harvard Square
Address: 16 Garden St.
Phone: 617-547-4800
Reservations: 800-535-5007
Fax: 617-234-1396
Website: sheratoncommander.com
Number of Rooms: 175
Gym/Spa Facilities: Yes
Parking: $18 per night
Pets: No
Business Services: No
Restaurant: 16 Garden Street
Bar: 16 Garden Street

$$$-$$$$

Neighborhood: Downtown/Theater District
Address: One Avenue de Lafayette
Phone: 617-451-2600
Reservations: 800-621-9200
Fax:
Website: www.swissotel.com
Number of Rooms: 501
Gym/Spa Facilities: Yes
Parking: $26 per night
Pets: Conditional
Business Services: Yes
Restaurant: Café Suisse
Bar: The Lobby Bar

TAGE INN

Located three miles north of downtown Boston off I-93's exit 29, the newly constructed Tage offers well-appointed rooms at half the in-town price. Some rooms easily accommodate families. Complimentary shuttle to local restaurants.

$$
Neighborhood: Somerville
Address: 23 Cummings
Phone: 617-625-5300
Reservations: 800-322-TAGE
Fax: 617-625-5930
Website: www.tageinn.com
Number of Rooms: 148
Gym/Spa Facilities: Yes
Parking: Free
Pets: No
Business Services: Yes
Restaurant: Soon
Bar: No

UNIVERSITY PARK HOTEL AT MIT

Not to be outdone by the Inn at Harvard, in fall 1998 MIT opened its own much more high-tech hotel between the campus and Central Square. About Sidney's Grille *Bon Appetit* wrote "It's almost shocking to pay this little for food this good, in surroundings this gorgeous."

$$-$$$
Neighborhood: Central Square
Address: 20 Sidney St.
Phone: 617-577-0200
Reservations: 800-222-8733
Fax: 617-494-8366
Website: www.univparkhotel.com
Number of Rooms: 210
Gym/Spa Facilities: Yes
Parking: $15 per night
Pets: No
Business Services: Yes
Restaurant: Sidney's Grille
Bar: Sidney's Grille

HOTELS & INNS

YMCAs and Hostels

BERKELEY RESIDENCE/
BOSTON YWCA
Accommodations for women,
nightly or long-term.
Neighborhood: *South End*
Address: 40 Berkeley St.
Phone: 617-375-2524

BOSTON INTERNATIONAL,
AYH HOSTEL
Dormitory style accommodations
require a membership in the sum-
mer.
Neighborhood: *Fenway*
Address: 12 Hemenway St.
Phone: 617-536-9455

GARDEN HALLS RESIDENCES/
BAY STATE COLLEGE
Summer-only hostel has rooms to
accommodate one to four people.
Five-night minimum required.
Neighborhood: *Back Bay*
Address: 260 Commonwealth Ave.
Phone: 617-267-0079

IRISH EMBASSY TOURIST HOSTEL
Very popular with international stu-
dents, this hostel near North Sta-
tion and New Boston Garden is
convenient to Faneuil Hall and
North End. Dormitory style plus
one private room.
Neighborhood: *Downtown/North End*
Address: 232 Friend St.
Phone: 617-973-4841

JOHN JEFFRIES HOUSE
Many of the 46 rooms in the "Flats"
section at the base of Beacon Hill
are used by patients and families of
the Massachusetts Eye and Ear In-
firmary, but they also welcome pleasure travelers.
Neighborhood: *Beacon Hill*
Address: 14 Embankment Rd.
Phone: 617-367-1866

YMCA CENTRAL BRANCH
Both double (bunk beds) and single
rooms available. Includes free use of
state-of-the-art fitness facilities.
Women guests summer only.
Neighborhood: *Back Bay*
Address: 316 Huntington Ave.
Phone: 617-536-7800

R E S T A U R A N T S

FANNIE FARMER NOTWITHSTANDING, BOSTON'S CULINARY TRADITIONS offer little to brag about. For centuries we made do with what we had—and what we had was codfish, beans, potatoes, and a legacy of British cooking. But around 1970 Bostonians awoke from 340 years of gastronomic slumber and discovered that fine dining could be more than Dover sole or a slab of prime rib hanging over the edge of the plate.

■ THE BOSTON STYLE

This ever-expanding universe has created a laudable solidarity and camaraderie among the city's chef-owners. The friendly relations have led to lots of cooperative efforts—establishing coops to buy cheeses, group support of certain organic farmers or livestock raisers—and the inevitable development of a "Boston style."

Boston restaurants tend to be fairly small and informal, favoring a trattoría or bistro model. While most menus fall within the rather loose definition of "New American" (local fresh-market ingredients adapted to dishes of Italian or French origin but with Latin American or Asian modifications), there are a few other generalizations to be made. Maybe it's our Irish heritage, but garlic mashed potatoes (sometimes combined with purées of other root vegetables) just won't go away. Portions, particularly of meat and fish, tend to be large. And we are definitely enamored of wood-fired ovens and open grills.

That said, two fairly upscale trends are discernible in Boston's current dining scene. Elegant "dining destination" restaurants have proliferated to the point where their refined dishes are now imitated by many of the trattorías and bistros.

Boston retains its ethnic enclaves. Italian-influenced dining is available all over the city, but most of the Neapolitan and Sicilian trattorías are found in the North End. Likewise, the greatest concentration of Chinese restaurants remains in Chinatown. But although Chinatown is increasingly Southeast Asian, the lion's share of Cambodian, Thai, and Vietnamese restaurants lie outside of Chinatown. Restaurants tend to cluster in specific neighborhoods, encouraging diners to browse before they make a commitment.

We were determined to limit the listings for this volume to 100 (we came close) but this meant leaving out several popular dining spots where everyone goes "because everybody goes there." In cases where we felt compelled to mention a famous restaurant that trades more on past than present accomplishments, we've tried to steer you to the best menu selections. Type of cuisine is a slippery signifier in Boston dining, thanks to continual cross-fertilization, but at the end of the alphabetical list is a cross reference by cuisine that can serve as a general guide. Some restaurants appear in more than one category. As Boston's patron saint of food, Julia Child, would say, Bon appétit!

■ NORTH END DINING

Long a stronghold of traditional Italian dining, the North End has metamorphosed into a continuously movable feast from fine trattorías to caffès that stay open until the wee hours of the morning. Most of the best dining rooms are small, don't take reservations or credit cards and encourage you to move along to the caffès for espresso and dessert.

■ SOUTH END DINING

South End is in the midst of artistic and culinary rebirth, anchored by a few upscale dininxg rooms and augmented by a myriad of small, chef-run restaurants that emphasize new twists on Italian, French, and Latin American cuisines. Much of the activity lies either close to the Boston Center for the Arts or to Massachusetts Avenue (arguably the hippest dining scene in the city). The South End is also a great area for brunch. Chinatown has been a diner's heaven since the days when Boston was a theatrical tryout town; more recently, newfound interest in Asian cuisines beyond the usual Cantonese and Szechuan has reinvigorated the restaurant scene here. This is where many of the young chefs from other areas go to eat on their nights off and where night owls head for post-midnight suppers.

■ NEWBURY STREET DINING

Back Bay is a Gold Coast that caters, all too often, to diners who wish to be seen as much as to get a good bite to eat.

■ CAMBRIDGE DINING

Harvard Square in Cambridge emphasizes light grill food, lots of herbs and fresh vegetables. Inman Square has emerged as an area where young sous chefs from other hot restaurants open their own places, with an emphasis on casual dining. Good but inexpensive ethnic dining, especially Indian, is the forte of Central Square, while Porter Square boasts a concentration of casual Japanese noodle and sushi bars in the landmark former Sears building on Massachusetts Avenue.

■ FANEUIL HALL MARKETPLACE EATERIES

The tourist mecca of Faneuil Hall Marketplace offers an assortment of real restaurants and one of Boston's best food courts is here in the central Quincy Market building.

> *Prices:*
> *Per person, for appetizer, entree, and dessert, excluding drinks, tax, and tip.*
> $ = $15 and under $$ = $15-30;
> $$$ = $30-50 $$$$ = over $50

Restaurant Listings

Alloro. *North End* 351 Hanover St.;
617-523-9268 $$$

The restaurants on each side have longer lines, but Alloro has better food and presents it with more class and a finely tuned palate: the shrimp and fennel appetizer has a sweet and salty crunch with the pungent anise flavor as a perfect foil. Pastas are modest, since they're intended as first courses. The family is part Italian, part Portuguese and so is the cuisine. Great soups, great breads, cheeses they age in their own cellar.

Ambrosia on Huntington. *Back Bay/South End* 116 Huntington Ave.;
617-247-2400 $$$-$$$$

Once a builder of "tall food," chef-owner Tony Ambrose now opts to emphasize complexity of taste over table-top architectonics (though the dining room retains its dramatic architecture). Perhaps more than other nominally French restaurants, Ambrosia displays strong Asian influences (Japanese, Thai, Vietnamese). You can start with a variety of sushi appetizers before moving on to fire-roasted duck with a soy-citrus glaze or halibut prepared in parchment and accompanied by risotto flavored with fresh chervil and sharp sheep's cheese.

Anago. *Back Bay* Lenox Hotel,
65 Exeter St.; 617-266-6222 $$-$$$

Chef and co-owner Bob Calderone has a penchant for luscious food—sturgeon he cures and smokes himself, squash bisque with a risotto croquette, roasted duck with späetzle and figs. Portions are generous, but leave room for the best pastries in the city. The warm but sparely decorated room seats about 100, and prices are lower than most Boston restaurants of this caliber.

Antico Forno. *North End* 93 Salem St.;
617-723-6733 $$- $$$

The wood-burning oven is essential for authentic southern Italian cuisine, and almost everything served here is kissed by fire. Look for hearty pastas in terra-cotta casseroles (Neapolitan pasta and beans, fusilli baked with spicy dry sausage in a tomato ragu), thin crust pizzas cooked hot and fast to keep the toppings pliable, roasted meats that are crisp outside and succulent inside. Simple, satisfying peasant food.

Aquitaine. *South End/Cultural District*
569 Tremont St.; 617-424-8577 $$$

The Parisian bistro, as imagined by American hipsters, sets the style for Aquitaine, where traditionally rich French provincial offerings have been lightened up with less cream and butter, and standards like cassoulet and choucroute take on a leaner look. Mostly French wines line the walls, floor to ceiling, hinting at lingering sippers who make up the end-of-the-evening crowd.

Artù. *North End* 6 Prince St.; 617-742-4336
   Beacon Hill 89 Charles St.; 617-227-9023 $-$$
Both locations are a tight squeeze, but superior grilled vegetables and smoky leg of lamb (also available as a sandwich at midday) compensate for the lack of elbow room. Everything is available for takeout.

Aujourd'hui. *Back Bay* Four Seasons Hotel, 200 Boylston St.; 617-351-2072 $$$$
The formal, top-flight French cuisine here is impeccable, and true gourmets will want to enjoy a dégustation menus (one for omnivores, another for vegetarians). Windowside tables overlook the Public Garden, though a better view of the room is available at the central banquettes. Service is attentive but not obsequious. Just make sure your cards aren't already maxed out.

Barking Crab. *Waterfront* 88 Sleeper St.; 617-426-2722 $-$$
With its outdoor picnic tables, beer by the pitcher, and buckets of steamers, mussels, crab claws, shrimp, this Fort Point Channel spot is Boston Harbor's only true New England–style fish shack. There's a great view of the Financial District, too. In July and August the wait can stretch to an hour before they stop taking names.

Mr. Bartley's Burger & Salad Cottage. *Harvard Square* 1246 Massachusetts Ave.; 617-354-6559 $
Every college town needs a joint with fat

burgers and sandwiches named for celebrities. The burgers rank among some of the greats—just avoid the "dinners" and salads. The two-fisted 14-ounce Macho Burger could make even a linebacker say "Uncle."

Bay Tower. *Downtown* 60 State St.; 617-723-1666 $$$-$$$$
The view from the 33rd story has always been unbeatable, but for years the cuisine was stalled by lower aspirations. That changed with new menus as swanky as the room. Look for classy treats like roasted sea bass dressed with osetra caviar or a duck risotto with a fig sauce. The raised lounge area offers an even better view of Boston Harbor, a smaller menu, and jazz (with a small dance floor) on weekend nights.

Ben's Cafe. *See* **Maison Robert.**

Biba. *Back Bay* 272 Boylston St.; 617-426-7878 $$$-$$$$
Lydia Shire (who first brought the gospel according to Alice Waters to Boston) and Susan Regis (1998 James Beard Foundation top Boston chef) share the top toques at this colorful room where creative food pairings are impeccably presented. Dishes with eclectic accents—a pizza with minty lamb and cumin, scallops with Tuscan black cabbage and black lentils—are balanced by wonderfully simple and traditional plates such as corn and lobster chowder.

Blue Diner. *Cultural District/Leather District* 150 Kneeland St.; 617-695-0087 $-$$
This faux diner has ambitions to be an artists' hangout—which it is, if you believe coders and website designers are today's artists. The diner food (meatloaf, eggs and bacon) seems to taste better at 3 A.M. when this is one of the few lively spots in town.

Blue Room. *Cambridge/Kendall Square*

One Kendall Square; 617-494-9034 $$$

Is it grill? Is it barbecue? Is it hip, or what? Chef/co-owner Steve Johnson believes in flavor bursts—crabcakes splashed with lime and served with perfect avocado, seared scallops and crunchy fried leeks—and in *bustle*. The tiny zinc tables are packed like Chiclets; the best seats surround the kitchen where diners can watch the cooks hop to. Order light, as portions are much bigger than the tables.

Bob the Chef's. *South End/Cultural District*

604 Columbus Ave.; 617-536-6204 $$

Situated on the border of Roxbury and the South End, Bob the Chef's excels at Southern soul food, a true jazz ambience (Berklee School of Music is a block away) and the most racially integrated scene in Boston. Count on "Soul Fish"—catch of the day dredged in cornmeal and flour and fried light and crisp in canola oil. You could learn to love collard greens here. There's live jazz later in the week, and the Sunday jazz brunch packs in folks from all over.

Boston Beer Works. *Fenway*

61 Brookline Ave.; 617-536-2337 $-$$

You could feed the whole family on the mixed plate of sausage, ribs, chicken and steak tips, though students from nearby B.U. often eat a whole plate each. Normally very loud, the noise level grows to DEAFENING before and after Red Sox home games. The house brews are light in style.

Brasserie Jo. *Back Bay* 120 Huntington Ave.; 617-425-3240 $$$

Alsatian-style brasseries are rare in Boston, which allows Brasserie Jo to thrive on novelty. Standby main plates like steak-frites and baked salmon are not always up to

their French counterparts, and the extreme popularity of Jo as a watering hole for conventioneers often stretches the wait staff a little too thinly. On the other hand, it's a great place to hang out at the bar and munch on sausages with a half liter of Alsatian beer.

Brew Moon. *Cultural District*

115 Stuart St.; 617-523-6467

Cambridge/Harvard Square

50 Church St.; 617-499-2739 $$

The Cal-American pub food (sesame seared tuna or fish and chips), a range of brews (including raspberry hefeweizen—a beer drinker's white zinfandel), and heavy-handed interior design sit well with Harvard students at one location and Theater District stage mavens at the other. Both places rock nightly: you may end up with a beeper and waiting an hour for a table.

Restaurant Bricco. *North End*

241 Hanover St.; 617-248-6800 $$

Bricco meets the challenge of re-inventing traditional cooking in the heavily ethnic North End by deft combinations of texture and flavors—for example, adding smoked red peppers and sharp-tasting braised broccoli rabe to sweet and chewy steamed mussels. Like a growing number of nova Italiana spots in Boston, Bricco even makes its own desserts.

Bristol Lounge. *Back Bay* Four Seasons Hotel, 200 Boylston St.; 617-351-2054 $$-$$$

The Bristol shares a kitchen and executive chef with Aujourd'hui, but its fare is lighter, more casual, more American. This place may serve the best burger in the city, and the classy but relaxed afternoon tea is a sure winner. In the winter there's light jazz

RESTAURANTS

by the fireplace and a Viennese pastry buffet on Friday and Saturday nights.

Brown Sugar Cafe. *Fenway*
129 Jersey St.; 617-266-2928 **$$**
Thai food as it's meant to be—vegetables with crunch, savory meats, no MSG. Bypass the merely good pad thai for gai gaprow of spicy minced chicken or beef on a hot pepper sauce laced with tender leaves of Thai basil. It's a short walk over an Emerald Necklace bridge from the back of the Museum of Fine Arts.

Bull & Finch Pub. *Beacon Hill*
84 Beacon St.; 617-227-9605 **$**
More than a half-million tourists have passed through the doors of this bar that inspired the "Cheers!" TV show. Once a hangout for state politicians (the legislature is two blocks away), it's now a great place to talk over Boston experiences with people from all over the world. Don't believe the hype about having Boston's best burger, but you didn't come to eat anyway, right?

Buzzy's Fabulous Roast Beef. *Charles River*
327 Cambridge St. (at Longfellow Bridge); 617-242-7722
Cambridge/Central Square 647 Massachusetts Ave.; 617-864-2333 **$**
Every night owl in the city eventually roosts at Buzzy's, which is open all night and where the best thing on the limited menu is the truly fabulous roast beef sandwich, available in many versions. Do like the locals and opt for an onion roll and horseradish. The coffee's fresh around the clock and before noon they sell muffins and a ham-and-egg sandwich.

Café Fleuri. *Downtown* Le Meridien, 250 Franklin St.; 617-451-1900 **$$$-$$$$**
As the more "casual" of the Meridien's restaurants, the Fleuri is nonetheless elegant with a dramatic high glass ceiling that bathes the café in light by day and provides a semblance of the outdoor experience by night. The menu is distinctly French, but the special attractions are a high-end, eight-station Sunday brunch buffet and a cool-weather Saturday afternoon chocolate buffet that is a wonder to behold.

Café Louis. *Back Bay* 234 Berkeley St.; 617-266-4680 **$$-$$$$**
Louis Clothier is perhaps Boston's finest purveyor of menswear, and the surprisingly casual "café"—already very successful—underwent a radical change when George Germon and Johanne Killeen of Providence's Al Forno took over and remade it in the image of some of their favorite restaurants in Provence. Still catering to well-heeled Back Bay shoppers, Café Louis has acquired an upscale, sunny disposition. You almost expect to see a Citroën limousine pull up to the door any minute.

Café 300. *Cultural District/Waterfront*
300 Summer St.; 617-426-0695 **$-$$**
Serving lunch and Sunday brunch in the basement atrium of a building in the Fort Point Artists Community, Café 300 believes that artists should eat good food too—like a saffron-infused mussel stew, or a roast pork sandwich with eggplant and peppers. Bypass fast food and eat here after visiting Museum Wharf, a block away.

Casablanca. *Cambridge/Harvard Square*
40 Brattle St.; 617-876-0999 $$-$$$
New owners have transformed the menu at this Harvard Square legend (couscous and burgers beneath Bogart murals) into a sophisticated take on Moroccan– North African cuisine. Simple dishes like grilled sea scallops with pistachio-basmati-lentil pilaf are balanced with French colonial delights like a signature duck cassoulet and a Pernod-laced bouillabaisse. Don't miss the rich Catalonian garlic soup drizzled with basil olive oil. The casual bar in back is louder and continues to offer excellent burgers for the less adventurous.

Casa Portugal. *Cambridge/Inman Square*
1200 Cambridge St.; 617-491-8880 $$
East Cambridge is a Portuguese neighborhood, and this homey neighborhood eatery serves the hearty comfort food of north-central Portugal. How could any cuisine that depends on onion, garlic, peppers, and homemade sausages go wrong? On a cold night opt for the calderirada (stewpot) of fish, shellfish, squid, peppers, and potatoes. The inexpensive plates are bounteous. There's a good Portuguese wine list, too.

Casa Romero. *Back Bay* 30 Gloucester St.;
617-536-4341 $$
With its Spanish rustic decor (dark pine furnishings and tile) and garden-level location, Casa Romero would fit nicely at the edge of Mexico City's Zona Rosa. This pioneer of Mexican cuisine in Boston serves truly criollo dishes—more Spanish than Indian—such as chicken livers in escabeche or pork tenderloin marinated in oranges and chipotle peppers. Yes, there are enchiladas and tamales, but the classic entrées are uniformly better. Skip the desultory wine list and sangria in favor of beer.

Chau Chow City. *Chinatown/Cultural District* 83 Essex St.; 617-338-8158 $-$$
Boston Chinese food used to be Szechuan-Mandarin, but Hong Kong has taken over in a big way. This restaurant draws countless well-heeled suburban Chinese Americans on weekends for excellent dim sum. Of the authentic Chinese restaurants, Chau Chow City is most accessible to those of us who don't speak or read Cantonese. Billed as a Chinese seafood restaurant, Chau Chow City leans heavily on crab, lobster, and scallops, since it can't obtain the Pacific fishes available to Hong Kong restaurants. Only half of the encyclopedic menu is available on a given night, so ask about the specials, which are the best bets anyway.

Chez Henri. *Cambridge/Harvard Square*
One Shepard St.; 617-354-8980 $$$
As urban chic and timeless as the little black dress, Chez Henri is a French bistro with a Cuban accent that shows in a few touches like mango salsa, black beans, Cuban sandwiches at the bar, and the signature duck tamales. But there's nothing Cuban about the grilled venison with honey-glazed shallots, red currants, and a purée of celery root and potato, or, for that matter, the braised rabbit. You might have to wait to get in (no reservations for parties under 6), but foodies on a budget can avail themselves of a terrific three-course prix fixe.

China Pearl. *Chinatown/Cultural District*
9 Tyler St.; 617-426-4338 $-$$
China Pearl draws the largest crowds in Chinatown for dim sum, with lines stretching down the stairs and into the street on weekends. During the noon peak of dim sum time (daily 8:30–3), as many as 60 varieties of these bite-sized plates are available in the two huge red-pink-gold dining rooms. With a different chef, the dinner menu is more predictable, though Biba chef Lydia Shire sings the praises of China Pearl's pork belly with preserved vegetables.

Cibo. *North End* 326 Hanover St.;
617-557-9248 $$-$$$
Cibo represents a new hybrid in the North End—a restaurant that's almost too stylish for words but serves stunningly presented traditional dishes—marsala, bolognese, puttanesca, piccata. The combination of culinary finesse and artistic plating can mean a bit of a wait, so order wine and dig into the excellent bread.

Claremont Cafe. *South End/Cultural District* 535 Columbus Ave.; 617-247-9001 $$-$$$
Owners Manuel Sifnugel and Paula Spina are Latino, which shows in the tapas menu, but the pastas and meat dishes are pure Mediterranean Rim. There's wit and imagination in both the decor and in such dishes as a polenta lasagna. Meats tend to be straightforward, as in roasted chicken, slow-roasted pork, and smoky seared steak. And you couldn't ask for a friendlier spot.

Clio. *Back Bay* Eliot Hotel,
370A Commonwealth Ave.; 617-536-7200 $$$$
Chef Ken Oringer is one of Boston's new stars and Clio, with its leopard-skin and beige decor, is a star too. Oringer cooks with finesse: seared day-boat scallops on the half shell dabbed with osetra caviar, side dishes of vegetables enlivened with shavings of white truffle, even a garlicky roast chicken that's far more than a gesture toward picky eaters. But elegance and excellence do have a price, both in waiting time and final tally.

Daily Catch. *Waterfront* 261 Northern Ave.; 617-338-3093
North End 323 Hanover St.; 617-523-8567 $$
At either location, Daily Catch is really about eating squid Sicilian style—with lots of garlic. It comes fried, stuffed, marinated, even ground and formed into meatballs. Squid tops the salads. The pasta is tinted with squid ink. Other fish entrées are available, but obey the signs ordering you to "mangia calamari." The North End location is sometimes called the Calamari Café.

Dixie Kitchen. *Fenway/Back Bay* 182 Massachusetts Ave.; 617-536-3068 $
The funkier notes implied by the "cooking with jazz" neon sign outside have been muted a bit since Louisiana-born Mary Gauthier left, but Dixie Kitchen still makes the best fried catfish in the city, even if the jambalaya has been toned down for Yankee palates. The "seafood jazz combo" is delicious Mississippi Delta cuisine—fried catfish, fried shrimp, and fried oysters.

Durgin-Park. *Market District*
340 Faneuil Hall Marketplace (north building); 617-227-2038 $-$$
Long before tourism was invented, Durgin-Park was serving such traditional New England fare as baked beans, broiled cod,

prime rib, and Indian pudding to the fishermen and longshoremen who worked in and near the markets. Yes, it's a huge tourist draw, but there's nothing phony about it. The only changes in recent years are friendlier waitresses and smoke-free dining areas.

East Coast Grill & Raw Bar.
Cambridge/Inman Square
1271 Cambridge St.; 617-491-6568
$$-$$$

Chris Schlesinger literally wrote the book on grilled food *(Thrill of the Grill)* as well as on salsas and chutneys, and, yes, he's related to the family whose name is on Radcliffe's library—the one with the famous cookbook collection. Virtuoso grilling is what he does best: study the specials board during your long wait outside. Be sure to try the Grilled Sausage from Hell.

East Ocean City. *Chinatown/Cultural District* 25-29 Beach St.; 617-542-2504 $$
Hong Kong dining is all about very fresh seafood, and here you'll watch dinner go from the tank to the kitchen in a bucket. But it's not just fresh—it's cooked perfectly, as attested by the tender conch in black bean sauce on a bed of sprouts and slivers of fresh ginger. Outstanding shrimp (swiftly stir-fried, tails chewy and sweet) brings shrimp-lovers from all over the area. Wonderful crisp chicken and duck, too.

Elephant Walk. *Fenway/Brookline*
900 Beacon St.; 617-247-1500
Cambridge/Porter Square 2067 Massachusetts Ave.; 617-492-6900 $$-$$$
The Somerville original is a bit slapdash in decor but the newer Brookline edition is classy in a tropical-chic style. In both spots, the once-separate Cambodian and French menus have met in a true fusion with chef Longteine de Monteiro in Somerville and her daughter Nadsa Perry cooking in Brookline. When French technique meets Asian spice, the results are explosive. Look for the likes of grilled salmon with yellow beets and plums on phyllo-wrapped leeks or delectable nom krourk—rice-paper pillows filled with rice flour, coconut milk, and scallions. Lemony lamb noisettes might show up with delicate jasmine rice.

Emma's. *Cambridge* 40 Hampshire St., Cambridge; 617-864-8534 $
Clinging to a corner in the dot.com/MIT hollow of Kendall Square, Emma's makes the ultimate contemporary crisp-crust pizza π (as in 3.1416...) with toppings like goat cheese, caramelized onions, and a flurry of fresh basil.

Figs. *Beacon Hill* 42 Charles St.; 617-742-3447
Charlestown 67 Main St.; 617-242-2229 $$
The original Charlestown location near the Navy Yard is a densely packed wild scene on any given night, while the more genteel Beacon Hill outpost is quieter by dint of architecture and fewer seats. At both, Todd English of Olives tries out bold, small trattoría plates that rely mainly on a wood-burning oven. The best grilled pizza in Boston is found at Figs—for a price. A lot of fun, but both places require stamina and a hearty appetite.

Forest Café. *Harvard Square/Porter Square/Cambridge* 1682 Massachusetts Ave.; 617-661-7810 $-$$
Ignore the bikers in leather and bleached blondes in pedal pushers at the bar. Look to

RESTAURANTS

your left and you'll see the dining area. The Oaxacan (mostly) food shows striking finesse and exploits the subtleties offered by a wide variety of chile peppers. Here you'll get the kind of enchiladas and mole verde your grandmother might have made if she grew up near the Monte Alban ruins. Some Veracruz influences (green olives and capers, for example) appear in the fish dishes.

Galleria Italiana. *Cultural District* 177 Tremont St.; 617-423-2092 $$$-$$$$
It has some serious competition, but this classy Abruzzi restaurant offers the best Italian dining in Boston. They serve breakfast and lunch—but come for dinner. Executive chef and co-owner Marisa Iocca has kept every one of her talented chefs de cuisine on a straight track for her native Abruzzi. The menu is balanced with just a few antipasti, a few salads, a few pastas, a few meat and fish dishes—all of them brilliant and small enough so you'll order every course. The pastas tend to be spectacular, like triangoloni simmered in vegetarian broth and served with tiny fava beans, browned garlic, and shaved truffles. Meat and fish are comparatively simple, like roast lamb with fingerling potatoes.

Giannino. *Cambridge/Harvard Square* 20 University Rd.; 617-576-0605 $$$
Giannino is hidden from view behind the Charles Hotel, but lovers of hearty Abruzzi cuisine find it soon enough. Plating is simple and elegant and portions are huge—though almost everything on the menu can be ordered in entrée or appetizer size. The braised and roasted meats are the real stars, like roast chicken over vegetables and white beans or an osso buco rich as Croesus. In warm weather, Giannino shares an outdoor plaza with the hotel's restaurant.

Ginza. *Chinatown/Cultural District* 16 Hudson St.; 617-338-2261 $$-$$$
Come after 1 A.M. (Ginza's open until 4) and you'll see parties of wealthy foreign students in heavily labeled clothes who've stopped by for sushi after the dance clubs close. The sushi favors Cal-Japanese, with items like B52 maki (yellowtail, crab stick and cucumber in a tempura roll) as well as more conventional sushi and sashimi. Traditional nabemono dishes are also good: shabu-shabu, yosenabe, ochazuke rice soup, and yakiniku-style chicken, meat, or fish.

Grillfish. *South End/Cultural District* 162 Columbus Ave.; 617-357-1620 $$
This noisy spot jumps with a mixed clientele that's part a *Who's Who* of South End gay couples and part suburban foodies who appreciate the snappy decor and the minimal treatment given to good fish. Rare tuna steak comes with a sauce dark with roasted onion bits; a Marsala sauce perks up quickly grilled scallops. Alas, expect to wait for a table and then wait for the food.

Grill 23 & Bar. *Back Bay* 161 Berkeley St.; 617-542-2255 $$$-$$$$
A stronghold of guys in expensive suits with no-limit expense accounts, Grill 23 is a consistent winner with its food. True, the cigar smoke rises around you, but it keeps rising, thanks to a great vent system. Perfect meat comes, in part, from dry-aging on the premises—and from knowing exactly how to cook it. For something lighter, look to the Arctic char. Predictably, the selection of vintage ports and single malts is superb.

Gyuhama of Japan. *Back Bay* 827-29
Boylston St.; 617-437-0188 **$$-$$$**
First-rate sushi is Gyuhama's claim to fame
—that and being close to the Hynes Convention Center. The front rooms are set up
with western furniture, the back with tatami mats and low tables. After midnight,
Gyuhama metamorphoses into a heavy
metal rock-and-roll club with sushi.

Hamersley's Bistro. *South End/ Cultural
District* 553 Tremont St.; 617-423-2700
$$$-$$$$
Gordon Hamersley's oversized bistro has
proved with a vengeance that the South
End can support upscale dining. Book way
ahead for a weekend table. The lemon roast
chicken ranks among the best in the world
(no kidding) and there's a full panoply of
French provincial fare from rabbit with
mustard to flaky fish to sauces of tomatoes
and lemon and thyme. You can dine outdoors on the plaza in warm weather. Inside,
it gets loud when it's full, but the little
room near the door permits conversation.

Henrietta's Table. *Cambridge/Harvard
Square* The Charles Hotel,
One Bennett St.; 617-661-5005 **$$-$$$**
The "fresh-market" theme (fruits, veggies
and breads for sale) would be a little heavy-handed if Peter Davis's American comfort
food weren't so good. The fare ranges from
familiar (meatloaf, chicken pot pie) to
pleasantly non-traditional (pan-seared
monkfish with a tomato vinaigrette). All
side dishes cost extra, which boosts the bill.

House of Blues. *Cambridge/Harvard Square*
96 Winthrop St.; 617-491-2583 **$-$$**
This first of the national chain of music

clubs stays true to its roots by booking the
blues (and a little gospel). It's truly more a
performance venue than a place to eat.
Still, the Sunday gospel brunch, an all-you-can-eat buffet of Southern food, is a great
show with decent grub. Buy tickets in advance for seatings at 10, noon, and 2. The
main stage is upstairs, but the downstairs
restaurant is where most of the real eating
gets done—gumbo, pizza with alligator
sausage, good jambalaya.

Icarus Restaurant. *South End/Cultural District* 3 Appleton St.; 617-426-1790 **$$$**
Chef/owner Chris Douglass puts on an ever-inventive menu with French soul, Asian
style, and American strut. And counter to
the style of Boston's most popular restaurants, Icarus maintains a genial fine-dining,
linen-tablecloth look along with a wide
range of healthy meals. Sure, you can get
seared venison steak bordelaise or grilled
sweetbreads on frisée with blood oranges,
but Douglass also offers a low-salt, low fat
Square Meal (on square plates, no less) as
well as a nightly Green Plate Special for
vegetarians. Even after a decade it's still the
top date spot in the South End.

Ida's. *North End* 3 Mechanic St.;
617-523-0015 **$$**
As old-fashioned as the neon sign intended
to lure customers from Hanover Street,
Ida's has been run for decades by the Bruno
family. They won't win points for trendiness, but this friendly little room of tiny tables still draws a pretty good crowd for
inexpensive, old-fashioned pastas and entrées featuring eggplant, veal, and chicken.
The roast veal is a real treat.

Iruña. *Cambridge/Harvard Square*
56 JFK St.; 617-868-5633 $$
Don't go out of your way for the paella, but this Basque outpost that's a favorite with long-time academics and graduate students offers some hearty pick-me-ups for a cold night (the garlic soup, carne guisada) and some light, inexpensive deals on many variations of the Spanish omelet. The minimal decor strikes the right tone of no-pretense, simple family food.

Jae's Cafe. *Cambridge/Inman Square* 1281
Cambridge St.; 617-497-8380
South End/Cultural Distsict
520 Columbus Ave.; 617-421-9405
Cultural District (Theater District) 212
Stuart St.; 617-451-7788 $$-$$$
Restaurateur Jae Chung has put together a Pan-Asian formula that Bostonians love—a mix of sushi, kimchi, stir-fry and even a few Thai skewers. It sounds like a mish-mash, but in practice it's coheres as a lively and bright cuisine favored by a youthful crowd. "Eat at Jae's and live forever," says a sign in the Cambridge location—and the diners act like they believe it. Be prepared for long lines.

John Harvard's Brewhouse. *Cambridge/*
Harvard Square 33 Dunster St.;
617-868-3585 $$
Cambridge's first brewery (1636) stood close to this site, but we'll bet it was a lot duller than the lively pub scene at John Harvard's. Head brewer Brian Sanford makes a crisp, sharply hopped IPA—the ale that's the brewmaster's benchmark. And the kitchen makes a dish of homemade sausage with spätzle that is the IPA's gastronomic match.

Julien. *Downtown* Hotel Le Meridien, 250
Franklin St.; 617-451-1900 $$$$
Contemporary French cuisine without gimmicks doesn't get much better than the Julien, where the heavy dishes of Escoffier receive up-to-date light treatment. The setting is imposing (the old Federal Reserve bank) but the voluminous wingback chairs and dimmed lighting make it almost intimate. Add warmly professional service and you can't go wrong—if you can afford it.

Kingfish Hall. *Market District* South Market, Faneuil Hall Marketplace; 617-523-8862 $$$
Restaurant legend Todd English puts his bold touch on seafood, though the best dishes are the ones that are the simplest—grilled or oven-baked fish, grilled prawns, skewered scallops. Half tourists (it's adjacent to Faneuil Hall) and half locals, Kingfish Hall also has a very busy barroom scene downstairs. Don't even think about reservations unless you're a party of six or more.

Koreana. *Cambridge/Central Square*
154 Prospect St.; 617-576-8661 $$-$$$
Perhaps Boston's most popular restaurant with Korean-born residents, Koreana's pine paneling and wood-pattern plastic table-tops may not suggest haute cuisine, but the kitchen delivers good bolgoki and fiery kimchi. One of the big draws for parties of four or more is the room with charcoal braziers built into the tables for on-the-spot cooking.

Lala Rokh. *Beacon Hill* 97 Mt. Vernon St.;
617-720-5511 $$-$$$
The key to deciphering a Persian menu is to mix and match main dishes with pi-

quant side dishes and relishes—kebab of Cornish game hen marinated in onion and lemon with a mango-tamarind chutney, for example. Restaurateur Azita Bina-Seibel and her waitstaff are especially helpful with this task, for they are evangelistic about the delights of the Persian table. Soothingly elegant Lala Rokh is a good place to learn, though you might find it sets a standard that few restaurants can meet. Reservations recommended on weekends.

L'Espalier. *Back Bay* 30 Gloucester St.;
   617-262-3023 $$$$
Chef and co-owner Frank McClelland is Boston's quiet culinary genius, and his Back Bay townhouse converted to an elegant restaurant is easily the most romantic spot in the city. Dining here often marks an event—a marriage proposal, an anniversary, closing a megamillion-dollar deal. A three- or five-course dégustation (approaching $70) is available Tuesday through Thursday, but the weekend menu is strictly a three-course prix fixe. Be sure to try foie gras, perhaps served on a quince, bacon, and onion tart. The vegetarian tasting menu is always a tour de force.

Locke-Ober. *Downtown* 3 Winter Place;
617-542-1340 $$$$
Calling Locke-Ober's menu "French" is an overstatement—it's more like "continental" circa 1875, when the place was founded as a dinner retreat for rich men on Beacon Hill. The exclusivity is gone, but the cigar-puffing robber-baron ways are not. A meal at the famous Locke-Ober offers the chance to see the old bulls of the vanishing Boston Brahmin breed in their natural habitat. Go at lunch to save money. Dress stuffy.

Maison Robert/Ben's Café. *Downtown* 45
   School St.; 617-227-3370 $$$-$$$$/$$
The Robert family introduced modern French dining in Boston nearly 30 years ago, and young chef Jacky Robert continues the tradition of innovation at this very formal dining room and more casual bar-café with outdoor seating. The oldtimers buried next door at King's Chapel (visible from the dining room) may be turning over in their graves as Jacky injects new Asian, Latin American, and Mediterranean blood into the classic French tradition. Gourmets on a budget might consider the prix-fixe at bistro-ish **Ben's Café** (under $25).

Marché Mövenpick. *Back Bay*
   Prudential Center, 800 Boylston St.;
   617-578-9700 $$
At this United Nations of themed food under a single roof, you grab a tray and a "passport" and walk around to the Italian section for pasta, to the Asian section for a stir fry, to the Mexican section for chimichangas, to the French section for ... you get the idea. Each dish on the tray comes with a "visa" stamp on the card, which becomes your bill at checkout. It's hardly high cuisine, but the food court approach makes a good solution for families where everyone wants something different.

Marcuccio's. *North End* 125 Salem St.;
   617-723-1807 $$$
Bold and brassy, Marcuccio's may spell a new direction for North End dining, in that the little old neighborhood ladies that you wouldn't expect to find in such postmodern decor come out singing the praises of chef Charles Draghi's veal dishes (especially the roasted veal with a sauce of endive,

RESTAURANTS

sweet onion, and lemon). The look is Pompeii, and the crowds on a Saturday night (no reservations) make it look like A.D. 79.

Masa. *South End/Cultural District*
439 Tremont St.; 617-338-8884 **$$$**
New England fare (especially good North Atlantic fish) gets Southwestern accents at this surprisingly sophisticated restaurant. Rarely do New England restaurants that make great margaritas also have good kitchens, but here the food is tasty and tequila's sun also rises. Imagine pan-roasted cod surrounded with smoked, peppery bacon and a sauce made of sweet corn and charred tomatoes and you'll get the drift.

Maurizio's. *North End* 364 Hanover St.;
617-367-1123 **$$-$$$**
Chef-owner Maurizio Loddo is nothing short of brilliant, and if you can snag a table where the kitchen is visible, you'll be astounded by Loddo's fluid yet lightning-quick economy of motion. His Sardinian upbringing shows in wonderful fish dishes such as a thick swordfish steak stuffed with olives, pine nuts, and basil, topped with a roasted plum tomato sauce. The place is small but they take reservations. Make one.

Milk Street Café. *Downtown* 50 Milk St.;
617-542-FOOD
The Park at Post Office Square;
617-350-PARK **$**
Just the ticket for catching a lunch break from shopping, Milk Street Café happens to be a dairy kosher operation. Best bets are the sandwiches (egg salad, tuna salad) and the soups. The seating rule on Milk Street is that "in fairness to other customers" you can't take a table until you've gone through the cafeteria line.

Mistral. *South End/Cultural District* 223 Columbus Ave.; 617-867-9300 **$$-$$$$**
Calculated at its inception as the place to be seen, Mistral is also a good place to eat (assuming you can get in), thanks to chef Jamie Mammano's inventive chops—like a brioche stuffed with foie gras and duck confit and drenched in a reduction with dried tart cherries. The menu also lists traditional bistro plates such as grilled rib-eye with horseradish whipped potatoes.

New Shanghai Restaurant. *Chinatown/ Cultural District* 21 Hudson St.;
617-338-6688 **$$**
Chef C. K. Sau aims to make New Shanghai the equal of any fancy room in Hong Kong, where he trained, and with white linens and an airy look, this restaurant definitely stands out from Chinatown's casual spots. Non-Chinese chefs from all over Boston come here to be inspired by dishes such as baby eels tossed in a glaze of oranges and hot peppers. Showing his Shanghai roots, Sau offers hard-to-find sliced lamb with scallions.

No Name Seafood. *Waterfront* 15, Fish Pier;
617-338-7539 **$-$$**
Easily the least fancy seafood house in Boston, No Name has a simple formula: Buy the fish off the boat and either fry or bake it. The menu is the same all day, though prices rise about 30 percent for dinner, so consider whiling away a rainy afternoon here with ice-cold beer and a hot bowl of the fish chowder, which has a little bit of everything that came off the boats that day. The barroom seediness (though very clean) is part of the charm.

No. 9 Park. *Beacon Hill* 9 Park St.;
617-742-9991 **$$$**
Co-owner and chef Barbara Lynch brings

both finesse and gusto to her interpretations of Mediterranean fare. Lynch made her reputation in Boston for her handling of duck, and the bird remains her signature. But her fish dishes are almost always an equally good bet. The bar at No. 9 Park is prime territory for meeting Boston sports figures and local politicians.

Oak Room. *Back Bay* Fairmont Copley
Plaza Hotel, 138 St. James St.;
617-262-2647 $$$$

For a truly lavish steak dinner at truly lavish prices, this is the place. The room was recently restored to the Edwardian splendor of its molded plaster ceiling, intricate dark woodwork, and blood red drapery. All portions are overwhelming, even the appetizers. Start with oysters Rockefeller before moving on to a perfect one-pound prime steak (or an immense slab of fish). Dessert soufflés (Grand Marnier, chocolate, Frangelico) must be ordered with the entrées.

Olives. *Charlestown* 10 City Sq.,
Charlestown; 617-242-1999 $$$-$$$$

Chef Todd English has made sure that Olives is Boston's most famous restaurant of the moment, and he delivers the goods with Italian-influenced New American cuisine. Pastas are hardly conventional—viz. an anchovy-potato mini-lasagna with a crusted tuna steak and a veal stock reduction. Ditto a tortelloni of asparagus in puréed asparagus sauce with crumbled feta and bacon. (The Olives plates have become ever more complex as English retires the simpler ones to Figs.) There's usually a long line when Olives opens and it just gets longer as the night wears on. You won't be able to converse over the din, but it's rude to talk with your mouth full anyway.

The Paramount. *Beacon Hill*
44 Charles St.; 617-720-1152 $-$$

A comfort-food destination since before World War II, the Paramount operates as a cafeteria-style diner during the day but switches to table service in the evenings. In keeping with the galloping refinement of the neighborhood, the Paramount has replaced its traditional chili and beef stew menu with stir-fry specials and plates that feature boneless chicken breast and cheeses with French names. But it's still the best cheap eating on Beacon Hill.

Parish Cafe and Bar. *Back Bay*
361 Boylston St.; 617-247-4777 $-$$

Some sandwich shops name their concoctions after celebrities. Here they are designed by celebrities—local celebrity chefs, that is—making for an eclectic, interesting selection. Lydia Shire's entry is lobster salad on pepper brioche, while Chris Schlesinger assembled ham and cheese on banana bread. Patio tables out front are a good place to watch the world go by.

Pho Pasteur. *Chinatown/Cultural
District* 8 Kneeland St.; 617-451-0247
682 Washington St.; 617-482-7467
Back Bay 119 Newbury St.;
617-262-8200
Harvard Square 35 Dunster St.;
617-864-4100 $-$$

Easily the best deal on Newbury Street and not a bad option in Chinatown or Harvard Square, Pho Pasteur shows remarkable consistency across locations. Service is fast and professional, and the dishes are hot, fresh, savory, and soothing. Noodle soups (phö) are always a good bet, but entrées like "pork with vegetable" or sliced catfish in casserole are uniformly excellent.

Pignoli. *Back Bay* 79 Park Plaza; 617-338-7500 $$$-$$$$

Susan Regis and Lydia Shire run this outstanding, if intensely upscale Eurochic spot on the flip side of the building from their other venue, Biba. Pignoli's roots are northern Italian, but interpreted through a New American lens. An artist friend summed it up: "My scallops cost $5 each—but they were the best scallops I've ever eaten. I'm happy." It can get very loud here.

Pizzeria Regina. *North End* 11 1/2 Thatcher St.; 617-227-0765 $-$$

It's hard to believe that this atmospheric little bar with the glaze of time is where the antiseptic Boston-area pizza chain began. Too bad they couldn't franchise the look and feel as well. It's the kind of neighborhood dive (finding it is the first challenge) where good thin-crust pizza *should* be eaten.

Pomodoro. *North End* 319 Hanover St.; 617-367-4348 $-$$

The room is tiny, the tables are tiny and the portions are huge. They're also wonderful and sunny, if hardly innovative. The eponymous sauce is one of the best tomato sauces in the neighborhood and a single serving of the cold roasted vegetable salad could feed two people for the whole day. Pomodoro is almost too intimate a place to eat with a merely casual acquaintance.

Pravda 116. *South End/Cultural District* 116 Boylston St.; 617-482-7799 $$-$$$

The late-night disco dance club in the back and the trying-too-hard bar in the front should not deter you from enjoying some of the best, most imaginative New American bistro cooking in the Theater District. It's perfect for enjoying an early dinner before a play, or a late dinner afterwards. Best dishes come off the wood grill.

Radius. *Downtown* 8 High St.; 617-426-1234 $$$$

Set smack-dab amid the anonymous towers of the Financial District, Radius is an extraordinary dining experience tailored for Those Who Have Made It (and can afford it). Chef and co-owner Michael Schlow lavishes extraordinary care on every detail of his plates, right down to shaping carrots with a melon baller. Every entrée is deeply sensual—slow-roasted sturgeon with Chinese mustard greens, for example. Expensive? Yes. And worth it.

Redbone's. *Somerville/Davis Square* 55 Chester St.; 617-628-2200 $$

Austin comes to Boston. Essentially a Texas roadhouse barbecue and blues house, Redbone's has an authenticity unmatched in the Northeast. And the price is right. Moreover, this is a beer-lover's heaven, with two dozen microbrews always on tap.

Rhythm & Spice. *Cambridge/Central Square* 315 Massachusetts Ave.; 617-497-0977 $$

This is the spot to go "easy in the Islands" —specifically the Lesser Antilles—with an excellent stewed goat curry, gundy (smoked herring) appetizers and a dizzying list of drinks made with rum. Late on Thursday, Friday, and Saturday nights they push back the tables and the place becomes a dance club to the bouncy hooks of roots reggae, soca, and zouk.

Rialto. *Cambridge/Harvard Square* The Charles Hotel, One Bennett St.; 617-661-5050 $$$-$$$$

Jody Adams—named top New England chef by the James Beard Foundation in 1997—has a quiet way with superlative food. The room has a swank feel, and the luxe olive and mushroom velvet banquettes break up the boxy space. Adams's dishes amount to an all-American interpretation of trattoría and bistro plates of southern Europe. Quail is deboned and prepped in a pepper marinade, then roasted and served with a salad of warm figs, watercress, and preserved oranges. If you don't have a reservation, you may be able to get a seat at one of the tiny bar tables. After all, it's the food you're after.

Rowes Wharf Restaurant. *Waterfront*
    70 Rowes Wharf; 617-439-3995 $$$-$$$$

Chef Daniel Bruce believes that food can only be as good as the ingredients, so he grows, forages, hooks, and/or hunts many of the ingredients himself, then prepares them with loving care. The rack of lamb with a Roquefort crust skin is as heavy as the food gets, yet the same kitchen also prepares a ginger-braised scrod in a carrot-vermouth-ginger broth laced with vegetables. The room feels like a library—except that it overlooks Boston Harbor.

Salamander. *Back Bay* Trinity Place, One
    Huntington Ave.; 617-451-2150 $$$$
Stan Frankenthaler may construct the most baroque taste experiences in Boston, but he is one of those rare chefs who can coax a single, complex effect from a long list of ingredients. At these new Copley Square digs, Frankenthaler augments his acclaimed Asian fusion dining room with a satay bar for light meals and drinks. Five- and seven-course tasting menus are available at dinner.

Salts. *Cambridge/Central Square*
    798 Main St.; 617-876-8444 $$$
Drawing on some surprising Eastern and Central European roots, chef Steven Rosen crafts a fresh and intense cuisine not quite like anyone else's. He smokes lamb with black tea and rosemary before roasting, and serves up wild sturgeon fillets with a golden horseradish sauce. There's great range here —from a delicate potato-chanterelle soup to a hearty duck prosciutto with fresh figs and marsala syrup. Reserve ahead—there are only 42 seats.

Santarpio's Pizza. *East Boston* 113 Chelsea
    St., East Boston; 617-567-9871 $
You like garlic? Extra garlic? Extra-extra garlic? Then hunt out Santarpio's, a classic pizza, sausage and beer joint in the Italian part of Eastie near the airport, replete with boxing memorabilia on the walls under the yellow haze of cigarette smoke. It's a short walk from the Maverick T stop on the Blue Line, or the first right after exiting the harbor tunnel.

Sel de la Terre. *Waterfront* 255 State St.;
    617-720-1300 $$$
Located right at the exit from the Aquarium T stop, Sel de la Terre offers country cooking, Provençal style, in a quietly elegant dining room. Chef Geoff Gardner used to be a baker, and his outstanding, crusty loaves are hard to beat. They're just about perfect for mopping up the last bit of bouillabaisse broth. (You can buy the breads to go at the boulangerie by the front door.) Sel de la Terre is also great for a substantial lunch.

Shalimar of India. *Cambridge/Central Square* 546 Massachusetts Ave.; 617-547-9280 $$

Northern Indian dishes dominate the menu at this best of many Indian restaurants in Central Square. Tandoori (no surprise) is the house specialty, and ordering the sampler plate guarantees a good selection of Shalimar's best dishes, including an outstanding lamb curry.

South End Galleria. *South End/Cultural District* 480A Columbus Ave.; 617-236-5252 $$-$$$

Posing as a Roman alleyway trattoria with its faux distressed plaster, South End Galleria is the more casual younger brother of Galleria Italiana. Chef Marissa Iocco concocts straightforward Abruzzi dishes for the dining room, while the lively bar side is one of the few indoor smoking venues in Boston.

Tanjore. *Cambridge/Harvard Square* 18 Eliot St.; 617-868-1900 $$-$$$

The Majmudar family operates two Indian restaurants in the suburbs, and in Tanjore —the city's best Indian restaurant, hands down—they've brought together the regional cuisines of India with a lengthy menu that makes cultural and culinary sense out of a rich gastronomic tradition. Don't be afraid to ask for help. In the afternoon and late at night, you can order tapas-sized nashta dishes.

Tapeo. *Back Bay* 266 Newbury St.; 617-267-4799 $$

As the name suggests, Tapeo specializes in tapas, and manages to do them with striking authenticity. This is a dandy spot to sit with a dry sherry and nibble on potato-onion omelets (tortilla española), grilled prawns, or slivers of manchego cheese. In colder weather, sit at the blue-tiled bar or by the fireplace in the pretty dining room.

Tia's on Long Wharf. *Waterfront* 200 Atlantic Ave.; 617-227-0828 $$

Tia's becomes something of a raucous drinking scene on weekends, but it's as civil a place as you can find to eat steamed lobster and clams on a summer afternoon. Stick to the basics: plain shellfish and beer.

Torch. *Beacon Hill* 26 Charles St.; 617-723-5939 $$-$$$

Torch is as tastefully classical as a little black dress—so truly French, so truly universal. Chef-owner Evan Deluty trained and worked in Paris, and he has graced Beacon Hill with an honest-to-goodness bistro that serves a fine hanger steak, great sliced duck breast and well-chosen, well-priced country wines. Deluty makes a fine crème brûlée but the best dessert choice is always the cheese plate.

Truc. *South End/Cultural District* 560 Tremont St.; 617-338-8070 $$-$$$

Chef Amanda Lydon turns out high-end French bistro fare here (albeit at bistro-plus prices), which is rare in Boston, where most chefs want to put their own, sometimes misguided stamps on tradition. If you're hankering for a classic coq au vin, pan-seared sweetbreads, a saffron-mussel cream soup, or the crunchy burnt-sugar crust of crème brûlée, Truc's your spot.

Turner Fisheries. *Back Bay* Westin Copley Hotel, Dartmouth and Stuart Sts.; 617-424-7425 $$$-$$$$

Turner Fisheries is elegant enough for a big night out, formal enough to get dressed up, and comfortable enough to let your hair down over a Sapphire martini. There are two ways to order: pick your fish and method of preparation, or opt for one of chef David Filippetti's fancier alternatives, like a shellfish medley in lobster broth.

Union Oyster House. *Market District*
41 Union St.; 617-227-2750 $$$-$$$$
John Kennedy ate here every Sunday morning when he was in town. So has almost every politician in Boston, as well as half the tourists who have visited Quincy Market. It claims to be America's oldest restaurant in continuous operation, and we doubt the menu has changed much in all those years. The best bet is to follow Daniel Webster's lead and stick to the raw bar for clams, oysters, and brandy.

The Vault. *Downtown/Financial District*
105 Water St.; 617-292-9966 $$$-$$$$
The two dozen wine selections by the glass might tip you off that this dramatically appointed Financial District dining room is owned by wine merchants. Rising star chef Rebecca Esty presents relatively straightforward plates of delectable meat- and fish-based dishes—a pan-roasted chicken breast over artichokes, baked halibut with braised leeks, a cioppino loaded with tuna, squid, mussels, clams and bits of lobster.

Warren Tavern. *Charlestown* 2 Pleasant St.;
617-241-8142 $$-$$$
The tavern dates from around 1780, making it one of Boston's oldest restaurants, but a recent menu overhaul has rescued patrons from pub food with such options as grilled lamb chops and a half-pound filet mignon.

The burgers are also still reliable. Pub crawlers flock here on Wednesday and Thursday nights for the live music.

West Side Lounge. *Cambridge/Harvard Square* 1680 Massachusetts Ave.;
617-441-5566 $$
The interior might look like a lounge from a circa-1955 jazz album (and some of that music might be playing in the background), but American club food was never this good or this unpretentious. You could start with briny steamed mussels, have a grilled club steak with "funky" potatoes (mashed potatoes with ripe olives), and finish off with a lemon tart.

White Star Tavern. *Back Bay* 565 Boylston St.; 617-536-4477 $-$$
One of Back Bay's best bargains, White Star proves that bar food doesn't have to be boring. The menu divides neatly into small and medium-sized snacking plates (like shrimp tempura), larger plates that can make a meal (penne with lobster and ham), and sandwiches at all hours. The tavern's fish and chips are among the best in Boston. White Star also has a wide selection of wines.

Les Zygomates Bistro & Wine Bar. $$-$$$
Cultural District/Leather District
129 South St.; 617-542-5108
Atmospheric and fun, Les Zygomates (French for the smile muscles) offers 30 wines by the glass, an excellent prix fixe bistro lunch, and more classics at night—cassoulet, poussin, lobster bisque, and (of course) foie gras. Wines are also available by the half glass, in case you'd like to concoct your own flight.

PRACTICAL INFORMATION

Note: Compass American Guides makes every effort to ensure the accuracy of its information; however, as conditions and prices change frequently, we suggest that readers also contact visitors bureaus for the most up-to-date information. See "Tourist Information" below.

■ TELEPHONE

Local calls in Boston and Cambridge require dialing all ten digits.

■ METRIC CONVERSIONS

1 foot = .304 meters (m)
1 mile = 1.6 kilometers (km)

1 acre = .4 hectares (ha)
degrees F = degrees C $(9/5) + 32$

■ TOURIST INFORMATION

Boston: Greater Boston Convention & Visitors Bureau.
Visitors' kit available by writing to 2 Copley Place, Suite 105, Boston MA 02116-6501 or calling (888) 733-2678 from outside Massachusetts, 617-536-4100 in state.

Boston Common Visitor Information Center. Stop by this information center at 146 Tremont St.. Or visit the **Prudential Center Visitor Information Center,** Center Court, Prudential Center.

Cambridge: Cambridge Office for Tourism. 18 Brattle St., Cambridge MA 02138; 617-441-2884. Or stop by the **Cambridge Information Kiosk** in Harvard Square.

■ WEBSITES

Boston CitySearch. *boston.citysearch.com*
Boston's premier online guide to entertainment and restaurant information.

Boston Globe site. *www.Boston.com*
Searchable electronic version of the "Calendar," which lists countless upcoming events. Handy restaurant review archives.

Boston Online. *www.boston-online.com*
Witty information on Boston, with crucial guide to public restrooms.

City of Cambridge. *www.ci.cambridge.ma/*
Details local services and also provides extensive information for visitors.

Greater Boston Convention & Visitors Bureau. *www.bostonusa.com*
Its website plugs its members but provides good links to other information:

Yankee Publishing. *www.NewEngland.com*
Blankets New England; especially good coverage of Boston and Cambridge.

■ CLIMATE

Meteorologists love Boston because something is always happening. Boston lies at the convergence of weather patterns sliding down off the Laurentian Shield in Canada, riding up the Ohio Valley and across the Great Lakes, and slipping up the Atlantic coast. All three atmospheric patterns are then further modified by the waters off Boston, where the Labrador Current and the Gulf Stream brush past each other.

Fall is like heaven on earth in Boston, with typically deep blue skies, a golden slant of light, moderately warm days, and moderately cool nights. The annual bird migrations pass through and the annual student in-migrations begin. Winter is mild by northern standards, with snow settling on the city one day and often melting off the next. Spring is sudden and exuberant, as daffodils, tulips, lilacs, and ornamental fruit trees proclaim the demise of boot weather. Summer is warm and indolent; temperatures by the waterfront remain comfortable on all but the hottest days, typically the cusp of July and August.

BOSTON CLIMATE
Average Daily Temperature Range (°F) and Precipitation (in.)

	High/Low	Prec./Snow		High/Low	Prec./Snow
JANUARY:	36/21	4.0/12.0	JULY:	82/65	2.7
FEBRUARY:	38/23	3.7/11.0	AUGUST:	80/63	3.7
MARCH:	46/30	4.1/7.0	SEPTEMBER:	71/58	3.4
APRIL:	57/40	3.7/1.0	OCTOBER:	62/48	3.4
MAY:	67/50	3.5	NOVEMBER:	51/39	4.2/2.0
JUNE:	77/59	2.9	DECEMBER:	40/27	4.5/7.0

GETTING AROUND

■ GETTING AROUND

■ BY PUBLIC TRANSPORTATION

The T is a web of subway and streetcar lines, with some trains beginning as one and ending as the other. It's unlikely you'll want to go anywhere the T doesn't. Service operates Monday through Saturday from 5 A.M. to 12:45 A.M., Sunday from 6 A.M. to 12:45 A.M. Weekday service is theoretically every 3 to 15 minutes, weekend service less frequent. T tokens are $1. The T's Visitor Passport provides unlimited travel on the T and buses for one day ($6), three days ($11) or seven days ($22). Passes are sold at the Greater Boston Convention & Visitors Bureau Information Center on Boston Common and at the Prudential Center. For other sales locations, or for specific information on routes and schedules, call 617-722-3200. Pick up a pocket map of the system at the service office at Downtown Crossing.

■ BY AUTOMOBILE

Are you *kidding?* Traffic is daunting and on-street parking spaces are hard to find, and often have brief time limits when you do find them. Thanks to computers, Boston and Cambridge hunt down violators (including those from outside Massachusetts). Acquire five tickets and your car will be immobilized with a Denver Boot. Walk, take public transportation, or hail a cab.

■ BY TAXI

A mark of Boston's advanced civilization is that you can hail a cab on the street. Drop fees and distance charges vary by municipality, starting at $1.25 for the flag drop and 10¢ per 1/8 mile. Taxi stands are usually found at large hotels, subway stations and the airport. (Airport cabs cost an extra $3 over meter rates to cover the cost of the tunnel toll and airport use fee.) Many taxi drivers may require directions to take you someplace off the beaten track. Using taxis is a good way to meet a cross-section of Boston's newest immigrants.

■ MAJOR FESTIVALS AND EVENTS

The old advice that the best way to get to know a family is to spend the holidays with them works for a city, too. Boston has all kinds of pocket celebrations in its neighborhoods, but the best way to get to know the city as a whole is to join the festivities for First Night, Patriots Day, and the Fourth of July.

■ FIRST NIGHT: DECEMBER 31

Semantics aside (a December 31 fest might be more aptly called "Last Day"), First Night is Boston's defiant midwinter party: a citywide, arts-driven New Year celebration. Since a group of artists dreamed up the first modest festivities in 1975, the franchise has spread to more than 130 other cities. Given that the cityscape is as much a player as the more than 1,000 paid artists, Beantown's First Night will most likely remain forever first.

In the broadest sense, First Night is a multicultural festival of both folk and fine arts played out in about 50 indoor and outdoor venues across the city and supported through the sale of First Night buttons. Activities begin at 1 P.M. with lots of events for children, and pick up after the 5:30 Grand Procession, a funky artists' parade the length of Back Bay down Boylston to Charles Street. Churches, concert halls, theaters, galleries, and colleges open their doors for everything from bluegrass to flamenco, Bach concertos to gospel music, poetry slams to juggling. But many of the 1.5 million or so participants ignore the weather and stay outdoors to view mini-performances in tony Newbury Street windows, ice sculptures in Copley Square and on Boston Common, and any number of un-cate-gorizable events/performances throughout the city streets. A countdown to midnight on the Custom House Tower clock signals a fireworks finale over Boston Harbor.

A full schedule of First Night event times and venues appears in the *Boston Globe* "Calendar" on the last Thursday of the year.

■ PATRIOTS DAY: APRIL

Patriots Day, celebrated on the third Monday of April, is perhaps the busiest holiday in Boston. For a day, the city expands its borders to take in the suburbs of Lexington and Concord, sites of the first skirmishes of the American Revolution. Patriots Day celebrations are about the irrevocable fact that the Revolution began here, with the events of April 18-19, 1775. One of the smallest but most moving commemorations occurs on the eve of the holiday, at Old North Church in the North End. The congregation gathers to mark 23-year-old sexton Robert Newman's climb to the steeple with the lanterns which would warn Paul Revere and William Dawes that the British were heading to Charlestown by boat or to Cambridge by bridge. (The first troops rowed over; reinforcements followed by bridge.) Each year, a descendant of Newman climbs 154 steps to the steeple and, as the vicar says, "the rest is history."

Reenactments of that history begin the next morning at the Lexington Common, where a bunch of exhausted Redcoats meet a ragtag colonial militia for the first encounter of the Revolution. By 5 A.M. a mostly local crowd has already walled off the Common ten deep, with the last to arrive setting up stepladders to see above the early birds. The call to alarm begins with a peal of church bells at 5:30. A Paul Revere impersonator arrives on horseback, and the militiamen come running out of the tavern. Columns of redcoats march up Main Street and confront the colonists on the Common. When the smoke clears, the patriots clear away their dead and chase the British toward Concord. (Onlookers then generally repair to one of the various pancake breakfasts at nearby churches.)

The scene shifts to North Bridge in Concord, where the colonials fare rather better. A few Redcoats twice advance partway across the bridge to fire and retreat. Then the Minute Men come marching across to fife and drum; they fire a volley, and the redcoats begin their flight down Battle Road (along Route 2A). The final reenactment occurs about a mile outside Concord at Meriam's Corner, a stream crossing where the orderly British march turned into a running rout. One of the best ways to follow this return route is by bicycle along the Minuteman Bikeway, a paved path that covers much of the original Battle Road.

More information is available from the Lexington Visitors Center, 1875 Massachusetts Ave., Lexington, 781-862-1450; or North Bridge Visitor Center, 174 Liberty St., Concord, 617-484-6156.

■ THE BOSTON MARATHON: APRIL

The only gunfire in another western suburb, Hopkinton, is the noon starter's pistol for the Boston Marathon, the world's oldest annual marathon. Organized since 1897 by the

Boston Athletic Association, the race winds 26.2 miles past 1.5 million cheering on-lookers before concluding at a stripe in the road on Boylston Street by the Boston Public Library.

It's hard to say who gets more psyched—the runners or their fans—and the race has made legends of a handful of Boston runners over the years. One of the most beloved is Johnny Kelley, who won in 1935 and 1945 and came in second seven times in the 58 marathons he completed (he entered 61). A dual bronze statue of an aged Kelley running hand in hand with a younger version of himself stands at the foot of Heartbreak Hill, the aptly named 20-mile mark where so many runners either fall behind or quit.

The Boston Marathon is almost two separate events. The last of the major marathons to relent and offer cash prizes, Boston has always drawn elite runners from around the globe. (Women began running Boston in 1966, gaining official status in 1972. Boston welcomed wheelchair athletes in 1975, the first major marathon to do so.) But Boston also routinely attracts nearly 10,000 amateurs, each of whom can tell a personal story of why he or she is running. Some are raising money for charities; others dedicate their efforts to the memory of a loved one. Still others see the Marathon as a struggle by which to measure themselves, hoping in some cases only to complete the distance or, in others, to improve a personal time that may be triple the winning time of just over two hours. The entire city, it seems, becomes a carbo-loading pasta party the night before and a celebratory beerfest the evening after the race is done.

Takes place third Monday in April. More information is available from the Boston Athletic Association, 131 Clarendon Street, Boston; 617-236-1652.

■ THE FOURTH OF JULY

Philadelphia may have a better claim on Independence Day than Boston, but that hasn't stopped the Hub from establishing one of the nation's best Fourth of July spectaculars. The elements are simple enough: a few hundred thousand people picnicking at a riverbank park waiting for a great band and world-class fireworks.

In a time-honored civic tradition, the Boston Pops Orchestra—under the successive batons of marchmaster Arthur Fiedler, movie-music-maestro John Williams, and now Keith Lockhart—plays a July 4 concert at the Hatch Shell on the Charles River Esplanade between the Longfellow and Harvard bridges. Never mind that seats within sight of the stage fill up before noon: commercial classical station WCRB broadcasts the music on 102.5 FM and the celebration is more about the crowd and the fireworks than the concert, anyway.

When Lockhart picks up his baton at 8 P.M., cool breezes have begun to dispel the day's heat and more than 300,000 people recline on their blankets for the show. Whatever else the Pops may play, everyone is waiting for Tchaikovsky's *1812 Overture,* complete with cannon fire and the ringing of church bells throughout the city. With the sound effects, the light effects begin: a half-hour program of fireworks bursting from barges in the middle of the Charles and exploding against the backdrop of the Beacon Hill skyline.

FESTIVALS AND EVENTS

■ EVENTS LIST

There's always something going on somewhere in Boston, but here are some of the major events Bostonians look forward to each year, listed chronologically. Dates may change, so check schedules in advance by calling the listed number or the Greater Boston Convention & Visitors Bureau at 617-536-4100/888-733-2678.

JANUARY

Chinese New Year. *Late January to March (depending on lunar calendar)* Celebration in Chinatown with parade, lion and dragon dances, firecrackers and more; 617-482-3292.

MARCH

New England Spring Flower Show. *Mid-March* Sponsored by the Massachusetts Horticultural Society, the nation's oldest annual flower exhibition is held at the Bayside Expo Center; 617-536-9280.

Boston St. Patrick's Day Parade. *Sunday before March 17* South Boston parade honors the Irish saint and the evacuation of Boston by the British. This event received national attention in 1995 when the U.S. Supreme Court ruled that the parade sponsors, the Allied War Veterans Council, may exclude Irish-American gay, lesbian, and bisexual marchers on the basis of freedom of speech.

APRIL

Battles of Lexington and Concord. *Third Monday in April.*

Boston Marathon. *Third Monday in April ; see page 306.*

Patriots Day Parade. *Third Monday in April ; see page 306* Parade starts at 9:30 A.M. at City Hall Plaza and ends at Paul Revere Mall in the North End for a reenactment of the start of Paul Revere's Midnight Ride.

MAY

Walk for Hunger. *First Sunday in May* The 20-mile walk, one of the oldest and largest pledge walks in the country, raises funds for food pantries, soup kitchens and homeless shelters. Sponsored by Project Bread; 617-723-5000.

Boston Brewers' Festival. *Mid-May* Featuring the best of about 100 brewpubs and craft breweries from around New England, the festival takes place at the Bayside Exposition Center.

Ducklings Day Parade. *Second Sunday in May* This Mother's Day event begins on the Boston Common and retraces the route of the ducklings in the children's classic *Make Way for Ducklings* by Robert McCloskey. Sponsored by Historic Neighborhoods Foundation; 617-426-1885.

Hidden Gardens of Beacon Hill. *Third Thursday in May* A self-guided tour of gardens that cannot be seen from the sidewalk. Sponsored since 1929 by Beacon Hill Garden Club; 617-227-4392.

Lilac Sunday. *Third Sunday in May* For many New Englanders, the stroll along Bussey Hill Road at the Arnold Arboretum, where more than 400 of the fragrant, multicolored lilacs are planted, is an annual tradition. The lilacs bloom early May to late June; 617-524-1717.

MAY *cont'd*

Annual Street Performers Festival. *Late May* The four-day festival features 50 of the world's top street performers at Faneuil Hall Marketplace.

JUNE

Boston Common Dairy Festival. *Tuesday, Wednesday, and Thursday of the first full week of June* Festival celebrates the Common's colonial pasturage role with farm animals, milking demonstrations, petting zoo; 617-734-6750. At the same time and in the dairy mode, the **Scooper Bowl**, a Jimmy Fund benefit, is one of the largest ice cream festivals in the nation. City Hall Plaza; 617-632-3300.

Dragon Boat Festival. *Early June* Teams race intricately crafted boats on the Charles from JFK Street to Western Ave. to commemorate the life of Chinese poet-patriot Qu Yuan. 617-441-2884.

Bunker Hill Weekend. *Weekend before June 17* Costumed reenactors, drills, firing demonstrations, talks, tours at Bunker Hill Monument; 617-242-5641. On Sunday, the **Bunker Hill Day Parade** steps off from foot of Bunker Hill, proceeds around the Monument and ends at the militia training field. This huge community event, with lawn chairs and picnics en route, takes all afternoon; 617-242-2646.

JULY

Boston Harborfest. *Week that includes July 4* Children's events, fireworks skyconcert over Boston Harbor, Chowderfest on City Hall Plaza; 617-227-1528.

Boston Pops Annual Fourth of July Concert and Fireworks *July 4* On the Esplanade. The Pops presents several other free concerts on the Esplanade during July; 617-266-1492. *See page 307.*

Bastille Day. *Friday before July 14* Block party around the French Library on Marlborough Street—*un bon temps* with food and dancing; 617-266-4351.

Religious festivals. *Mid-July through end of August* Festivals with parades, music and food honor patron saints from the Old Country every weekend in the North End; 617-635-4455.

Annual Festival Betances. *Third weekend of July* Honors the Puerto Rican patriot Dr. Ramon Betances with music, dancing, food, sports, and other events. Most occur on Plaza Betances, Villa Victoria, 100 W. Dedham St.; 617-927-1700.

AUGUST

Annual Civil War Encampment. *First weekend of August* Fort Warren on Georges Island features 300-400 people in period costumes; 617-727-7676.

Caribbean-American Carnival. *Mid-August* With activities centered on Franklin Park, this longstanding celebration of Caribbean culture features live music, dancing, and ethnic foods.

SEPTEMBER

Art Newbury Street. *Third weekend of September* Stroll the art galleries of elegant Newbury Street; 617-267-7961.

South End Open Studios. *Third full weekend of September* Includes the studios at the BCA, the largest concentration of artists in New England; 617-426-5000.

TOURS

OCTOBER

Fort Point Arts Community Open Studios. *Third weekend of October* Features more than 100 artists in 23 buildings; 617-423-4299.

Head of the Charles Regatta. *Next to last weekend in October* The world's largest two-day rowing event, with 2,000+ boats, 4,000 athletes; 617-864-8414.

DECEMBER

Annual Christmas Performances *Throughout December* Boston Ballet's *Nutcracker,* at the Wang Center, 617-695-6950, and Ballet Theatre's version at the Emerson Majestic, 617-262-0961; Handel's *Messiah* performed by the Handel & Haydn Society, 617-266-3605; Langston Hughes's gospel play, *The Black Nativity,* at Tremont Temple, 617-442-8614; *The Christmas Revels* at Sanders Theatre, Harvard, 617-621-0505.

Crafts at the Castle. *First full weekend in December* High-quality juried crafts exhibition benefits Family Service of Greater Boston; 617-523-6400.

Reenactment of the Boston Tea Party. *Sunday closest to December 16* Begins at the Old South Meeting House and ends at the Tea Party Ship and Museum on Congress Street Bridge; 617-338-1773.

First Night. *December 31* See page 308.

■ TOURS

Some programs are seasonal; check with the tour operator.

■ BUS & TROLLEY TOURS

Beantown Trolley. Narrated tours with unlimited all day reboarding. 617-927-1174

Blue Trolley. Narrated trolley tour with 20 boarding/reboarding stops. 617-876-5539

Boston Duck Tours. Tours aboard an authentic renovated World War II amphibious landing vehicle begin at the Prudential Center and conclude with a "splashdown" in the Charles River for a water side view of Boston. 617-723-3825

Discover Boston. Narrated trolley tours are available in several languages. 617-742-1440

Gray Line/Brush Hill. Bus tours include Boston and Cambridge; Cambridge/Lexington/Concord; Plymouth; Salem. 781-986-6100

Old Town Trolley. Narrated Boston city tour with free reboarding. Also offers Boston and Cambridge brewpub tours, and "JFK's Boston." 617-269-7010. Cambridge trolley tours also available. 617-269-8137

Boston Park Rangers. Year-round free walking tours and interpretive programs on Boston's parks. 617-635-7383

Cambridge Historical Society. A limited number of walking tours of Tory Row and other areas of Cambridge. 617-547-4252

Chinese Historical Society of New England. Offers occasional guided tours of Chinatown and has a walking tour brochure available. 617-338-4339

Freedom Trail. 90-minute tours from Boston National Historical Park Visitor Center, 15 State St.; 617-242-5642

Harrison Gray Otis House. A guided tour of the house precedes a walking tour of Beacon Hill. 617-227-3956

Historic Neighborhoods Foundation. Walking tours include Chinatown, North End, the waterfront, sunset strolls of Beacon Hill and a Saturday duckling tour. 617-426-1885

Massachusetts Audubon Society. Offers occasional Boston Urban Education Programs, including Birding by Ear at Fresh Pond Reservation and Mount Auburn Cemetery. 617-259-9500

MIT Information Center. Campus tours depart from the Information Center at 77 Massachusetts Ave. 617-253-4795

Minute Man National Historic Park, North Bridge Visitor Center. Offers guided walks. 617-484-6156

■ FERRIES AND WATER TOURS

A. C. Cruise Line, Inc. Whale watching cruises and cruises to Cape Ann. 617-261-6633

Airport Water Shuttle runs back and forth between Logan Airport and Rowes Wharf from 6 A.M. until 8 P.M. ($10). L Late June through Labor Day, Cruise runs hourly 10-4 except noon on weekdays, 10-5 except 3 P.M. on weekends.

Free water taxi service from Georges Island goes to Bumpkin, Gallops, Grape, Lovells, and Peddocks Islands. Round-trip fare is $8 for adults, $6 for children under 12. 617-227-4321

Lovejoy Wharf Ferry operated by MBTA mornings and early afternoons on weekdays shuttling from Lovejoy Wharf (adjacent to the Fleet Center, off Causeway Street) to the Charlestown Navy Yard (home of the USS *Constitution*) to Long Wharf and back to Lovejoy. The ferry continues running until early evening between Lovejoy Wharf and the Charlestown Navy Yard. Tickets are $1; T passes are honored.

New England Aquarium. Whale watch expeditions led by experienced naturalists. 617-973-5277

Odyssey. Lunch, dinner, and moonlight cruises of Boston Harbor. 800-946-7245

Spirit of Boston. Lunch, cocktail, and dinner cruises of Boston Harbor. 617-457-1450

■ WALKING TOURS

Black Heritage Trail. Two-hour tours leave from Robert Gould Shaw Memorial, Memorial Day to Labor Day. 617-742-5415

Boston by Foot. 90-minute walking tours include The Heart of the Freedom Trail, Copley Square in Back Bay, The Waterfront, Beacon Hill, The North End, Boston Underground. Also offers a 60-minute guided tour of the Freedom Trail for ages 6-12 called Boston by Little Feet. 617-367-2345

TOURS

Charlestown Navy Yard. Guided tours of the Navy Yard focus on invention and ingenuity. 617-242-5601

Chinese Historical Society of New England. Offers occasional guided tours of Chinatown and has a walking tour brochure available. 617-338-4339

Freedom Trail. 90-minute tours from Boston National Historical Park Visitor Center, 15 State St.; 617-242-5642 **Historic Neighborhoods Foundation.** Walking tours include Chinatown, North End, the waterfront, sunset strolls of Beacon Hill and a Saturday duckling tour. 617-426-1885

Massachusetts Audubon Society. Offers occasional Boston Urban Education Programs, including Birding by Ear at Fresh Pond Reservation and Mount Auburn Cemetery. 617-259-9500

Minute Man National Historic Park, North Bridge Visitor Center. Offers guided walks. 617-484-6156

BICYCLE TOURS

Earthbikes. Guided 2-hour historic tours on weekend days throughout summer by reservation only. 617-267-4733.

A SELF-GUIDED TOUR OF JOHN F. KENNEDY'S BOSTON

Few Boston figures since the Revolution have had as profound an effect on the nation as the grandson of John "Honey Fitz" Fitzgerald and son of ambassador and financier Joseph P. Kennedy. John Fitzgerald Kennedy lived here as a child and again as a young man, drawing on Boston idealism and representing the city to the nation. Boston knew Jack Kennedy as one of its own.

KENNEDY CHILDHOOD SITES

Kennedy was born on May 29, 1917, in the second-floor master bedroom of 83 Beals Street, Brookline, a house marked simply with a plaque the town erected in 1961. The modest nine-room Colonial, which Rose Fitzgerald Kennedy remembered as "just right, beautiful and comfortable," is now designated the **John F. Kennedy National Historic Site**. It was repurchased and restored by the Kennedy family after the assassination and is open for guided tours from early May through Columbus Day. Part of the tour is a tape of the President's mother talking about the family's life here. 617-566-7937.

The family was growing quickly, so in 1921 they moved to a bigger house nearby at 51 Abbottsford Road.

The future president was baptized and served as an altar boy at **St. Aidan's Roman Catholic Church** on Freeman Street and attended the Noble and Greenough Lower School next door (now a high-rise apartment complex) and the Edward Devotion School on Harvard Street.

JFK AT HARVARD

The family soon moved to New York, but Kennedy came to Cambridge to attend **Harvard** in 1936, living in room 32 in **Weld Hall** as a freshman. Harvard later subdivided the room and delights in telling half a dozen freshmen a year that they're dwelling in JFK's old room. That year he lost his first election when he ran for freshman class president. Room F-14 in **Winthrop House**, where Kennedy lived as an upperclassman, has been preserved and now is used by visitors to Harvard's John F. Kennedy School of Government on JFK Street next to JFK Park.

CONGRESSMAN KENNEDY SITES

After winning the 1946 Congressional election, Kennedy dwelled briefly at the **Bellevue Hotel** (now condominiums) at 21 Beacon Street, Boston, before moving to Apartment 36 above the **Capital Coffee House** at 122 Bowdoin Street—his legal voting address until his death. He often treated himself to lobster stew at the **Union Oyster House** on Union Street, where he would sit alone with outspread newspapers in Booth 18 in the upstairs dining room from noon until 5 on Sundays.

PRESIDENT KENNEDY SITES

JFK chose what is now called the Kennedy Room of the **Omni Parker House** hotel to tell Boston Democratic Party leaders that he would run for President, but his formal announcement came at **Faneuil Hall.** In that election, he cast his vote at **Old West Church.**

Just before his inauguration, Kennedy returned to the **State House** to speak on January 9, 1961, recalling that both of his grandfathers had served in those chambers. An eight-foot-tall **bronze statue** of him, dedicated May 29, 1990, stands on the West Wing lawn.

In his State House address, Kennedy said that "God willing, wherever I serve, this shall remain my home." But, in truth, John Fitzgerald Kennedy no longer belonged to Boston—he belonged to history. The man and the President alike are memorialized for all time at **The John F. Kennedy Library and Museum** at Columbia Point. *(See page 209).*

A TOUR OF BOSTON DOMESTIC ARCHITECTURE

JACOBEAN/COLONIAL
Paul Revere House
19 North Square, Boston; (617) 523-2338
After moving into this 1677 home, Revere added another story, but the oldest surviving wood-frame building in Boston has since been restored to its original appearance. Its English architectural origins are apparent in the Tudor details and massing, and the interior furnishings are authentic to the period. The house is open daily for house tours.

GEORGIAN
Longfellow House (Reopens in 2002)
105 Brattle St., Cambridge; (617) 876-4491
This very formal and elegant Georgian home (built in 1759) served briefly as George Washington's quarters after its Tory owner, John Vassal, fled; it was later occupied by Henry Wadsworth Longfellow. While the interior reflects mid-19th-century taste, the symmetrical, hip-roofed, freestanding mansion with classical moldings and pilasters is typical of homes built in England and America ca. 1750-70.

FEDERAL
First Harrison Gray Otis House
141 Cambridge St., Boston; (617) 227-3956
Built in 1796 and designed by Charles Bulfinch, Otis's first house has been restored to reflect home life in the early 19th century. The signature Federal home today serves as headquarters of the Society for the Preservation of New England Antiquities. Open for house tours.

VICTORIAN

Gibson House

137 Beacon St., Boston; (617) 267-6338

This Italian Renaissance Revival home was built in 1860 as part of the first block to be developed in the newly filled-in Back Bay. Because only the Gibson family ever occupied this home, their furnishings (many from the 1860s) remain intact, providing a complete tableau of life in Victorian Boston. When built, the very modern home boasted gas lighting and coal-fired central heat.

ECLECTIC

Beauport

75 Eastern Blvd., Gloucester; (978) 283-0800

Started in 1907, this classic summer "cottage" of over 40 rooms typifies those built along the New England coast at the turn of the century. While a source of architectural commissions of the period, these mansions were neo-anything and everything, depending on the owner's nostalgic preference. While Beauport's exterior resembles a fairy tale castle, the interior contains rooms decorated to represent myriad historical periods and literary themes.

MODERN

Gropius House

68 Baker Bridge Rd., Lincoln; (718) 227-3956

Built in 1937-38, the Gropius House is one of the finest examples of Modernist design in America. Walter Gropius, founder of the Bauhaus, designed this home for his family while Dean of Harvard Graduate School of Design. The Gropius' furnishings are still in the house, which stands in the lovely suburb of Lincoln, 15 miles west of Boston.

—Holly Cratsley, Boston architect

RECOMMENDED READING

■ NONFICTION

Campbell, Robert. *Cityscapes of Boston: An American City Through Time.* Boston: Houghton Mifflin, 1992. Historic photos juxtaposed with contemporary shots by Peter Vanderwarker highlight the changing face of the city. Campbell may be one of America's best architecture critics.

Connelly, Michael. *26 Miles to Boston: The Boston Marathon Experience from Hopkinton to Copley Square.* New York: Parnassus Imprints, 1998. This chronicle details the Boston Marathon from the runner's perspective.

Dickson, Harry Ellis. *Arthur Fiedler and the Boston Pops.* Boston: Houghton Mifflin, 1981. The Associate Conductor Laureate of the Boston Pops gives a chatty account of Arthur Fiedler and the founding of the Esplanade concerts.

Fischer, David Hackett. *Paul Revere's Ride.* New York: Oxford University Press, 1994. Although the screen rights have been sold, don't wait for the movie. This book is an engaging account of the facts behind Revere's midnight ride and the subsequent skirmishes that took place west of Boston.

Goodwin, Doris Kearns. *The Fitzgeralds and the Kennedys: An American Saga.* New York: Simon and Schuster, 1987. Traces the two families during the century in which they rose from poverty and obscurity to glory and unimagined political power—culminating with JFK's inauguration.

Lukas, J. Anthony. *Common Ground.* New York: Knopf, 1985. Pulitzer Prize–winning account of Boston's school busing crisis told through the lives of three families affected by it.

McCord, David. *About Boston.* Boston: Little Brown & Company, 1973. Not since Walt Whitman has a poet so loved his city.

Morison, Samuel Eliot. *One Boy's Boston.* Boston: Northeastern University Press, 1983. Growing up privileged in Boston and liking it—the account of a great historian descended from Harrison Gray Otis.

O'Connell, Shaun. *Imagining Boston: A Literary Landscape.* Boston: Beacon Press, 1990. Boston through the eyes of its literati.

O'Connor, Thomas H. *Boston A-Z.* Cambridge: Harvard University Press, 2000. Preeminent city historian relates tales of Boston's people, places, and events.

Schama, Simon. *Dead Certainties.* New York: Knopf, 1991. This re-examination of the murder of Dr. George Parkman in 1849, which shook Boston society, raises fundamental questions about the nature of history.

Shand-Tucci, Douglass. *The Art of Scandal.*

New York: HarperCollins, 1997. New biography of Isabella Stewart Gardner casts her as a patron of bohemians and a champion of artists, liberated women, and gay men.

Tharp, Louise Hall. *Mrs. Jack.* Boston: Little Brown & Company, 1965. Gossipy biography of the fascinating Isabella Stewart Gardner.

Wakefield, Dan. *Returning: A Spiritual Journey.* New York: Doubleday, 1988. The journey centers on King's Chapel and touches on many other Boston sites.

Weitzman, David. *Old Ironsides: Americans Build a Fighting Ship.* Boston: Houghton Mifflin, 1997. Written and illustrated by Weitzman for a juvenile audience, the meticulous drawings also appeal to adults.

White, Jasper. *Jasper White's Cooking From New England.* New York: Harper & Row, 1989. The dean of New England cooking in Boston helped define the New Boston style.

Whitehill, Walter Muir, and Kennedy, Lawrence. *Boston: A Topographical History, Third Enlarged Edition.* Cambridge: Harvard University Press, 2000. The definitive history of Boston as revealed by its changing landscape.

■ FICTION AND POETRY

Barnes, Linda. *A Trouble of Fools.* New York: Delacorte Press, 1987. The first in a series of mystery novels featuring wise-cracking cabbie-cum-detective Carlotta Carlyle.

Bernays, Anne. *Professor Romeo.* New York: Weidenfeld & Nicolson, 1989. The title says it all in this book about Harvard.

Carroll, James. *Mortal Friends.* Boston: Little Brown & Company, 1978. *The City Below.* Boston: Houghton Mifflin, 1994. Sweeping family sagas set in Boston. Carroll uses the city setting as well as—or better than—any novelist we know.

Forbes, Esther. *Johnny Tremain: A Novel for Old and Young.* 1943. New York: Dell, 1987. A tale of growing up in Revolutionary times.

Hawthorne, Nathaniel. *The Scarlet Letter.* 1850. New York: Penguin Books, 1983. Hester Prynne may well be the greatest heroine in American literature. On the night of February 3, 1850, Nathaniel Hawthorne read the ending to his wife: "It broke her heart and sent her to bed with a grievous headache, which I look upon as a triumphant success," he wrote to a friend the next day.

Healy, J. F. *Blunt Darts.* New York: Walker and Co., 1984. Jeremiah Healy's first detective novel features sharply observed cityscapes and several Boston "types."

Heilbrun, Carolyn (pseudonym Amanda Cross). *Death in a Tenured Position.* New York: Dutton, 1981. This cult mystery has private eye Kate Fansler investigating the murder of Harvard's first tenured woman English professor.

Higgins, George. *The Friends of Eddie Coyle.* New York: Knopf, 1972. Small-time hood Coyle just can't get out of the life. Notable for Higgins's command of the spoken Boston idiom.

Kilmer, Nicholas. *A Man with a Squirrel.* New York: Henry Holt and Company, 1996. Murder mystery set on Beacon Hill and the antiques row of Charles Street is rich in local color.

Lowell, Robert. *Life Studies* and *For the Union Dead.* New York: Farrar, Straus and Giroux, 1956. Growing up privileged in Boston and hating it—from the brilliant poet related to James Russell Lowell and Amy Lowell.

McCauley, Stephen. *The Easy Way Out.* New York: Simon & Schuster, 1992. *The Man of the House.* New York: Simon & Schuster, 1996. Gay and straight characters interact in cuttingly funny novels set in Cambridge.

McCloskey, Robert. *Make Way for Ducklings.* New York: Viking Press, 1941. Beloved children's classic.

Miller, Sue. *The Good Mother.* New York: Harper & Row, 1986. Sexual and marital politics, as seen from Cambridge.

Neely, Barbara. *Blanche on the Lam* (1992), *Blanche among the Talented Tenth* (1994), and *Blanche Cleans Up* (1998). New York: St. Martin's Press. African American domestic who lives in Roxbury and works in the whiter parts of Boston solves crimes. Smart and sassy mystery series.

O'Connor, Edwin. *The Last Hurrah.* Boston: Little Brown & Company, 1956. Fictionalized account of Irish political machine recalls the days of James Michael Curley.

Parker, Robert B. *The Godwulf Manuscript.* New York: Delacorte Press, 1974. The first in a long series of mystery novels set in Boston and revolving around the first-person observations of the detective Spenser.

Senna, Danzy. *Caucasia.* New York: Riverhead Books, 1998. This coming-of-age story of sisters born to a white mother and black father is set in the South End in the 1970s.

Shute, Jenefer. *Sex Crimes.* New York: Doubleday, 1996. Set along the hipper sides of Newbury and Boylston Streets, Shute's novel captures the streetscape and the scene alike.

Updike, John. *Roger's Version.* New York: Knopf, 1985. Updike's updated version of *The Scarlet Letter.*

West, Dorothy. *The Living Is Easy.* New York: Arno Press and The New York Times Press, 1969. The quest for upward mobility and respectability set in the African-American neighborhoods of South End and Roxbury after World War I.

RECOMMENDED READING

I N D E X

COMPASS AMERICAN GUIDES

Critics, booksellers, and travelers all agree: you're lost without a Compass.

"This splendid series provides exactly the sort of historical and cultural detail about North American destinations that curious-minded travelers need."

—*Washington Post*

"This is a series that constantly stuns us; our whole past book reviewer experience says no guide with photos this good should have writing this good. But it does."

—*New York Daily News*

"Of the many guidebooks on the market, few are as visually stimulating, as thoroughly researched, or as lively written as the Compass American Guides series."

—*Chicago Tribune*

"Good to read ahead of time, then take along so you don't miss anything."

—*San Diego Magazine*

New from Compass:

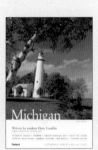

Georgia
$19.95 ($29.95 Can)
0-679-00245-6

Gulf South
$21.00 ($32.00 Can)
0-679-00533-1

Michigan
$21.00 ($32.00 Can)
0-679-00534-X

Nevada
$21.00 ($32.00 Can)
0-679-00535-8

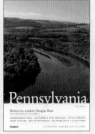

Pennsylvania
$19.95 ($29.95 Can)
0-679-00182-4

Southern New England
$19.95 ($29.95 Can)
0-679-00184-0

Vermont
$19.95 ($27.95 Can)
0-679-00183-2

Compass American Guides are available in general and travel bookstores, or may be ordered directly by calling (800) 733-3000. Please provide title and ISBN when ordering.

  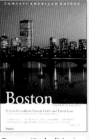 

Alaska (3rd edition)
$21.00 ($32.00 Can)
0-679-00838-1

Arizona (5th edition)
$19.95 ($29.95 Can)
0-679-00432-7

Boston (2nd edition)
$19.95 ($27.95 Can)
0-679-00284-7

Chicago (2nd edition)
$18.95 ($26.50 Can)
1-878-86780-6

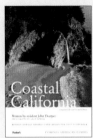 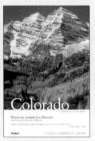  

Coastal·CA (2nd ed)
$21.00 ($32.00 Can)
0-679-00439-4

Colorado (5th edition)
$19.95 ($29.95 Can)
0-679-00435-1

Florida (1st edition)
$19.95 ($27.95 Can)
0-679-03392-0

Hawaii (5th edition)
$21.00 ($32.00 Can)
0-679-00839-X

  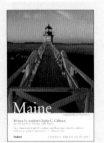 

Idaho (2nd edition)
$21.00 ($32.00 Can)
0-679-00231-6

Las Vegas (6th edition)
$19.95 ($29.95 Can)
0-679-00370-3

Maine (3rd edition)
$19.95 ($29.95 Can)
0-679-00436-X

Manhattan (3rd ed)
$19.95 ($29.95 Can)
0-679-00228-6

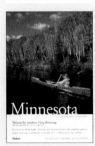 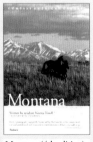 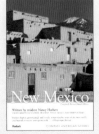 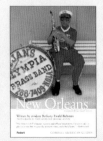

Minnesota (2nd ed)
$19.95 ($29.95 Can)
0-679-00437-8

Montana (4th edition)
$19.95 ($29.95 Can)
0-679-00281-2

New Mexico (4th ed)
$21.00 ($32.00 Can)
0-679-00438-6

New Orleans (4th ed)
$21.00 ($32.00 Can)
0-679-00647-8

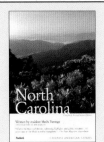

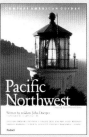

North Carolina (2nd ed)
$19.95 ($29.95 Can)
0-679-00508-0

Oregon (3rd edition)
$19.95 ($27.95 Can)
0-679-00033-X

Pacific NW (2nd ed)
$19.95 ($27.95 Can)
0-679-00283-9

San Francisco (5th ed)
$19.95 ($29.95 Can)
0-679-00229-4

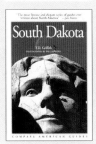

Santa Fe (3rd edition)
$19.95 ($29.95 Can)
0-679-00286-3

South Carolina (3rd ed)
$19.95 ($29.95 Can)
0-679-00509-9

South Dakota (2nd ed)
$18.95 ($26.50 Can)
1-878-86747-4

Southwest (3rd ed)
$21.00 ($32.00 Can)
0-679-00646-X

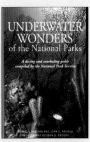

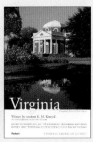

Texas (2nd edition)
$18.95 ($26.50 Can)
1-878-86798-9

Underwater Wonders of the Nat'l Parks $19.95
0-679-03386-6

Utah (5th edition)
$21.00 ($32.00 Can)
0-679-00645-1

Virginia (3rd edition)
$19.95 ($29.95 Can)
0-679-00282-0

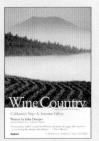

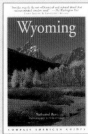

Washington (2nd ed)
$19.95 ($27.95 Can)
1-878-86799-7

Wine Country (3rd ed)
$21.00 ($32.00 Can)
0-679-00434-3

Wisconsin (2nd ed)
$18.95 ($26.50 Can)
1-878-86749-0

Wyoming (3rd edition)
$19.95 ($27.95 Can)
0-679-00034-8

■ ABOUT THE AUTHORS

Journalists and critics **Patricia Harris** and **David Lyon** review restaurants online for *Boston Citysearch* and write extensively on art, travel, and food. They are frequent contributors to *Yankee Magazine's Travel Guide to New England,* and their articles have appeared in a range of publications from *American Craft* and the *Boston Globe* to *Food Arts* and *Expedia.com.*

■ ABOUT THE PHOTOGRAPHERS

Joel Sartore *(pictured at left)* is a contract photographer for *National Geographic.* He has won many awards, including being named a Pulitzer Prize finalist.

Robert Holmes has twice received the Travel Photographer of the Year Award from the Society of American Travel Writers and has 18 books in print, among them several in the "Day in the Life" series.

New Englander **James Marshall** has been taking pictures the world over for the past 20 years. Along the way produced and edited *Hong Kong: Here Be Dragons; A Day in the Life of Thailand;* and *Planet Vegas: A Portrait of Las Vegas.*

Comments, suggestions, or updated information?
Please write:
COMPASS AMERICAN GUIDES
5332 College Ave., Suite 201
Oakland, CA 94618